Praise for
Slow Birding

"Joan Strassmann, an expert on the evolution of behavior, has written a wonderfully accessible account of the rewards of really watching birds and how fascinating even the most familiar species are. She shows us how biologists have revealed intriguing behaviors, what everyone can discover by careful observation, and how joyful and patient 'slow' birding can be."

—Doug Futuyma, Distinguished Professor Emeritus,
Stony Brook University and author of *How Birds Evolve*

"I highly recommend *Slow Birding* to novice and advanced birders alike. Strassmann invites us all to sit and watch the common birds near our homes and favorite parks to better understand and value their amazing lives. Put your check lists aside for just a moment and make your own discoveries about your feathered neighbors."

—Bridget Stutchbury, Distinguished Research Professor and author of
Silence of the Songbirds

"*Slow Birding* is the book for the curious and observant bird watcher of all ages. I wish I had a copy of this book when I started my own adventures into urban birding as a kid in Budapest in the early 1980s. Books like this, where popular beliefs on bird behavior are supported or rejected based on scientific papers and personal insights are supplemented by quotes from friends and colleagues, might even recruit a few more and much needed scientists who focus on natural-history driven questions in STEM."

—Mark E. Hauber, PhD, DSc, and author of *The Book of Eggs*

"In *Slow Birding*, Joan Strassmann brings together the best of avian behavior, ecology, and natural history that few outside of academia will ever hear about. Focusing on birds that many of us might see in our backyards or in a local park, Strassmann highlights the amazing but underappreciated lives of some of our favorite birds—such as Blue Jays and American Robins—as well as those of recent interlopers to many countries around the world—such as House Sparrows and European Starlings. She shows, with engaging prose and a deep scholarship, that we don't have to travel to the far corners of the Earth to witness the wonders of behavioral ecology or appreciate the important ecological roles of our feathered friends. *Slow Birding* shows that birdwatching need not focus on amassing a big life list—that there's joy and wonder in eavesdropping on the extraordinary daily lives of one or a few species."   —Scott Edwards, PhD, Harvard ornithologist

"From serendipitous discoveries to long-term field studies, Strassmann takes us on a journey through the worlds of ornithology and behavioral biology using backyard birds as her guide. She weaves together a collection of stories about natural history, the scientific method, and the importance of place into an enthralling narrative about her own experiences with some of her favorite American birds. With each chapter devoted to a single species, including an engaging set of activities for readers to do in their own backyards, *Slow Birding* is appropriate for novice and skilled birders alike, as well as those simply interested in learning more about the fascinating lives of the birds around them."   —Dustin Rubenstein, author of *Animal Behavior*

"In the frenetic world we live in, where even birding has become a competitive sport, *Slow Birding* reminds us of the simple joy that comes from observing the birds around us—not checking them off a list, but really watching and appreciating the nuances of their daily lives. Strassmann weaves together the stories of these familiar species and of the scientists who unlocked the mysteries of their behavior. A superbly crafted and enjoyable read!"

—Douglas J. Emlen, University of Montana regents professor of biology and author of *Animal Weapons: The Evolution of Battle*

"Like all the best nature books, *Slow Birding* is about much more than its titular topic. Yes, it is about birding, but it is also about history, geography, psychology—and most of all, how to see, really see, the ordinary things around you. Strassmann cleverly combines sharp observations of common species with suggestions for ways to learn more about birds like American Robins (check out how different individuals hunt down worms) and House Wrens (put up a simple nest box). She also shows us the dedicated scientists who painstakingly unravel the lives of these and other supposedly unremarkable species. You don't have to be obsessed with lists and rarities—*Slow Birding* will show you your own backyard as you have never seen it before."

—Marlene Zuk, author of *Paleofantasy* and *Dancing Cockatoos and the Dead Man Test*

"There are birders who race around trying to see as many species as possible, and there are birders who are more interested in the behavior and history of the birds they see every day. Joan Strassmann is one of the latter, and here in *Slow Birding* she provides a manifesto of this approach, combining carefully researched and well-written essays describing the biological history and recent scientific research of sixteen common North American birds with dozens of suggestions for how to enhance your appreciation of the birds around you. I highly recommend slow birding, both the book and the philosophy it represents.

Reading it will convince you to follow Strassmann's suggestion and pull out a lightweight, easily carried chair, sit down with your binoculars, and watch; you may never bird the fast way again."

—Walt Koenig, retired senior scientist, Cornell Lab of Ornithology

"Joan Strassmann has provided guidance on how to make the most of your time in the field—or living room—by pointing out what to look for and how to make the experience most meaningful. Just as a course in art appreciation can enhance your visit to a museum, slow birding can enhance your time with birds. Her mode of expression also makes this book a pleasure to read. This quote is an example of how she mixes science with empathy when writing about snow geese: 'Avian cholera is a disease of density, passed from one bird to another, with the potential of killing nearly a tenth of the population every year, creating goose heartbreak when one's partner for life dies.' *Slow Birding* is a book to appreciate and return to."

—Ellen Ketterson, Distinguished Professor of Biology,
Indiana University and author of *Snow Birds*

"Slow down birders and savor the soap opera, all the sexual infidelities, sibling rivalries, inheritance disputes and instances of parents playing favorites, unfolding right in your own neighborhood. That's the advice of veteran naturalist Joan Strassmann, a world's expert on the evolution of social behavior. In writing that is always informative, occasionally lyrical, Strassmann provides character sketches and social histories of some of our most commonly sighted winged dinosaurs. Along the way, she introduces readers to the ornithologists who devote their lives to unlocking the secret lives of birds and explains how they construct and test the hypotheses that transform suspicions and birder-gossip into publishable facts. Incidentally, I plan to get copies for all my friends who started birding during the pandemic and recommend the book to all the young people (high-school to post-grads) who ask me how to become an animal behaviorist. As an aside to Joan: When can I expect *Slow Birding for West Coasters*? Also eagerly awaiting *Slow Entomology*."

—Sarah Blaffer Hrdy, author of *The Woman That Never Evolved* and *Mother Nature*

Slow Birding

The Art and Science of Enjoying the Birds in Your Own Backyard

JOAN E. STRASSMANN

Illustrations by Anthony Bartley

A TarcherPerigee Book

tarcherperigee
An imprint of Penguin Random House LLC
penguinrandomhouse.com

Most TarcherPerigee books are available at special quantity discounts for bulk purchase for sales
promotions, premiums, fund-raising, and educational needs. Special books or book excerpts also
can be created to fit specific needs. For details, write: SpecialMarkets@penguinrandomhouse.com.

Bird feathers illustration © aksol / Shutterstock.com
Watercolor distressed vintage background © Apostrophe / Shutterstock.com

Library of Congress Cataloging-in-Publication Data

Names: Strassmann, Joan, author.
Title: Slow birding: the art and science of enjoying the birds in your own backyard /
Joan E. Strassmann; illustrations by Anthony Bartle.
Description: New York: TarcherPerigee, Penguin Random House LLC, [2022] |
Includes bibliographical references and index.
Identifiers: LCCN 2022017481 (print) | LCCN 2022017482 (ebook) |
ISBN 9780593329924 (hardcover) | ISBN 9780593329931 (epub)
Subjects: LCSH: Bird watching—United States. | Bird feeders—United States. |
Birds—United States—Identification.
Classification: LCC QL682.S77 2022 (print) | LCC QL682 (ebook) |
DDC 598.072/34—dc23/eng/20220528
LC record available at https://lccn.loc.gov/2022017481
LC ebook record available at https://lccn.loc.gov/2022017482

Printed in the United States of America
4th Printing

Book design by Laura K. Corless

To David Queller, with love

Contents

Slow
Birding

Preface

Why not Slow Birding? After all, we have Slow Food, a movement that began in Bra, a village thirty miles south of Turin, Italy.[1] Carlo Petrini and collaborators began this movement with the publication of the "Slow Food Manifesto" in November 1987. It argued above all for the return of taste in food, replacing the fast food that was spreading through Italy. The movement reached beyond just food, encompassing a slower, more thoughtful life that celebrated local varieties and local recipes.

In 2005 Jessica Prentice coined the word "locavore" and, along with Dede Sampson and Sage Van Wing, challenged San Franciscans to eat only food harvested within a one-hundred-mile radius of their city during that August. From there the locavore movement grew. A focus on the local is a focus on quality, for local foods are more likely to be picked at their prime with a minimum of environment-destroying transport costs.

Slow Birding brings these ideas to birding. All too often, birding is something done racing around in automobiles, stopping for moments to pick up a species here and there, then driving on. I call it "motor birding," the birding equivalent to eating fast food.

What if instead we stayed close to home and watched the birds that intersect our lives? What if we learned more about our birds, building our knowledge more slowly through daily observation? It may take some practice to get more out of local birds. It may be hard at first to learn to watch birds instead of ticking them off a list. This book will help.

This book's origins go back more than thirty-five years, when I first introduced students to the careful observation of bird behavior. Birds are among the most noticed of animals, but that notice seldom goes beyond identifying and listing. I encouraged my students to watch birds carefully as a way of enriching their understanding of animal behavior.

Early each April, I took my Bird Behavior class across the Rice University campus, in Houston, Texas, where I taught until 2011. First we stopped right across the street from Anderson Hall, and I pointed out the Great-tailed Grackles. The students took note of the huge difference in size between males and females and wondered why some males frequently pointed their beaks to the sky. None of them liked the piercing shrieks those males made.

We walked on. I stopped when I heard a Northern Mockingbird singing. The students learned to use their binoculars as they looked for him. This was their second bird.

We entered the main quadrangle and walked past the statue of Willy, Rice's founder. I knew better than to take the students out the Sallyport archway in the main building, since that is reserved for graduation. Instead we walked between the main building and the physics building toward the heavily wooded northeastern corner of campus where the Yellow-crowned Night Herons nested in a group of about twenty live oaks that were nevertheless not too close together.

I figured that even the most unprepared student could quickly learn to recognize these three species. All their assignments were open-ended. They spent at least four hours in the field observing birds, and then we met for an hour or so to discuss their discoveries. I encouraged them to take careful notes, timing and counting as much as possible.

The first assignment was to watch Great-tailed Grackles, Northern Mockingbirds, and Yellow-crowned Night Herons for at least an hour each and to write about how each species used time and space and how it differed between the sexes. It was a bit of a trick question since there are no obvious visible differences between males and females of mockingbirds and night herons. In that assignment they also had to think of something else they wanted to know about the birds.

The weekly meetings of this class were fascinating as I watched the students become better and better at observing. I saw their curiosity increase. I saw them ask original questions and answer them. The last assignment was to simply answer a question about one of the bird species with numeric data and a statistical test.

My students had no special equipment beyond binoculars, pencils, notepads, and a way of keeping time, yet they learned to appreciate what these three species of birds did in a profound way.

If we all took a little more time with the birds that are around us, then we, too, might appreciate their actions and begin to understand the biological underpinnings of bird behavior. This is the origin of *Slow Birding*. I shared the excitement of simply watching birds close to home in a way that makes a list of ten carefully observed birds more exciting than a list of a hundred seen quickly with only names and numbers. It is what I did with my students beginning in 2010 with a blog, also called *Slow Birding* (https://slowbirding.wordpress.com).

Part of what I want to do is share what animal behaviorists have figured out about birds. This helps Slow Birders tie what they see to what has already been discovered about the birds, enriching the experience. I bring my long experience in animal behavior to play as I tell these stories, often about research by people I know. I also hope to help bird-watchers become citizen scientists who document where birds are and what they are doing for the professional community through portals like eBird and iNaturalist. We need to know what is happening to the life on our planet in these times of great change.

With this book I chose to focus on a circle whose twenty-mile radius centers on my St. Louis, Missouri, home. My husband and I moved to Washington University in St. Louis more than ten years ago. I describe five of the places within that circle where I spend a lot of time observing. The heart of the book is the stories of sixteen common birds and the researchers who study them. Each chapter is followed by suggested activities for Slow Birders. Now that the book is done, maybe I'll also have more time myself for sitting and patiently watching the birds that flit through our landscape and our lives. Perhaps I'll bring with me a picnic made from local farmers market foods.

Introduction

A force in us drives us to the untamed. We dream of the wild, not the domestic, for it is wildness that is unknown. The force toward wilderness does not wait for a weekend or a vacation. It can be a daily need, a desire to connect with the wind, to live facing the unexpected.

What will bring us wildness in the places we live, domesticated with warmth and culture? For some, icy branches scratching together will suffice. A glimpse of a gibbous moon or a pomegranate-stained evening sky might help. But more than these, more than perhaps anything else, are the birds. These winged dinosaurs that have given up stored fat, hollowed their bones, and made many other compromises for flight—these organisms connect us with here and there, with then and now, as they chatter outside our windows or soar past our lives.

It is not news that birds are our closest connection with wildness. Birds are everywhere, and not only city birds like pigeons, starlings, and House Sparrows. Brightly colored Northern Cardinals, Blue Jays, and American Robins; melodious Song Sparrows, Northern Mockingbirds, and House Wrens; and stealthy Cooper's Hawks and Screech

Owls may all be found commonly where we live. They give us a connection with wildness because they can leave. They are birds that we may see locally but that can also fly far away to places we have not visited. This book is about how to bring birds more profoundly into our lives.

As I write this at my home desk, a baseball cap on to keep the morning sun out of my eyes, I hear a male Carolina Wren proclaiming his winter territory next door. I hear a European Starling, whose ancestors were here long before most of mine, proclaiming its winter shelter under the neighbor's eaves. Earlier a Tufted Titmouse scolded from the elderberry, desiring the peanut feeder but fearing me. Under the dead brown-eyed Susans, a White-throated Sparrow scratched backward. I could not tell whether it was a male or a female, but I could see it had a tan eye stripe, not a white one. These four winter birds penetrate my consciousness because I expect them. Because I know them, I am also aware when a surprising bird arrives. But there is so much more to enjoying birds than this.

What do people interested in birds do? Writing a list of the birds they have seen is a common beginning. This list might be in a little yellow notebook, and you might put the date and place along with the species. Slowly your list will grow. You will learn to identify more and more birds. The list might become an end in itself, and before you know it, the list grows. You will learn early on that the more new places you go, the more new birds you will see.

Birding can then quickly become divorced from outdoor pleasure. After all, it is most efficient to motor from one good birding spot to another, picking up the few birds here or there and moving on. A leisurely walk along a path is likely to turn up many individuals of the same few species, with only a few new ones interspersed. Before you know it, you have become a lister, a motor birder who checks the rare-bird alerts as well as who has seen more than you on online lists. Birding can so easily become a competitive enterprise where you strive to see more birds than the next person, or more in this county, or on a sponsored big day of birding. You can find trips all over the world that will present birds to help get your life list over a hundred, five hundred, then a thousand. You are on your way toward seeing as many of the ten thousand bird species on the planet as you can.

Adventure birding can be thrilling, as you see new colors, hear new songs, and meet new birders. But what have you really learned of the birds you see? Does that sighting of a Great Potoo in Costa Rica that lets you add it to your life list really satisfy? How much do you want to understand this bird, or will you simply move on to the next visual trophy that's not on your list? I suppose there is nothing wrong with this kind of birding. It gets you outside to new places, often with interesting people. It employs bird guides all over the world. It takes you to sights unimaginable. I would not give up a dawn sighting of parrots and macaws eating orange clay at a remote cliff up the Tambopata River in Peru, or the Malabar Hornbills that came to Eldhose's lodge in Thattekad, India. But these trips are rarities. There is another way to approach birds that may ultimately be more satisfying.

I call it Slow Birding. Just as the Slow Food movement turns the focus from ever more exotic food to the local, Slow Birding turns the focus to the birds at home. At first it might seem that there is nothing new to Slow Birding. After all, many birders put out a few feeders and see what birds come in. Even the most extreme travel birders will have a yard list, perhaps even partly viewing it as another way to compete. Birders may also have what they call their patch, a place near home where they bird most frequently. More recently there is a five-mile-radius birding challenge. Stay within five miles of home, perhaps at places you reach only by walking or biking, and see what birds are there. Clearly Slow Birding by other names is becoming interesting, but I would like to introduce something new.

Even local birding has tended to focus on lists. Where did you go? When did you go? What birds did you see, and how many did you see? All numbers—supremely valuable numbers in the right hands. But what these numbers leave out is nearly all of a bird's life. What are the birds doing? What can you learn about the birds? What if, along with your binoculars, a guide app, and a list app, you also brought along a folding chair? What if you followed the advice of famous ornithologist Margaret Morse Nice and sat still and watched?

This is what I mean by Slow Birding. Sit and watch the birds. You might draw them or take notes on what they are doing. Then when you see those birds again, they will seem like old friends. Doing this takes advantage of local birding and resighting the same birds repeatedly. It adds depth to your experience of those birds. It means that the goals of local birding are very different from the listing goals of motor birding.

But this advice could be given in an article, a blog, or a half-hour podcast, and you have in your hands an entire book. Why? Because this is a guide to Slow Birding that depends on the slowest birders of all: the professional ornithologists who have spent their own lives discovering the lives of individual birds. The thesis of this book is that if you tie in the biological stories that go with the birds, they will be much more rewarding to watch. These are not the birders' stories of where birds occur, how to see them, or even what the American Ornithological Society has done with splitting or lumping various species.

These are the stories of the birds themselves, obtained over months, years, and even decades by professionals who have given their lives to birds. Ellen Ketterson knows more than anyone about how testosterone and its fellow hormones influence the behavior of Dark-eyed Juncos. From Karen Wiebe I learned of the tenuous lives of Northern Flickers as they defend their cavities and hunt for ants. Charlie Thompson has been taking teams of undergraduates out to census House Wrens in the "Wren Wagon" for more than forty years. Robert Rosenfield climbed thousands of trees to document every Cooper's Hawk action as their numbers recovered from near extinction by the pesticide DDT. Enid Cumming braved wolves, bears, and moose in the most ancient of Canada's boreal forests to watch Yellow-rumped Warblers in their most native territories. These are but a sampling of the ornithologists who have shared their work here, through their writing and through live interviews with me.

As with the birds, the discoveries these ornithologists have made are myriad. How do American Coots tell their own chicks from those someone else laid in their nest? How do Snow Geese flourish in spite of annual cholera outbreaks that kill thousands of them? How have the suburbs benefited Northern Cardinals? How do American Robins detect earthworms? Each bird has a story, and a question to be answered. Each bird contributes to our understanding of life.

These stories would not be complete without telling something of the tools that make the discoveries possible. My favorites are the tiny ones, like the sensors strapped to even the tiniest migrating birds. Others are molecular, like DNA fingerprinting that brought paternity analyses to humans and birds alike. Some are exactly the same as what we use to document our own lives, like the cameras stuck in nest boxes. Many are simple and old, like, perhaps the most important of all, those colored leg bands so that individuals can be distinguished.

The tie to Slow Birding is that it is the local birds that we can watch most easily. They are also the ones that become routine if they are simply counted. Ornithologists often write in a way that is not particularly accessible to the rest of us, but I can translate.

I have chosen to tell the stories of sixteen birds that are common inside my St. Louis circle, with its twenty-mile radius. They are also generally common in much of the United States. I focus on five places and follow each place-specific chapter with chapters on three or four birds seen at that location, though many of the birds could be seen at all of the locations.

Since Slow Birding is also about place, I have included chapters on these specific places. It is important to understand place. It is also important to learn how to discover the natural and human history of your places, so I have included some advice on this kind of discovery. But this should not diminish the value of learning about St. Louis itself. We are the heart of the nation, at the junction of the two biggest rivers, the Mississippi and the Missouri. We have prairies and forests. We are the site of the greatest Native American settlement north of Mexico, Cahokia. We also have Superfund site stains of the Manhattan Project. One of my much loved sites, Tyson Research Center, has Quonset bunkers covered in concealing forest where munitions were hidden during World War II. Perhaps removing them would be expensive, but all have electricity going to them. Why? My place might interest you even if it is not your place. Discovering how I discovered the history of my place may help you with discovering the history of yours.

Home

Home. A shelter with beds for all, a place to cook, eat, tell stories, do homework, store our clothes and books, hang our art, and use a bathroom. How can these simple ingredients have such an emotional tie for us? I think it is because home is embedded in the environment. Sounds are a profound part of that environment, especially natural ones. So I might say that birdsong defines home.

I'm likely to wake to the formal notes of Northern Cardinals, the policing cries of Blue Jays, the intense notes of Northern Flickers, or the chatter of House Sparrows. I slowly got to know the other birds of my home, the whistles of a passing flock of Cedar Waxwings, the hoarse voice of the Fish Crows nesting down the block, the clear repetition of a Carolina Wren, and the clicking sounds of a Cooper's Hawk. And there are others. Many others.

If you know the birdsong that defines your home, you can never lose it. If home becomes song, then no landlord can push you out. You can maintain the feeling of home. Though it might not include a bed, it will be somewhere you can revisit.

My home is in St. Louis, the city that opened the West and sold furs from the North to traders headed south to New Orleans down the Mississippi, from where they would be shipped to Europe. It is a city that has been important ever since Native Americans built the mounds across the river in Cahokia and also all through what would become northern St. Louis more than a thousand years ago. I like to say that St. Louis became big before America became selfish. This means we have a wonderful zoo, great museums, and state parks that have no entry fees.

My home is more precisely in an independent city adjoining St. Louis proper, called University City, founded as a planned city by the publisher, insecticide salesman, and shyster/visionary Edward G. Lewis. Lewis wanted to move his magazine publishing to a choice spot and had to buy the adjoining eighty-five acres to do so. He bought the land in 1902 and incorporated the city on September 4, 1906, with himself as mayor. His idea for the city was that it would follow the natural hills and valleys of the land, with minimal fill. The neighborhood to the north of us, University Heights, has curving streets and variably sized lots that fulfill that dream. Our street is in an area called West Portland Place and is a simple grid of streets, though the hills mostly remain.

In 1871 the eastern section of our street was named after the natal city of my father, Berlin. But in 1918 it lost that name because of strong sentiments against the Germans. The name of a military general, Pershing, was deemed more suitable. The efforts in 2014 to bring back Berlin as the street name failed.

Our house was built in 1921 of solid brick, three structural rows coated inside with plaster on a lot that's 50 by 135 feet. The clay that our bricks were fired from was dug locally, probably from within three miles of the house, perhaps from pits in Dogtown. The thick walls help our home stay warm in winter and cool in summer. It has giant radiators because it was built soon after the 1918 flu epidemic. Some then thought that keeping windows open was good for health, and the radiators had to keep up.

We wanted to make this small piece of St. Louis as wild as possible. First we dug a small pond, with a deep end of three feet and a shallow end where the toads could easily hop out. We surrounded it with slabs of native limestone and put a row of limestone boulders to curve across the back, separating a wild meadow from our vegetable garden. We planted the slope in front and the curb strip with little bluestem and other grasses, with asters, echinacea, and other prairie plants.

On one side in front we planted blueberry bushes. I imagined children going to Flynn Park Elementary two blocks away plucking a blueberry or two to suck on, though the blueberries ripen long before school opens in fall. Or they might pick a brown-eyed Susan for their teacher. In the fall our little hill turns purple with asters. American Goldfinches hang from drying flower heads picking out the seeds.

There is a patio in back where we eat in the summer at a metal table my sister handed down to me. It is shaded by a native dogwood that an American Robin nested in last year. Under it is bloodroot, columbine, and wild ginger. To the west is that small pond we dug, now inhabited by goldfish, toads, dragonflies, and other animals. Once a Great Egret and a Little Blue Heron visited it, and I have a photograph to prove it. Around the pond are cattails, irises, blazing stars, and ever more rudbeckia. In the summer Ruby-throated Hummingbirds and American Goldfinches flit through the plants. In the winter Northern Cardinals show red against the bare branches, and the American Goldfinches have lost their brilliant color.

The heart of the backyard is my vegetable garden. I grow mostly leaves and herbs, along with tomatoes, peppers, eggplant, beans, squash, and okra. The squash is mostly for the blossoms, which I stuff, dip in batter, and sizzle in olive oil. The leaves include mustard greens, collard greens, kale, arugula, and lettuces. Herbs are rosemary, sage, lots of basil, parsley, oregano, thyme, tarragon, and cilantro. Mint is kept in the front because it is too aggressive and would take over the garden the way the lemon balm is doing. I also have garlic, both for the heads and for the sprouts.

On this summer day, the House Wrens are going in and out of the nest box my husband, David Queller, gave me for my birthday in May. It is mounted in the backyard on a concrete post with a hook on top left over from a clothesline, with the other end once attached to a similar hook coming out of the garage. The male wren sat on the electric wire running just above the nest box to our house. He trilled away, clearly unhappy that I was picking pole beans only feet from his nest.

A Carolina Wren sings from the ridgeline of our neighbors' garage, maybe twenty feet from this nest box. These neighbors, Jay and Pam, are good friends. We have both House Wrens and Carolina Wrens in our backyard. I have seen them scuffle in the elderberry on the edge of our patio. But Carolina Wrens choose more open places than boxes for their nests.

Starlings nest under the eaves of the home Holly and Curtis bought a couple of years ago just to the west of us. From the thick layer of white droppings outside, I guess that nest was successful. Also, right after they fledged, I often heard the dry buzz of begging juvenile starlings.

Every day there is something going on with the birds at home. There is the day the Northern Flickers urge their babies out of the nest with repeated long calls. There is the day the same flickers fail to chase the starlings out of the hollow across the street and have to find another down the block. There is the ongoing tension between Carolina Wrens and House Wrens. Does it matter that one migrates and the other does not?

In winter we have Dark-eyed Juncos and White-throated Sparrows with their mournful song. I saw them at home for the last time this year on April 8. They had been here since October 24. The White-throated Sparrows were here for longer. I last saw them on May 15 at nearby Heman Park. I first saw them at home on October 24.

We put out feeders of sunflower seeds, peanuts, and suet in the winter. The sunflower seeds that fall to the ground attract these species. The suet brings in the Downy Woodpeckers and the Northern Flickers, when the European Starlings are not in the way.

I've talked about some of the birds in our small yard. I looked at what I have logged on eBird and saw I have logged seventy-three species right in my own garden.

Keeping a journal of the birds at home helps. Here is a section of mine.

April 18, 2020: The chimney swifts are back! Saw about 6 of them pivoting over our house.

April 19, 2020: The juncos are gone. When did I see the last one? I always know the first. But when was the last?

Lots of evening drama. A pair of flickers tried to take over the starling hole in the tree across the street. The flickers copulated, and then the male flew off. The female stayed at the hole, staring down the starling. She did not move. I only could see her sharp yellow beak. The flicker sat at the hole. The male starling fluttered a few meters above. The flicker stayed maybe 20 minutes, then moved up the trunk and to the side.

Across the street a Cooper's Hawk landed on Carol and Roger's house two doors east, then leaped over to the neighbors', the family that had the dream of grandparents down the block until he took an unfortunate medicine, went on oxygen, then ultimately both went to a retirement center, where he finally decided to go off the treatments and died.

The hawk didn't know this. It jumped to the ground. We went back to watching the flicker until we went in for dinner.

May 12 our daughter saw a Cooper's Hawk fly up from the pond. Was it hunting goldfish?

Wherever your home is, learning the birds and what they do will help keep it in your heart forever.

HOME ACTIVITIES
FOR SLOW BIRDERS

1. **Create a home bird list.** Start a list of the birds you see at home. Do it on eBird so that the world can benefit and you can easily pull it together. Ornithologists the world over use eBird, from Cornell University's Lab of Ornithology, to understand where birds are and how that changes with habitat and time. It is a record we can all contribute to. You might also want the satisfaction of a home bird journal. Just remember to write down the date, time, and weather for every observation. I record the temperature and whether it is sunny, cloudy, raining, or snowing. If you live in an apartment, you can list birds you see out the window or outside your apartment. The key thing is that you record what you see in one small, frequently attended place.

2. **Install a bird feeder.** Put out a feeder near your home or on your balcony. I usually put out peanuts, black-oil sunflower seeds, and suet. I add a hummingbird feeder when they arrive in the spring. In the winter I throw a couple of cups of sunflower seeds on the ground for the Dark-eyed Juncos, White-throated Sparrows, and Mourning Doves. I diminish feeding in the summer, when the birds can find natural food more easily. A feeder can work on a balcony. We had one on our balcony when we lived in Berlin for a year doing fellowships at the Wissenschaftskolleg zu Berlin. There we were able to attract the lovely Eurasian Bullfinch, along with Great Tits and others. It is really satisfying to pool your observations with those of others by joining the Cornell Lab of Ornithology's Project FeederWatch (https://feederwatch.org). It has lots of advice on what to put in your feeders and how to watch the birds.

3. **Put up a birdhouse for small birds.** A House Wren discovered and used our little house. Afterward, the squirrels started to enlarge the opening, so we bought a large metal washer to go around the opening. Cavity-nesting birds love birdhouses.

4. **Make your garden bird-friendly.** The British call it a garden, not a yard, which I like. The Audubon Society has lots of suggestions for plants that are good for birds. There are three things you can do to make your garden better for them. First, plant native plants. Find out what works in your area, plant appropriately for sun or shade, and remember to leave the dead stems standing, since there will be many insects, including beneficial bees, hibernating in them. Plant native trees also, a mix of deciduous and evergreen. Second, have a water feature. We have a small pond, but a birdbath works too. Be sure there is a way out of the water for toads or other animals. Even a wet puddle is better than nothing. It is best if the water feature has a drip, though our pond is still. Third, have a brushy area for birds to shelter. Easiest is to pile trimmed twigs and stems in a corner rather than compost them. This will provide shelter for the birds on the coldest nights. On your balcony you could plant native flowers and put out water. Even a vase or trayful of dead stems might attract some birds.

5. **Spend time outdoors or at the window.** Home is where we spend most of our time. If a bird does something you have not seen before, it is likely to be at home. We eat on our patio whenever possible. Watch what the birds do. You can record these observations in a bird journal for your home. This will be much richer than only listing the birds you see at home. If you have nesting birds, noting the time of various activities is important and is something you can put in your eBird observations. If you do not have a garden, find

one nearby, perhaps in a park, and make it a practice to visit, not to simply walk through but to sit a while.

6. **Invite others to see your natural garden.** Once you have improved your garden or balcony to be more inviting to birds, use it as a teaching moment. Invite others to see what you have done. Inspire others to expand their own natural environments to make their gardens better for birds, bees, and other insects and wildlife.

Blue Jay

Mighty Oaks from Little Blue Jays Grow

It is a mystery to me why the Blue Jay cannot claim to be the state bird of a single state. Blue Jays are gorgeous, with their jaunty crest and bright blues intensifying to near purple and a cerulean that puts the Cerulean Warbler to shame. Northern Cardinals, Western Meadowlarks, and Northern Mockingbirds are each the state bird for six or more states, but no one wants the noisy Blue Jay. Maybe they are too bossy as they police the skies, calling to one another, perhaps warning of a Cooper's Hawk swooping low, or a Barred Owl sleeping deep in a spruce, or your cat, who—dare I say it—should not be outside unleashed. Sometimes Blue Jays shriek at each other for social reasons apparent only to themselves, fooling the bird-watchers hoping to spy a more exciting cause for the noise. Did blue as a color of law enforcement come first from Blue Jays?

I have long watched and loved Blue Jays. This year I stepped out into the chilly blue dawn on January 1 wondering what bird I would hear or see next. It is a custom among birders to celebrate the first bird of the year, so I did not want the moment to go by unappreciated.

Before long, I heard a Blue Jay call as it flew across the front yard. It would be the year of the Blue Jay.

Perhaps my most exciting sighting of Blue Jays was farther north, close to the northern edge of their range. Whitefish Point in Michigan reaches into Lake Superior, pointing toward Canada. On a surprisingly cool day, June 9, 2009, tendrils of mist twisted over the water, sometimes obscuring and sometimes opening the pounding shore to my eyes. Out of these vapors Blue Jays flew, pummeling across the water in clumps of five or six, then moving into the trees to rest after crossing the great lake the Ojibwe called *gichigami*. Every time I looked away, another group flew into view, their blue punctuating the haze. I counted more than eighty Blue Jays on that foggy day during a boreal flora mini course I was taking from Ed Voss at the University of Michigan Biological Station. Then, I did not know the glacial connection between lakes, Blue Jays, and forests.

Blue Jays are the most American of birds, occurring in every state, though they are rare west of the Rockies. Blue Jays occur only in southern Canada, so the birds I saw crossing Lake Superior did not come from much farther north. At the southern extreme, there have been a few observations of Blue Jays on the northern border of Mexico.

Another way of looking at where the Blue Jays are is to look at a map of oak trees. A map from 1884 by Charles Sprague Sargent that shows the distribution of oaks, *Quercus*, might as well be a map of Blue Jay distributions, at least for the eastern two-thirds of the country.[1] This is not a coincidence, as we shall see.

Despite their neglect in the state-bird sweepstakes, Blue Jays are among the birds we are most curious about. Biologists Justin Schuetz and Alison Johnston asked what birds we google most often, and Blue Jays placed sixth, after Wild Turkeys, Bald Eagles, Common Ravens, Mallards, and Ospreys.[2] Blue Jays were not only near the top of birds googled; they were also among the birds people most often see, as reported in eBird. People reported seeing only Mourning

Doves, Northern Cardinals, American Robins, and American Crows more often than they reported seeing Blue Jays. I suppose this means that Easterners log more eBird observations, since Blue Jays are not common in the West.

We seem to have a love-hate relationship with Blue Jays, probing into their secrets but not honoring them with a state. One reason might be the way their intelligence interacts with their officiousness and brazen curiosity. I had a favorite Blue Jay back when we lived in Houston and my children were little. We called him the money bird, though we could not know for sure if he was male. The money bird simply appeared in our lives. This Blue Jay swooped out of the live oak in our front yard and onto my hand and pried my fingers apart with his beak, seemingly knowing I had just taken some change from the car. I opened my hand, amazed to have a bird on it, and he pushed the pennies aside, then flew off with a quarter and a dime clamped in his beak. We had a tame money bird! Over the next few years he visited often, accepting silvery coins or perching on my garden fork as I paused from turning over the soil in our vegetable garden. Some of our youngest son's earliest memories come from holding out his soft fingers for the scratchy feet of the money bird, giggling at the tickling touch. I wondered if our money bird would ever bring his children over to partake in the joys of shiny coins, but he did not. I also did not figure out why Blue Jays and others in the Corvidae family like shiny things so much. There are many reports of collections made by Blue Jays, crows, and magpies. We never did find our money bird's collection, but he always flew south with his loot, perhaps to a stash in a hollow tree.

I imagine this bird must have been coddled by a human as a fledgling and then survived the transition to independent living. The money bird visited us for about six years before vanishing. When I hear Blue Jays calling to one another, I think of the money bird, smart enough to take our silver coins but not smart enough to spend them.

Of course, the money bird did not eat the coins he pilfered. What

Blue Jays eat and what they want to eat are a major part of the story of how they have changed the environment, and with it our very climate. But first I will tell a story of what Blue Jays do not eat. Well known to naturalists is a black-and-white photograph of a Blue Jay that has just eaten a monarch and looks positively ill. What is the story behind this famous image? It is by Lincoln Brower, who worked on monarch butterfly migration. Brower wanted to understand how monarchs were protected from predation. He chose Blue Jays to test whether monarchs were truly distasteful.[3] Monarch caterpillars eat milkweed leaves, which contain toxins like the resinous galitoxin and cardiac glycosides. Monarch caterpillars can tolerate these toxins and sequester them in their bodies, so they, too, become toxic.[4] Brower wondered if the monarchs were toxic to Blue Jays and, if so, how quickly Blue Jays learned to scorn monarch caterpillars.

It is hard to catch adult Blue Jays before they have learned not to eat monarch caterpillars. So Brower took another approach. He caught wild adult Blue Jays and got them to unlearn their rejection of monarchs in aviaries. To do this he had to develop tasty monarchs that the Blue Jays would like. This could be done only by letting the caterpillars grow up on something mild. Brower chose cabbage. However, the caterpillars were completely unwilling to eat cabbage and died. So Brower painted the cabbage with a dilute extract of milkweed. This fooled the caterpillars. With them, Brower developed a line of cabbage-raised monarchs for his experiments that he maintained in the lab for five generations.

At first Brower's captive Blue Jays refused the monarchs, but hunger made them explore. Once they realized these monarchs were tasty, they feasted on them. After the Blue Jays regularly viewed monarch caterpillars and adults as food, it was time for the experiment: presenting them with milkweed-reared monarchs. Would the Blue Jays get sick on caterpillars reared on milkweed?

The hope was that they would get sick after eating the monarchs and then from that learning experience avoid them entirely. The experiment was a success. Blue Jays enthusiastically swallowed the monarchs but then got sick between eight and fourteen minutes later. Brower describes it vividly:

> Ingestion of these was followed uniformly by violent retching and vomiting . . . excessive bill-wiping, crouching, alternate fluffing and flattening of the feathers, erratic movements about the cage, jerky movements of head, wings, and thoracic regions, partial closure of the eyes, eating of sand, twitching, and a generally sick appearance.[5]

After that, no convincing would get them to try another monarch caterpillar or adult. By the way, all the experiments were done on frozen then thawed caterpillars and butterflies, so no need to worry about the insects themselves suffering fear in these experiments.

Blue Jay behavior on eating monarchs reminds me of the first time my baby daughter tasted brussels sprouts. Her disgust might not have been as graphic as that of the Blue Jays, but if she had feathers I think she would have ruffled and then flattened them in a whole-body display of disgust. Me, I love brussels sprouts, and so does she now.

There are plenty of other delicious insects for Blue Jays to eat, but insects are not their principal food. Acorns are. Oak trees depend on animals to disperse their acorns. It is a mutualism, an interaction in which both parties benefit, and one that has changed the continent as the glaciers receded.

How the Blue Jays changed our continent might best be understood if we start small, with that first acorn one might pick up on an autumn walk, like the one I found recently nestled among fallen leaves. It still had its cap on, making it look like something a child might design for a fairy garden. The acorn had simply plopped down from the oak tree overhead. Unlike a maple seed, it had no wings to make it spin even a few feet away from its mother tree.

Instead, acorns rely on birds and, to a much lesser extent, mammals like squirrels to bring their young to a place they can grow. And many of these birds are in the crow family, including Blue Jays. Blue Jays carry acorns out from under their parent tree to locations that can be miles away. This is a story of paying attention to the whole environment, not just one bird.

In 1936, while a famous early ecologist, Joseph Grinnell, was studying pocket gophers in California, he pondered the challenge of the oaks around him.[6] How did seedlings get to mountain slopes higher than any parent oak tree? After all, acorns roll downhill. He looked up from his pocket gophers and saw the local jays, in this case California Scrub Jays, busily flying up the mountain carrying acorns far above the tree line. These jays carried thousands of acorns and buried them in individual winter caches in the soil and rocky slope. Grinnell then imagined bands of oaks of different species migrating up and down the mountains over millennia, rising with warmer climates and receding with colder ones.

The jays that buried the acorns did it for their own benefit as a food source for the future. Acorns buried high up would be covered in snow through the winter but available for eating as the spring snows melted. They would be available long before other food sources. If the jays remembered and ate all their acorns, there would be no benefit to the oaks. But they did not. Some acorns were always left to hatch in the new year and form new oak trees. The jays are smart enough to cache and smart enough to find most of their acorns but not quite smart enough to find all of them.

Not that long ago Blue Jays had a much, much bigger landscape to fill than the mountain scree above western forests. It is not hard to extend Grinnell's idea of a few Blue Jays moving acorns up and down a mountain to millions of Blue Jays moving acorns far north to the thousands of miles of land laid bare as glaciers retreated after the last ice age. Much of the northern hemisphere, including Michigan, was under the great Laurentide Ice Sheet that reached its maximum extent twenty-two thousand years ago.[7] The glaciers melted away around only eleven thousand years ago. As they melted, the glacial waters formed Lake Michigan, Lake Superior, and the other Great Lakes—lakes the Blue Jays now fly across. The state even today is rebounding from the unimaginable weight of the glaciers. The rate of uplift around Sault Ste. Marie at the juncture of the Upper and Lower Peninsulas of Michigan and not far from Whitefish Point is about a foot every century—nothing we can see, but easily measurable.[8]

We have some idea of the landscape laid bare by retreating glaciers if we consider the bare gravels at the bases of current melting glaciers.[9] First to colonize the bare rocks are the lichens, that ancient marriage of rock-binding fungi and oxygen-capturing algae. Next come the tundra plants, the sedges and ferns seething into moist, empty crevices. As the glaciers puddled, a meadow-like landscape of grasses, flowers, and sedges flourished. Trees followed, beginning with spruces and pines that adapted to the cold and to nutrient-poor soils.

How do we know these things? We know where the ice was and how it retreated from striations on rocks, caused by stony debris dumped in glacial patterns.[10] We know what plants grew in an area in the past from pollen records stored undisturbed over the centuries in the mud at the bottom of lakes. A core, carefully taken to preserve the order of deep samples, can show centimeter by centimeter when different plants arrived. Sedges, ferns, birches, ragweed, sunflower-family plants, and others reveal themselves by their pollen. And then comes the surprise—oaks moving north and reaching Lake Michigan as early as ten thousand years ago, only shortly after the ice retreated.[11]

But how could oak trees move hundreds of yards north per year? Once an acorn gets to a spot, it cannot immediately transmit new acorns farther north but needs first to grow into an oak tree. A red oak might have a generation time of forty or so years.[12] One way to see if Blue Jays could move the oaks and beeches hundreds of miles north along with the receding glaciers is to study how Blue Jays move acorns today, following on the observations of Joseph Grinnell.

The way to do this is to find a site with a group of oaks in an open landscape where the Blue Jays can be followed as they take acorns from the oaks. To observe Blue Jays harvesting and caching acorns, students Susan Darley-Hill and Carter Johnson at Virginia Tech University watched and counted.[13] They chose a stand of eleven pin oaks (*Quercus palustris*) right on campus. This clump of trees was in a typical university neighborhood, with campus buildings and fields and nearby residential neighborhoods, fields, and woodlands. They color-banded nine Blue Jays so that they could follow individuals. What they wanted to find out was how many acorns the trees produced and what happened to them. To get at the numbers of acorns moved, the students counted acorn caps left under trees when the Blue Jays took the nuts. This is a good measure because Blue Jays generally remove the caps before they take acorns. The rough cap would stick in their throat and also take up space, meaning they could carry fewer acorns. The cap is where the acorn attaches to the tree, and almost seems to have evolved to be detached.

Darley-Hill and Johnson found that Blue Jays took about four minutes collecting acorns before flying off with them. It wasn't so easy to count all the acorns a Blue Jay packed away in its mouth and throat for caching, but they got the numbers for thirty-seven trips and found that the birds took between one and five acorns at a time, averaging just over two nuts per flight.

Another hard thing the investigators wanted to know was how long and far Blue Jays flew. Darley-Hill and Johnson found that flights to a cache the Blue Jays knew about that was 0.6 miles away took about fifteen minutes. Once the Blue Jays arrived at a cache site, they disgorged all the acorns into a pile. From that pile, they picked up individual acorns and buried them tip-first in holes so each held only a single acorn. This might have made them harder to find, but it made it less likely that an incidental acorn thief would get all the acorns.

These few observations of what exactly the Blue Jays did with the nuts could be scaled up to the entire population by evaluating the acorns themselves. The investigators estimated that the eleven oak trees produced 246,000 acorns, and the Blue Jays carried away 54 percent of the acorns, or 133,000 in all, mostly avoiding only the weevil-infested nuts. That is a lot of acorns. Even if only a few are flown miles away for caching, a blank landscape can quickly become forested in oaks planted by Blue Jays.

But before we get too enamored of the idea that Blue Jays brought our oak forests north as the glaciers retreated, it is important to remember another possible candidate, one that can no longer sing for itself: the Passenger Pigeon. Canadian professor Bob Montgomerie thinks that Passenger Pigeons were much more responsible than the Blue Jays for moving the oak forests north. After all, an estimated three to five billion Passenger Pigeons were in North America at the arrival of the first Europeans. But alas, we cannot evaluate their impact today. They are not plants and so do not produce pollen we could discover in cores. They did not cache acorns, so their movement would have to have been quite different from that of Blue Jays. Here we will continue the Blue Jay story.

These studies have shown that Blue Jays move acorns around a lot, burying them in ways that allow any acorns they forgot to germinate. For a behavior that is such an important part of a Blue Jay's life to evolve, there must be a clear benefit to the Blue Jays. Also, that benefit has to be to the individual bird that buried the nut, because that is the bird that paid the cost of the action. We know Blue Jays eat acorns, and we know they hide them. All that remains to show for a complete story is that they are smart enough to find the acorns they bury. Do they really have the memory for it?

Paul Callo and Curtis Adkisson, also at Virginia Tech University, teamed up to see exactly how good Blue Jays are at finding nuts they have hidden.[14] They caught fifteen Blue Jays and put colored leg bands on them and kept them with food and water in an outside aviary measuring twenty by ten by eight feet. When they wanted to test whether the jays could remember their caches, the researchers put them into a test cage with a one-way mirror. Blue Jays are smart and might not go to their caches if they knew they were being watched, even by a species as different from Blue Jays as we are. But they were presumably not smart enough to understand one-way mirrors. The test aviary had tree stumps, branches, and cinder blocks in it, so there were lots of places for hiding. The investigators also put a grid of tabs of colored electrical tape on the ground so they could better estimate exactly where the birds were.

For the experiments, they made sure the birds were hungry by not feeding them for twenty-four hours. These hungry birds should be motivated to discover the bowl of fifteen peanut halves to eat and cache. The hidden scientists watched each bird in the cage for an hour, noting where it cached the peanuts. Then they took the Blue Jay out and waited until the next day, when they put the bird back in the cage. Did the bird preferentially go to its caches and retrieve its nuts? They were expected to retrieve some for eating, and indeed they did, usually discovering and eating three peanuts. They went straight to their hidden nuts without hunting around, indicating they remembered where they were. We can apply the findings of this small laboratory experiment to the wild caches Blue Jays work so hard to conceal. Clearly, Blue Jays have the brains to remember.

There are many other kinds of laboratory experiments on Blue Jays that explore their intelligence.[15] But I most like to think of Blue Jays outside. When I hear that the Blue Jays have found a roosting owl or have become alerted for some other reason and fly through the neighborhood with their screeching warning, I like to remember that they have airlifted the oak trees north in tiny acorn packages as the glaciers retreated. They also bring these seeds into lands that have been logged and abandoned. When I hear Blue Jays screaming at the beginning of my daily bird walk, it seems that all is as well as it ever was in this dangerous world.

Perhaps someday a state will rethink having a Northern Cardinal or American Robin as its state bird. After all, Connecticut, DC, Georgia, Illinois, Iowa, Maryland, and New Jersey all have oaks as their state tree. Why not match the tree with the bird? Or go a step further. Our national tree is the mighty oak. Why should the national bird not be the mighty Blue Jay instead of the Bald Eagle?

BLUE JAY ACTIVITIES
FOR SLOW BIRDERS

1. **Record the Blue Jays you see.** Every walk you take outside can include Blue Jays. I record my bird walks on eBird, either using the mobile app as I go or keeping notes and entering my observations into eBird later. I keep track of how long I walk and how far. I am careful to note how many Blue Jays I see, along with all the other birds. Binoculars are always helpful, but Blue Jays can be seen easily even without them. If you participate in the Audubon Society's Christmas Bird Counts or the Cornell Lab of Ornithology's Project FeederWatch or their other activities, Blue Jays are likely to be part of what you see. Christmas Bird Counts focus on a circle fifteen miles in diameter. There are about 2,500 counts in the United States each winter. Breeding Bird Surveys are in the spring. One census for the Breeding Bird Survey consists of short counts at fifty stops half a mile apart along roads in the breeding season. At each stop the expert birders listen and look. There are more than 4,000 Breeding Bird Survey routes in North America. I am not a good enough birder to participate in a Breeding Bird Survey, though maybe I can tag along as an observer. But I have participated with others more expert than me in Christmas counts, where all levels of birders are welcome.

2. **Follow Blue Jays' calls to find hawks and owls.** Blue Jays hunt down predators like Great-horned Owls and Cooper's Hawks and pester them until they fly away. Sometimes I can follow the noise and find the predator. If you try this, you might have to take a long time peering into the deepest dark interior of a tree. Sometimes the shape of the owl, hawk, or even cat is hard to make out, so give it some time.

3. **Record all the Blue Jay sounds.** Blue Jays have many different calls, from the familiar warning call to one that sounds like a rusty pump handle to mimicking local hawks. Among themselves they have a quiet chatter that certainly means something. See how many sounds you can record and categorize from your neighborhood Blue Jays. See how often they make each sound. What is the rarest?

4. **Watch a Blue Jay.** Most of all, I like to simply watch Blue Jays. What are they doing? Have they found an acorn? Are they moving it into their especially extended throats? How long can I follow an individual Blue Jay, taking careful notes just as Grinnell did? Grinnell used two kinds of notebooks: a field notebook that he carried with him and wrote in outside and a field journal into which he wrote more in the evening, relying on the field notebook for details (see https://americanornithology.org/joe-grinnells-notes/).

5. **Study the acorns.** Pick up a handful of acorns under an oak. If you were a Blue Jay, how many would you have selected for caching? Can you tell those with weevils from those that are sound? An acorn infested with weevils will be lighter and will have at least one small hole. You can break them open to see the weevils. How difficult is it to get that cap off for easy carrying? Can you cache a few acorns yourself, pounding them into the ground or burying them under a few leaves? Have you noticed any oak seedlings away from any oak trees?

American Robin

Earthworm Whisperer

American Robins are for everyone. They are colorful, ever present, and often on the ground where even toddlers can see them. Robins look sturdy, like the kind of bird a child would draw. Their upright stance on the ground makes them look fat, but that is just their feathers. No bird can be fat and still fly.

Robins never come to seed feeders, though on the coldest winter days they might come to a suet feeder. But just because robins are common does not mean they are not worth our attention. They might be the best bird of all for learning to really watch birds. Robins have many calls and a subtle difference in head color between males and females, and they fight right in front of us over territory boundaries invisible to us.

American Robins can be found all over the country most of the year, though the birds we see in summer are probably not the same ones we encounter in winter, for they do migrate a little. American Robins are the state bird of Connecticut, Wisconsin, and my childhood home state of Michigan. American Robins are the ninth most googled bird. Among eBirders, American Robins are the third most encountered bird, after Mourning Doves and Northern Cardinals.

I am not the only one in my family to pay attention to robins. I asked my husband to imagine a bird he had seen here in St. Louis recently so I could test out Merlin Bird ID, the app from the Cornell Lab of Ornithology. I asked him the Merlin questions, beginning with where and when he saw it, the answers being here and today, something that could be true any time of the year in St. Louis. The next question asks which of seven size categories from sparrow to goose, with robin and crow in the middle. He chose robin-sized. The next question asks for main colors, and he chose buff/brown and orange. The last question asks where the bird was, and he chose on the ground.

My husband was thinking of an American Robin! Sure enough,

Merlin correctly identified it. Later, I asked my son to think of a bird and went through the same questions. He also thought of an American Robin, and Merlin also guessed it. Try it yourself and see if your companion is not also thinking of a robin.

Robins like our city yards and small parks because they hunt for earthworms best in fields of short grass.[1] Those worms are important to robins to feed to their young, so robins don't even start nesting until the humidity is high enough to bring the earthworms close to the surface. But they are still under the surface, so how do the robins figure out where to peck? What are robins doing as they hop along the ground in our yards or on the forest floor?

How American Robins find worms is a question that sounds like a seventh-grade science fair project. But it is a legitimate scientific question, one that Canadian professors Bob Montgomerie and Patrick Weatherhead decided to address. Weatherhead told me the story.

> *Bob and I were sitting on the porch at the biology station [Queens], quite possibly with an adult beverage in hand, chatting and incidentally watching robins foraging on the lawn. That led to speculation about how they find worms in the soil. It appeared to us that when they cocked their heads, they were listening for whatever sounds worms make when moving through soil. It happened that someone had published a study that concluded that head cocking allowed robins to focus visually on worm movement. That study had not been designed to rule out hearing, however, so we decided to investigate. We conducted experiments with robins in aviaries where we controlled the sensory information available to the birds.*

The experiments that they designed ended up in an elegant and clear paper entitled "How Robins Find Worms."[2] What they wanted to know was whether robins heard, saw, smelled, or felt the vibrations of the worms. They described the behavior they wanted to understand like this: "Foraging robins run several steps at a time, cock their heads to one side for up to a few seconds, then lunge at the ground, often driving their bill well into the soil where they grab an earthworm, pull it to the surface and consume it or take it to feed their nestlings." This sure seems like the robins are listening to worms, but only an experiment would tell for sure.

Montgomerie and Weatherhead actually used mostly mealworms because they stay put, are shorter than earthworms, and are easily purchased and grown in oatmeal. They verified this approach with a preliminary study that showed robins like to eat mealworms.

They used trays of soil marked in a grid along their edges so that they could put the worms in precise spots and record exactly where the birds probed. They set up their apparatus, introduced the robins to it, then videotaped. The robins were in an outside aviary, and their regular food in the cages (diced apples, raisins, mealworms, and moistened dog food) was removed an hour before the experiment to give them an appetite. They studied four robins: three males and a female. After the experiments were done, they let the robins go.

In the first experiment, they tested whether robins could smell the worms. They killed the worms by freezing them to ensure that their odor would not be affected, then buried them in the trays half an inch deep. If the robins could smell the worms, they would peck more often than random where the worms were buried. But the robins pecked at random, hitting a square with a dead mealworm only two times of seventeen first strikes. By contrast, when there were live mealworms, thirty-five of thirty-nine first strikes were in squares with the live mealworms. If they didn't pull up the mealworm on the first strike, they got it on the second. Clearly, American Robins are not finding worms by smell.

In the next test, Bob and Pat asked whether the robins felt the worms' vibrations. To test this, they used two trays of soil arranged so that the robins would stand on the tray with no mealworms but feed from the other one where the mealworms were—much like lining up at a buffet. This meant they could not feel any vibrations through their feet. The birds had no trouble finding the living worms in the other tray, so they did not need to feel vibrations to find the worms.

The third test attempted to remove visual cues for worms. The worms are underground, but Bob and Pat worried that the worms' movements might slightly disturb the soil, enough that a robin could see it. To study this, they buried mealworms in the soil half an inch deep, then laid down a sheet of cardboard covered with another half inch of soil. The cardboard would conceal any soil movement made by the worms. In this case, the birds still found the worms more often than expected by random chance, though one of them spent most of the time trying to remove the cardboard. Bob said, "We have some striking videos showing a robin launching itself into the air and driving its bill down exactly where the worm was below the cardboard."

This left the final test, but how were they going to block worm sound? First they tried playing white noise from a speaker beside the tray. But that did not deter the robins' ability to find the worms. So then they took a tiny, inch-wide speaker, put it in a cloth bag, and buried it an inch deep in the middle of the tray, facing upward. The birds did not strike the soil as often, perhaps because they detected fewer worms. When they did, they hit the worm with the first strike less often than when sound was unimpeded, 59 percent of first strikes compared with 90 percent. So the most important cue proved hard to mask, but the speaker in the soil at least diminished their ability to find worms, indicating that sound, indeed, is how robins find worms.

So Bob Montgomerie and Pat Weatherhead were right to think that the earlier scientist had not ruled out sound. Bob Montgomerie summed it up:

> *As I recall, we initially debated about sound versus sight, and everyone we talked to, including a leading sensory physiologist, said the robins*

were almost certainly using sight, turning their heads to focus their foveae [the sharpest, central part of the eye] on the ground where the worm might be. Based on all that, we started these experiments reasonably skeptical about the birds' ability to hear the worms. When that physiologist died a few years ago, the person giving the eulogy said that the results of our experiment were one of the most interesting scientific puzzles and findings that the physiologist had encountered. In the end Pat and I concluded that the birds were initially locating the worms by hearing, then tilting their heads to focus their foveae on the spot where they thought they heard the worm.

But worms are mostly for babies, not adults. What the adults live on is fruit.

If you see a fruit tree of some sort in the fall, you will often see American Robins and Cedar Waxwings gobbling down fruit. There are other temperate-zone birds that eat fruit, but these are the professionals. If you are wondering exactly what fruit American Robins eat, you could turn to the US Bureau of Biological Survey records, as Nathaniel Wheelwright did. Wheelwright is a professor at Bowdoin College in Maine. Most of his local work is on Savannah Sparrows, but what he really loves is work in the Monteverde, Costa Rica, field station where he studies the reproductive ecology of tropical trees. He has published a calendar-notebook for us to keep track of natural observations.[3]

The records of robin stomachs that Wheelwright studied are from 1885 to 1950.[4] Wheelwright looked at three things: the volume of food in the stomachs, the different kinds of food in the stomachs, and how much of that was fruit. The data for his study were somewhat biased, since the point of the original survey was to understand the impact of robins on crops, so birds were often shot in orchards or other agricultural fields. This meant that fruit would have been overrepresented in the birds' diets and indeed made up most of the stomach contents. But during the breeding season, roughly April through June, fruit fell precipitously to less than 20 percent of the stomach contents by volume. Of the insects, beetles were overrepresented, but that information could also be biased because the beetles' wing covers are highly visible and indigestible. The commonest fruits in robin stomachs were *Prunus* (often as cherries), 23 percent of all fruits in the robins from the eastern United States. For families of plants taken, the commonest were 34 percent Rosaceae, including *Prunus*, followed by 10 percent Anacardiaceae (the poison ivy family), 6 percent Vitaceae (grapes), and 5 percent Cornaceae (dogwoods).

It is not easy to switch from a mainly fruit diet to a mainly insect one that's necessary for developing eggs, so researchers were curious how robins did this. In a laboratory study of American Robins, Douglas Levey and William Karasov found that the difference between eating fruit and eating insects has to do with how long the food stays in the digestive tract.[5] Since fruit is low in nutrients, a bird eating fruit has to eat more of it. This works only if the fruit passes through the gut more quickly than the birds are eating protein-rich insects and worms. And that is just what they found. Levey and Karasov added both neutral liquid and solid markers when the birds were eating fruit or insects. For fruit they found that the liquid marker was expelled at forty-eight minutes on average, with the first liquid appearing in only twenty minutes; while in the insect-fed birds, the average was sixty-five minutes with the first liquid appearance at fifty minutes. The solid markers had similar patterns. This seems like a fairly easy adaptation to a new food: simply hold it in the gut a different amount of time.

But when robins are hunting worms and insects, they are generally not letting them reach their guts at all because they feed their young with the prey. For the first four days of chicks' lives, their parents feed them regurgitated food, mostly worms and insects. By their thirteenth day, the chicks leave the nest but continue to be fed for at least three weeks.[6] Both parents feed the chicks, though the male feeds the first chicks that leave the nest while the female concentrates on the chicks remaining in the nest for a day or two. Then, if she begins a new batch of eggs in a new nest, the male takes main charge of the fledglings. He works so hard to care for them, one imagines they are all his progeny. But no, and this leads us to an example in which common knowledge turned out to be incorrect, an example counter that of the way robins find worms.

This is perhaps the most famous case of everyone being wrong about birds. Females were assumed to be faithful to their mates since they stayed close together and cared for the young together. Males were also assumed to be faithful. Perhaps you have watched an American Robin pair defend its territory or tenderly tend their demanding young, bringing them food or lifting their fecal sacs out of the nest. Robin fathers are excellent providers. And they mate daily during the egg-laying period. Any careful observer of their behavior should not be criticized for believing that fidelity reigns in robin unions.

But by the time Karen Rowe embarked on her Ph.D. thesis on American Robins, it was known that over 90 percent of birds mate and have young outside the pair bond, even though behavioral monogamy is nearly the rule, especially in songbirds. So it would no longer be a surprise if American Robins were not entirely faithful. Even the techniques for assessing paternity had become quite straightforward since they were first developed in the mid-1980s. Rowe caught robins at their nest, put colored bands around their legs, and drew a drop of blood. Then she waited for the chicks to hatch and did the same to them. She took those precious capillary tubes of blood, extracted the DNA, and used a variable genetic marker to see if the markers in the parents matched those in the chicks. The ancestry and health genotyping service 23andMe gives us this kind of information in a much more detailed way. Really, all she would need is a few highly variable genetic markers. In her case, Rowe used three microsatellite markers that had been originally identified in Swainson's

Thrushes, a bird that is closely related to American Robins. The technique is a simple one that sees if the variants in the offspring match the variants in the putative parents. One should match mom and the other should match dad. If they don't match the female, someone else laid eggs in the nest. If they don't match the male but do match the female, another male mated with her.

The expectation is that in exchange for all that paternal care, the least the female robin could do is be faithful to her mate. But natural selection doesn't work that way. Each parent will do what is in their own best interest even if it doesn't seem fair. If a female that mates with another male has more babies than a female that is faithful, then any genetic tendency to infidelity will be passed on and will spread in the subsequent generations. But if a female that is unfaithful leaves fewer progeny, then the trait will not spread. And the same argument can be applied to males.

Sneaking a mating with a male not one's mate is easy because in birds copulation takes only a few seconds. In robins copulation is typically performed in the trees. Male birds do not have a structure like a penis (except in ducks and a few other birds), so the female has to willingly move her tail aside to copulate.

Males therefore have to be very attentive to guard against outside matings, if his female is so inclined. Rowe and Weatherhead reasoned that a male will be too busy caring for fledglings of the first brood to guard the female while she produces a second brood. So this would give her a chance to mate with others if she so chose.[7] This gave Rowe a hook to her study beyond simply reporting on how faithful robins are to their mates and adding one more example to the more than a hundred species where extra-pair paternity had been recorded.

Rowe did this research at a ten-acre Illinois Christmas tree farm in 2003 and 2004 during breeding seasons that lasted from mid-April to mid-July. That birds with close neighbors are more likely to mate outside the pair bond was known for other species, so Rowe estimated the proximity of others by looking at the number of other robin nests within fifty-five yards of each nest under study.

In the two study years, Rowe was able to genotype 212 young from 74 different nests and found that in all cases, the mother that tended the young was the genetic mother according to the DNA. For the nests where Rowe succeeded in capturing and genotyping the father, he was not the genetic father of 68 of 148 nestlings, or 46 percent. There was at least one chick from another male in 34 of the 52 nests, or 65 percent of nests. This is a very high rate of mating outside the pair bond. It says that most males are caring for at least one chick that is not their genetic progeny. Because they had sampled most of the population, the researchers could further say that the males mated with females other than their mate from nests about seventy-five yards away.

But what about the original hypothesis? Did males busy with the first brood lose parentage to neighbors because the female was beginning a new brood? If the first nest failed, then the male should have had time to guard the female while she produced a new brood. He would not be busy caring for the first brood fledglings. But it turns out that the female actually produced fewer extra-pair young in the second nest, 7 percent compared with 33 percent in the first ultimately unsuccessful nest. If the first nest was successful in their sample, they had 46 percent extra-pair young, compared with 40 percent in the second nest.

So it seems there is no hope for their original hypothesis that males busy with the older chicks while females start a new nest will be less able to guard females in a way that reduces the number of chicks fathered by another male. Maybe she was not motivated to stray. The reason awaits future experiments.

Another hypothesis Rowe and Weatherhead considered is based on another measure of male quality. It is called interclutch interval, the measure of the time between when the first brood left the nest and the second brood was started. Under the mate-guarding hypothesis, the shorter the interval, the less well the male could guard the female. But it could also be that a shorter interval indicates a higher-quality male. Rowe and Weatherhead found support for this idea. The sooner a new nest was started after the first batch fledged, the less likely the female was to mate with males other than her partner.

Clearly, family life in American Robins is complicated. But some of the complications could have come from the study site itself. Nests in the pine plantations, in this case a Christmas tree farm, were more dense than those reported by others in more variable and natural vegetation, between two and six times more dense at twelve to twenty nests an acre. But density variation within the study site did not account for fidelity rates. Nor did male mate guarding appear to be important. The authors conclude that it seems females are in charge of extra-pair mating.

Science is a social enterprise, so I always like to read a research paper's acknowledgments section. In this case I saw that my friend Sarah Kocher worked on this project as an undergrad. She is now a professor at Princeton and works on bees. I contacted her to see what she had to say about her time in the field studying robins with Karen Rowe:

This was my first foray into behavioral ecology. I took a class with Pat Weatherhead and realized how much I adored animal behavior. I signed up for a summer project with one of his graduate students, Karen Cavey (now Rowe), and it literally changed my life. It was pretty typical birding fieldwork. Waking up at 4:00 a.m. to go out to our site, search for nests, set up cameras to record behaviors, mist nets to capture birds, band them and draw blood for paternity analyses, and a field spec to measure the intensity of each bird's plumage. Once I had finished that first cup of coffee, I genuinely loved every minute of it. It was because of Karen and her amazing mentorship that I realized that I really had a passion for studying animal behavior, and that summer was the first time I really started to seriously contemplate graduate school as a viable path forward. This study also happens to be how I met my partner, Julien. He came to the field site one day to bring Karen lunch, we started talking, and I guess the rest is now ancient history. So yes, this project literally changed my life! How exciting to think it may one day end up in a book written by you—that seems like a wonderful way to close the loop. :)

Isn't that a wonderful story? She met her husband working on robins as an undergraduate in that Christmas tree farm.

Now that we know the chicks in a nest were not all fathered by their mother's partner, we might wonder about exactly how much care the males give. I don't know of a study that has looked at whether males with rogue chicks provide less care, but I do know of related studies. One has to do with whether males give less care when they think the chicks are of lower quality. That might sound a bit counter-intuitive, that the weakest chicks might receive less. But even the strongest chicks have very high mortality rates, so parents might invest in them just to have someone survive. But how might they realize they have great chicks? Researchers have looked at this in two ways. One way involves egg color.

Robin eggs are blue, ranging from the deep turquoise of a tropical sea to the pale blue of a dawning sky. Philina English and Bob Montgomerie wondered if fathers would take better care of bluer eggs.[8] This would be the case if the egg color indicated higher-quality chicks because they received more nutrients in the egg. The color comes from the pigment biliverdin and could signal female health. Such an effect had been reported for European Starlings, and English and Montgomerie found it improbable. They expected to find no such effect in American Robins.

English and Montgomerie looked at entire clutches of different color intensities with a particularly ingenious experiment. They made fake eggs of clay and painted them with acrylic to be bright or dull, with all the eggs in a given nest of the same color. The females hopped right on these clay eggs and incubated them as if they were real.

At the time the eggs should be hatching, the investigators replaced the clay eggs with chicks taken from faraway nests, so the birds would think the young hatched from those clay eggs. Robins might be smart, but not for things of which they have no experience. This is a great experiment because English and Montgomerie have manipulated both egg color by using fake eggs and hatchling hardiness by using chicks from other nests. Would the parents think the bluest egg would hatch out the best chick, making it worth caring for even more in the future?

Then they videotaped how much the male and female fed the chicks. Sure enough, the male fed the chicks more often at the nests with brilliant eggs, nearly two times as often as the pale-egg nests. But this was true only at the crucial beginning of the chicks' lives, when they were up to three days old. By six and nine days, the feeding was no longer different between nests that had dull and bright eggs. Perhaps chicks that survived to the sixth day no longer needed extra food. One thing in biology, and really all science, is that any given experiment usually explains only a piece of the story. In this case, the brightness of eggs matters, but only for males and only early on. Still, it is strong support for the hypothesis that males use egg-color brightness as a signal of chick quality and that they reward those high-quality chicks with extra morsels in their crucial early days.

Robin fathers may often care for one or more chicks that are not their own, but there is one thing they do not do naturally: care for chicks of other species. In this, robins are somewhat special, since most species cannot tell Brown-headed Cowbird eggs from their own and rear the alien chicks. Robins expel cowbird eggs. Brown-headed Cowbirds are a native bird originally limited to the Great Plains, but they have expanded with agriculture and the cutting of eastern forests. They never build their own nests, instead laying their eggs in the nests of other songbirds. Many people revile cowbirds, but they are native and natural, and it is illegal to remove their eggs from nests.

Rebecca Croston was interested in the cost of actually rearing a cowbird had the robins not rejected the egg, so she did experiments that placed cowbird chicks that were either newly hatched or three days old in American Robin nests.[9] These she compared with robin chicks that had been similarly added to the nests of other robins.

Croston found that the cross-fostered robins did just fine in their adoptive nests, while the cowbirds did not do as well. Only 50 percent of cowbirds survived, versus 90 percent of cross-fostered robins. This may have to do with the amount of fruit in the diet (30 percent), the early switch to whole food, or to losing food competitions to their robin nestmates. The nests with additional cowbird chicks fledged fewer robin chicks than did the unmanipulated controls, so even though cowbirds don't do well in robin nests, they do exert a cost on the robins, one that robins can avoid by simply rejecting cowbird eggs in the first place. I wonder if the poor success of cowbirds in robin nests could also mean that cowbird females lay their eggs infrequently in robin nests. It is an interesting pattern that cowbirds are more likely to parasitize nests of birds smaller than themselves where their chicks have a better chance at the food.

Who would have thought that this commonest of all birds would be so interesting? Its robustness is clear, as is its adaptation to environments we have changed. Of all the birds in this book, this might be the easiest one to get out and watch! I see American Robins nearly every single day no matter which of my nearby places I visit. This very morning in midsummer, the young are largely independent, their baby spots fading. There was a storm last night that brought down a huge red oak in Flynn Park. I looked among the leaves to see if a robin's nest had come down with it but did not find one. I guess from the tens of robins on the wet grass that it was a bit late for nesting, but the birds were intently plucking up worms.

AMERICAN ROBIN ACTIVITIES
FOR SLOW BIRDERS

1. **Tell males and females apart.** It was not until embarrassingly recently that I learned to tell male and female robins apart. They are not always distinguishable, except in the breeding season. I learned to identify juveniles with their breast speckles soon enough, but the slightly duller color of most females, particularly their less black heads, took me a long time to recognize. Learn them, describe all the differences, and maybe even draw or paint them. If you are lucky, you might even see a robin with a color mutation as I once did. That bird was leucistic, with white splotches interrupting the normal pattern.

2. **Watch them.** Robins may be the easiest bird of all to watch because they spend so much time on the ground. Start by using a notebook and a pencil or pen. I like to use pencil because water or alcohol won't wash lead away. Later you might want to use a tape recorder or even a laptop, but paper is less complicated. Sit down with a notebook and try out the three main ways of observing animals, famously categorized by Jeanne Altmann, a retired professor from Princeton well-known for watching baboons in the Amboseli basin in Kenya, in 1974.[10] The three methods are called "ad lib," "scan sampling," and "focal animal observation." Start with ad lib. This is the easiest but potentially the most biased and difficult to quantify. Spend five minutes just writing down everything you see robins doing around you. You might see one pulling a worm. Another might have flown into a tree calling a robin shriek. A third might be fighting with a fourth over an imaginary boundary. Or more likely, they will just be hopping around. Write it all down.

   To do scan sampling, look from one side of your field of view across to the other, taking in for a brief moment one bird and writing down what it does. Then move on to the next robin. Do another scan at a measured time later, maybe five minutes. This gives a better sampling of what the robins do than does the ad lib sampling, where you can't get everything on every bird.

To do focal animal observation, choose a robin and watch just that robin for a pre-chosen amount of time, perhaps five minutes. Write down everything that bird does in that time. Then move on to the next robin you see and do the same thing. At the end, you can compare the kinds of information you gathered with these different techniques. Of course, in this summary there is the expectation you can see more than one robin from your spot.

3. **Listen to them.** The American Robin's song may be the most familiar of all birdsong to you. But they actually sing in a lot of different ways and they also call. Use your smartphone and Merlin from the Cornell Lab of Ornithology to record and identify birdsong.

4. **Observe nest behavior.** Robin nests are common and often low through much of the eastern United States. If you can find one, set up your chair far enough away that you will need binoculars to watch the nest. You might even decide to hide your presence with a simple bird blind, a kind of tent that lets you watch without showing yourself; they are also called hunting blinds.

Once you are situated, watch the nest. How often do the parents visit the nest? Can you see if it is the male or female coming in? If there are eggs in the nest, one parent (usually the female) will be incubating the eggs and the other may bring her food. When there are chicks, they will be noisy, and feedings may be more often.

Keep track of the nest history: when it was started or when you first found it, the intermediate stages, and when the chicks fledged. Then maybe you can watch the fledglings. You can join NestWatch (https://nestwatch.org) and help the world know about your birds.

5. **Track fruit eating.** Robins love to eat fruit. Watch them in a fruit tree. How do they choose the berry they eat? Do they eat all in an area before moving on? Do they spit some out? Do they fight with other birds?

6. **Track worm eating.** Robins love worms, which they feed to their babies. Watch them hunting for worms. How many times do they hop between worms? How often do they cock their heads as if they are listening or feeling for vibrations? Do they look with their left eye or their right? Do different robins have different cadences?

7. **Prompt escape behavior.** Try to see how close you can get to a robin, not by walking right at it but with a parallel walk, edging ever closer. Do this ten times, estimating the number of feet between you and the robin before it flies off. Repeat this in a forest and see how much more skittish robins are in the woods. Robins, like many animals, have to balance the dangers of predators with their need for food or nesting material. They may be more skittish when there are trees for a predator to hide behind.

8. **Migration and winter behavior.** Robins migrate south in the fall but not too far. See if you can count the numbers in your area at the same time and exact place each day. Where are they and what are they doing? If they are in flocks, see if you can count the numbers in the flocks and whether they are males or females. Try using the scan sampling method when you watch.

House Wren

Strategies for Success

There is no reason to suppose that a smaller bird would have a simpler life than a larger one, but nothing prepared me for the secrets of House Wrens. I suppose they look like they have something to hide when they scuttle under a log or into a leafy tangle, chattering a threat. But before I discovered House Wren mysteries, I watched the birds in my own backyard.

Two years ago a House Wren family took up residence in our backyard nest box. House Wrens find cavities for their nests and were happy to accept the one I provided, since they are common in city gardens.[1] I loved hearing the bubbling House Wren song from our backyard.

It is a universal bird truth that a female can lay only one egg a day. So if she plans on rearing five chicks, she will lay eggs for five days. If the mother wants all the chicks to hatch at the same time so she can rear them together, she simply refrains from incubating them until they are all laid, since they start developing only when warmed.

My backyard nest probably had six eggs, the average for second broods. Then the eggs needed about thirteen days of incubation, tight against the mother's skin, bare for this heat transfer because her feathers fall out. After that the chicks needed fifteen days of feeding before they could leave the nest, bringing us to the middle of August.

As I drank my coffee on the patio on August 10, I saw a tiny face peering out of the dark nest box and down at the leafy tangle of pole beans. I wondered if that was it, the last bird, or the first bird, or even a parent. I couldn't really tell, but the hesitation suggested that it was a chick facing its first leap. And once a chick leaves the nest, it never goes back. From then on it will shelter in the shrubbery, still begging and receiving food from its parents.

By August 12, no one visited the box anymore, so I figured the babies had taken the plunge. I took the box down from the concrete clothesline post. I looked inside. At first glance, it was empty. But wait! There was a single tiny egg still in the nest, an egg that never hatched. It was so tiny, tan with brown, almost maroon coloring more toward the broader end. Somehow it survived intact as its sisters and brothers stomped all over it, jostling for the insects the parents brought back, thousands of them over the couple of weeks they were in the nest.

An egg that never hatched holds promise unfulfilled. I gently picked up the egg and weighed it on my kitchen balance. It weighed 0.05 ounces, hardly more than a feather. I carefully opened it and discovered only liquid. No chick had developed in this egg.

House Wrens are anything but rare, occurring all through the Americas, and numbering about 160 million.[2] They are the songbird in the New World with the largest range. More than three million sightings of House Wrens have been recorded on eBird. I have seen and recorded them myself in eBird over three hundred times.

In North America, House Wrens migrate from the northern two-thirds to the southern third of the continent. They are common enough that if you think you saw this tiny little bird with a tail held at a right angle to its body disappearing into the brush, you probably did.

The oldest paper I found on House Wrens is by James Graham Cooper, who lived from 1830 to 1902.[3] He was an early western naturalist famous for paying attention to exactly where animals and plants lived and why they lived there. J. G. Cooper's paper on House Wrens is fewer than two full pages in the *Bulletin of the Nuttall Ornithological Club*, published in 1876. He observed unbanded House Wrens in his own backyard, where he saw a pair nesting in a box on top of a twelve-foot-high post.

Half a century later, in 1913, Samuel Prentiss Baldwin began to work on House Wrens after using traps to control House Sparrows. He banded a lot of birds with aluminum bands from the American Bird-Banding Association.[4] House Wrens were Baldwin's focus because they were so common in his nest boxes. From 1914 to 1937, Baldwin and his assistants banded 11,214 House Wrens. Besides banding birds, Baldwin and his assistants, including budding ornithologist Charles Kendeigh, watched them.

In his first paper in 1921, Baldwin debunked the idea that "most birds mate for life and each year return to the site of the previous nest to rear their young."[5] He reported that a pair he had banded reared a brood together, then separated, and each reared a new brood that same summer of 1915, a summer of war and turmoil in Europe. But what Baldwin wanted to know was whether this behavior of divorce and remarriage, as he put it, was common or rare in House Wrens.

Baldwin's next case is a story that began on July 4, 1917, three months after the United States had entered World War I. He found box 51 occupied by parents 44008 and 44009, which were finishing rearing their first brood, the only brood they reared that year, at least in his boxes. The following year Baldwin found 44008 back at box 51, but this time with mate 44100. The next year, on June 17, 1919, these two birds were again together, in box 19, two hundred feet from box 51. By 1920 Baldwin failed to recover any of the parents or chicks from any of these nests. Either they nested elsewhere or had perished.

Baldwin's stories go on for a total of five broods whose complex stories make it clear that House Wrens often switch mates both within and between years. From the nests he watched, Baldwin was also able to calculate that incubation is thirteen or fourteen days and fledging is after about fourteen days. If he had not banded the birds and caught them repeatedly, Baldwin would not have been able to document all this mate switching.

As the years went on, Baldwin compiled his thousands of observations to generate a more complete view of his population of House Wrens. Charles Kendeigh also continued to work increasingly on the House Wrens. Even today, if you look at the *Birds of the World* chapter on House Wrens, one paper keeps coming up, by Kendeigh and Baldwin, published in 1937, the year before Baldwin died. This paper, published in *Ecological Monographs*, talks about abundance in passerine birds in the title but is really all about House Wrens.[6] They document relative numbers of males and females, number of broods, young raised, nest initiation dates, whether they had more than one mate at a time, and population. A careful Slow Birder could observe many of these behaviors in their own backyard.

The next big study I found was by the cheerful Charlie Thompson. I talked to him on September 15, 2020, from Leland, Michigan, where I was getting some time to walk along the beach looking for Petoskey stones after teaching remotely through Zoom. What Charlie wanted to do was a long-term study in nest boxes, just like his hero David Lack had done with Great Tits (related to our chickadees) in Oxford. A long-term study avoids the vagaries of a given year, reveals patterns over a bird's lifetime, and makes rare but important events detectable. And the nest boxes reduce predation, which stymies long-term studies.

Thompson put nest boxes on poles with metal sheaths, protecting the eggs or chicks from a snake's gullet. The Illinois State Wren Crew has been checking nest boxes since 1980 at the Mackinaw Reserve, about twenty miles northwest of Bloomington, Illinois. More than forty years! Why, my daughter was born in 1980, and I've switched study organisms from wasps and bees to tiny amoebae.

If you want to find Charlie Thompson between early April and early September on a Monday, Tuesday, Wednesday, or Sunday between 6:00 a.m. and noon, you will need to go to the reserve, for he will be on wren duty. Scott Sakaluk takes the team on the other days and has since the 2004 spring season, when this famous cricket wrangler fell in love with a bird.

On Mondays and Thursdays they census all 820 nest boxes to determine the nesting stage. The other days of the week they catch, band, and weigh unmarked adults or babies and bleed previously uncaught individuals because they can use the DNA in blood to identify chicks' parents. They use an ancient database program written in dBASE4 where they enter each day's observations, and according to nest condition and location in the study plot, it spits out a list of tasks for each nest for the following days. When one of their teammates, Keith Bowers, moved to the University of Memphis, one of the first things he did was re-create the dBASE4 program in Excel, which he could use with any computer.

Forty years of data can answer lots of specific questions about what wrens do. They can reveal the answer to Charlie's first question, inspired by David Lack:[7] Do House Wrens lay the number of eggs that result in the largest number of chicks they can actually rear? Lack famously hypothesized that this was the case, that birds lay the number of chicks they can rear to adulthood, and not a chick more nor a chick less. Lack's hypothesis, as it is called, is one of the most famous of all ideas about behavior. It has been tested in many species, most of which do not support the idea at its simplest level.[8] Parents in most of the forty-two studies that Eric VanderWerf looked at could rear more chicks. Whether they paid other costs like earlier senescence is not easy to answer in most birds.

House Wrens are a great species with which to address this classic question because essentially the whole population in an area can be coaxed into nest boxes and because they generally lay a lot of small eggs, usually between five and eight. This makes it easier to add or subtract an egg without completely changing nest dynamics, as would be the case if the birds laid only a couple of eggs. Mark Finke, Dona Milinkovich, and Charlie Thompson identified 560 nests they could use for this study and then treated them in one of four different ways. They had two control treatments. The first was to simply do nothing to the nests. But it could be that any manipulation has a cost, so the second control they did was to switch chicks from one nest to another without changing the total number of chicks. The two experimental treatments were to either add or take away a single chick of about the same weight as the chicks in the nest naturally. Lack's hypothesis predicts that the nests with the natural number of eggs would rear the most chicks to fledging.

The result was that there was no indication that more chicks led to fewer chicks reared to fledging. The House Wrens could rear more babies than they had naturally produced and everyone turned out fine. Furthermore, there was no sign that the parents suffered from the extra work, at least if they looked at their success in rearing a second brood that same summer. I thought Thompson would have been disappointed by this result, but he told me otherwise: "I actually hoped to disprove hypotheses, so I wasn't really disappointed. I am reminded of a reviewer's comment on an NSF proposal I submitted back in the 1990s: 'Thompson has told us what doesn't limit clutch size, when is he going to tell us what does?' My thought at the time was that I had always thought disproving hypotheses was the way progress is made in science." Charlie Thompson is clearly the ultimate Slow Birder, returning day after day, year after year, to the same population of House Wrens and documenting their lives.

Does Thompson's finding mean that the House Wrens of Mackinaw should be laying more eggs? Yes, is what the experiment tells us. And that is what they published. But it is not the last word. After all, in the experiment, they added eggs to the nest so the wrens got extra chicks to rear without having to lay more eggs. What if there is a cost to producing the extra eggs?

To look at this, Christine Hodges, Keith Bowers, and the rest of the Wren Crew did more experiments.[9, 10] Instead of increasing the number of chicks to be reared, they tricked the females into laying more eggs. They did this by removing eggs after the first egg, so the female would continue to lay, ultimately causing them to lay four extra eggs. The control wrens did not lay any extra eggs.

And then they found a cost. The females who laid more eggs were not as likely to start a second clutch in the same season. Those that did produced smaller clutches. And the following year, the females that had been tricked into laying extra eggs produced fewer eggs and fewer fledglings. So it seems that the measurable cost to females is actually from laying those tiny eggs.

David Lack died March 12, 1973, of non-Hodgkin's lymphoma at sixty-two, so he could not have known about what I think of as the biggest behavioral discovery of all, something that has changed our view of songbirds. It is no wonder that it was hard to discover, for when watching a nest of House Wrens, or nearly any other songbird, what you see is a devoted couple rearing a clutch of noisy, hungry young. Their begging is incessant. From my seat on the patio, I could tell when a parent arrived at the nest box by the pole beans by the sounds of the chicks' begging. It looked just like a monogamous family with oh so many young, and loyal parents trying to keep them fed, warm, and alive. It is easy to think that mothers and fathers have the same interests and the same dedication to their helpless chicks.

But mothers and fathers do not have identical interests. Natural selection operates on them separately, favoring traits in each that increase the spread of that trait in the next generation. A trait that caused the father to swallow an extra morsel to increase his chance of surviving to the next year might be favored. Or he might take a little time out from parental duties to see if he could mate with a female next door. Any chick he fathered outside the pair bond would be a real bonus, costing only the act of mating and not the cost of rearing the chick. Likewise, the female might eat those extra morsels. Or she might find a genetically more fit male next door and mate with him, putting her genes in an environment that made them more likely to spread in the next generation. It is a complex dance between the partners who have evolved to care for the chicks assiduously so they survive, but have also evolved to profit from other opportunities and to preserve themselves to live another year.

In House Wrens it turns out that males and females explore other breeding options while sticking to their social partner for rearing chicks. Males arrive first on a nesting ground, identify possible nest cavities, and advertise them to the later-arriving females. When females make their choice of a mate, they are choosing him, his nesting site, and the caterpillars and insects of the territory that will later nourish the young. It is a package deal, perhaps not as different from humans as we like to think. They court each other and settle down to family life. But either might still keep an eye out for a quick mating opportunity nearby.

But why would a male, the one whose nest box a female has occupied, tolerate a female that philanders with a neighbor? I suppose there are a lot of answers. First, he may not know. Second, he may have no other, better options than to keep caring for these young, given that most males father at least some of the young in their nest.

To see whether House Wrens philander with their neighbors, Scott Johnson and Brian Masters of Towson University teamed up with the Wren Crew and used data from two time periods, 1991–1993 and 2004–2006. During that time the Wren Crews at the Mackinaw River had observed, banded, and bled 521 broods from 270 unique females.[11] This included an impressive 3,291 eggs laid, of which 3,123 hatched, producing 2,345 young available to be bled for parentage studies. It turned out that 15 percent of the chicks were the product of an extra-pair liaison by the female.

Female wrens are not going to mate with a neighbor just for the thrill of it. After all, there are potential costs to doing so. Her own mate might retaliate in some wren-like way. She may be infected by a disease or parasite by mating with another male. She could be picked off by a predator while mating, or simply lose time from foraging. It is worth remembering that a bird is nearly always hungry. So for philandering to evolve in wrens, there should be a benefit, and with any luck, patient researchers should be able to figure out a way to detect it.

A likely benefit would be that the neighbor is of higher genetic quality, meaning that his progeny would also be better. They might be stronger, or sing more mellifluously, or be more resistant to illness. An alternative to a genetic hypothesis could be that males might tolerate a neighbor foraging on his territory if he had mated with them. Keith Bowers, the University of Memphis professor who modified the wren checklist program for Excel, tried to figure this out.

The Bowers group discovered that females were less faithful to their mates if they were mated to young males in their first season or to males more than three years old.[12] Males in the sweet spot of two to three years old had females that were more faithful. This might seem puzzling because age is not a genetic trait, but in a short-lived species like House Wrens, just living longer is a sign of genes that enhance survival, something females should desire for their progeny.

Maybe females always try to mate with other males, but males in their prime are better at preventing it. It could be that all females would benefit from more tolerant neighbors for foraging, something this study did not look at. As is so often the case in science, getting one piece of the puzzle answered leads to new questions. Science is usually slow.

Scott Johnson and his group had another question. They wanted to know when females were most likely to mate outside the pair bond. Was it at the beginning of egg laying or at the end? Johnson did this study on the ranches of Sheridan County, Wyoming, with nest boxes.[13] They watched 93 nests with 681 eggs in 2002 and 2003 and numbered the eggs as they were laid, one per day. They weighed all the eggs and discovered that the first-laid eggs were heavier. Then in 2006 and 2007 they did DNA tests and weighed the chicks so they could know which were laid first. They determined paternity in 79 broods and found that 63 percent had only within-pair offspring and 3 percent had only extra-pair offspring. In 34 percent of broods there were both kinds of chicks, and so extra-pair young could be compared in the same nest with within-pair young. They found that those extra-pair chicks were laid early in the sequence. So it seems that females mate with others at the beginning of the nesting season.

Some males go one step further and attract two females to two different nest boxes on their territory.[14] Johnson and L. Henry Kermott put two or three nest boxes with twenty-five to forty meters between them in each of ten to fifteen locations on the Quarter Circle A and Gallatin Ranches near Big Horn, Sheridan County, Wyoming. The investigators compared the rate of polygyny in 1987, when they added no nest boxes, with that in 1985 and 1986, when they added nest boxes.

They discovered that even when they added no nest boxes, a few males, three to be exact, out of thirty-one, attracted second females to second natural cavities. Males in the years with nest boxes attracted more, eight of fifteen. But at least this shows the behavior is natural, not an artifact of the nest boxes.

Johnson has a lot of research to be proud of now that he has retired to Sedona, Arizona, so I asked him which of his many studies gave him the most pleasure. His answer surprised me. It was a study he published in 2008 in the journal *Behaviour* on an intriguing question: How do males know the eggs have hatched?[15] This is a question that gets inside the mind of the male and has immediate behavioral consequences. After all, the female does all the brooding, keeping the chicks warm, and the male is responsible for bringing in the food. So it is crucial for him to know when to start bringing the food to hungry newborn nestlings.

Johnson and his team considered four hypotheses. First, the females might signal to their mates that the eggs have hatched. Of course, they do chirp at each other in ways with more meaning than we can understand. Second, the male might hear the chicks directly. Third, he might observe changes in the female's behavior, perhaps bringing food to the chicks herself or removing the eggshells from the nest. Finally, he might need direct proof of hatching; he may enter the nest box and behold his chicks.

To test these hypotheses, Johnson and his team found twenty-six nests, banded the adults with color bands, and began to videotape from about ten feet from the nests during all daylight hours, with cameras good enough to see both the adults' leg bands and the prey items they brought in. They added a little perch to the nest boxes so the birds might pause there and give the camera more time to record the birds. Normally a perch is not a good idea, because it helps predators. The cue they looked for was the change to consistent feeding trips, indicating the male knew the chicks had hatched.

It turns out that the female does not sing or behave differently after the chicks hatch, so Johnson and his team ruled out that hypothesis. Johnson said: "At many nests the males actually saw females carrying eggshells out of the box or food into the box, but surprisingly that did not stimulate males to start bringing food to the young. Instead, in all but three cases, the males did not start bringing food to the nest until they actually had a chance to detect the young themselves by sight, sound, or perhaps smell."

This study is careful and interesting because it gets at the mind of the male and what makes him change his behavior to care for chicks when before he had been only bringing food to the brooding female and rarely entering the nest cavity. That he requires direct evidence of the presence of hatchlings for a behavioral shift lets us imagine what goes through his mind when the speckled eggs have broken and tiny, naked chicks beg for food.

Sometimes the nest boxes themselves can be useful in understanding House Wrens, since cavities are naturally in short supply. Males fight for the best cavities, and the most successful ones can even claim a territory with more than one nest site. But this creates a dilemma for researchers interested in separating male quality from territory quality in the choices females make. Natalie Dubois and her team at Michigan State University's Kellogg Biological Station did a really cool manipulation that achieved just this separation.[16] They put in a transect of nest boxes along a forest edge and grouped them in sets of three that were only about twenty feet apart, so a male could dominate all three boxes in a set. The sets were three hundred feet apart, so any given male could control only three boxes. Then the team plugged the nest entrances of two of the three nest boxes, so the males had only one box to claim when they set up their territories. After the males had set up their territories and claimed the one box with an opening, the experiment began. Dubois removed the stoppers in the other nests from half the territories, giving these males a bonus of two more possible nesting sites. They made sure that the territories without stoppers were equivalent to those with stoppers by pairing them up according to the date the male arrived.

What would the females do? It turned out that females whose mates had extra nest boxes laid on average half an egg more. They also produced slightly more sons. So the way that Dubois and her team interpreted this is that the females considered their mates to be of higher quality if they had empty nest boxes in their territory and therefore laid more eggs, figuring that the males could care for the extra young and that they were worth the females' extra effort. These males could not actually have been of higher quality, since it was the human experimenters who bestowed the extra nest boxes by opening their entrances, something the males could not have predicted.

One of the big advancements in ornithology is the increased appreciation of what female birds can do. One surprising thing is that females sing, something that used to be thought to happen only in birds that stay in the tropics and don't migrate.

Charlie Thompson says he has heard females singing only four or five times ever. Scott Johnson and Henry Kermott were very surprised to find female song. Johnson said it was one of the cool things they discovered because they went out every day and spent hours and hours carefully watching House Wrens.

From 1985 to 1989 on a couple of ranches in Wyoming, Johnson and Kermott recorded songs of males systematically in the morning during the time males set up territories.[17] Females they recorded by chance as they recorded the males. Out of the seven pairs they recorded, they heard six females sing. They said females sang in variable ways, with some songs short and sounding like a "human squeal" and others longer and more like male songs in their composition. Females sang when soliciting copulation or when males were absent. During the incubation stage, the females sang near the nest, particularly if males did not. The females also sang if the male paired with an additional female in another nest box. One female sang in an attempt to evict a female from a nest box. Another female, that they called OC-733, sang male-like songs near the male and when she exited the nest box while she was building the nest. She kept working at it and singing, even lining the nest with feathers, singing in alteration with the male. Ultimately both birds disappeared without ever properly nesting. But don't think she was a total oddball, because the next two years, 1987 and 1988, she came back to the area and produced normal broods, interestingly with no singing at all. Were her hormones out of whack that first season?

Cara Krieg discovered that female song was common in her southeastern Michigan population and figured out why females sang in her population.[18] She considered three possibilities: that females sang to communicate with their mate, to solicit him for mating, or to defend against other wrens that might threaten her eggs or young. Krieg checked the wren boxes nearly every day during 2012 and 2013 and noted song when it occurred, being careful not to count the chattering alarm calls that wrens so often make when people are nearby.

She found that 72 out of the 108 females sang at some point. Of these, 29 percent sang spontaneously. But even more, 65 percent sang in response to a recorded playback of either a male or a female, or another species. The spontaneous song occurred mostly when the females had just started laying eggs, particularly on the second day of egg laying. Females sang back a lot when there was a recording playing, particularly of a female. It seems like female song caused other females to sing in response, particularly in the egg-laying stage. This is important because it also turns out that singing females lost fewer eggs to marauding neighboring females who might come in and stab and kill the eggs. So females sing to tell other females to stay away, and singing females are better at keeping the egg-stabbers away. Clearly the female House Wrens viewed other females as a threat and a greater threat than other males.

I had a nice conversation on Zoom with Cara Krieg. She is a busy new assistant professor at the University of Scranton, in Joe Biden's hometown and a place that is reviving after a long coal depression. She set up House Wren boxes in nearby Lackawanna State Park to keep up with her research passion.

One of the experiments that Krieg did turned the females on one another in ways so fierce that Krieg wonders if she would have done the experiment had she known. The experiment was simple. She removed the nest boxes of half the females early in the season, hoping to increase competition. And so it did. But the wrens did not stop at singing battles. They invaded the existing nests of other females and punctured their eggs in attempts to take over the nest boxes. And it turned out that the boxes were what the females cared about, not the males. Sharing a male was fine. But sharing nest boxes was not possible, so the other had to go or a female could not breed that season. Many House Wrens only survive to breed in one season, so it was no wonder they turned their sharp beaks to the tiny eggs of their rivals.

Female song is not so easy to find, but Krieg was lucky. She happened to be recording males when one day she realized that there was a female singing as she recorded. She could see her, so there was no doubt about the unusual song. Krieg could then use this recording of a female song to trick other females into thinking their territories were being invaded. It followed her beliefs about being a biologist: take down all the information you can, because who knows what might turn out to be useful later.

Krieg also learned to distinguish some of the songs. When the male is courting and has no female, just a lovely empty nest box in which he has begun a nest with a few twigs, he sings and sings. If his song is successful and a female comes to inspect the home he is so proud of, his notes get squeaky and high, and Krieg knows what is going on. She can even watch him lead the female to his box, should she not already have found it.

Once the female has accepted the nest box, has finished building the nest, and is incubating eggs, exposing her naked skin to warm the eggs, then the male uses song to warn her. Krieg's own work was an example of this. She needed to band the females and later the babies. The males had already been banded. Time and again she would sneak up to the nest to put a net over the entrance to catch the brooding female only to have the male warn her, so the female fled at the last minute. There was no way these birds could understand Krieg would take a drop of blood, weigh the bird in a sling, put a couple of leg bands on, and then let them be. And of course they also could not know that was it not for Krieg, there would be no fancy nest box to use.

I asked Krieg if she used eBird in her research, and she said she did. It is a huge help, she said, telling her when to get ready for the birds in the spring. She could watch them moving north along with the records of the eBirders.

House Wrens may be dull looking to some, but I love their brown feathers speckled with black. More than that, I love their attitude. They are noisy and busy, and they stop at nothing to rear the best babies they can. They have two broods a year. They switch partners readily, even cheating on each other early in the season. But when there are babies in the nest, they get tended to. Mom keeps them warm when they cannot do it themselves. Hang a wren box and for a few months of the summer the entertainment will be constant. If I had a summer free, perhaps I would join Cara Krieg or Charlie Thompson on their House Wren projects and travel from box to box myself, banding, watching, and also hearing all the other northern springtime birds.

HOUSE WREN ACTIVITIES
FOR SLOW BIRDERS

1. **Learn their song.** House Wrens are easy to miss, but their fluid melody is a wonder to listen to. Once you know their song, they will seem to be everywhere, and you can patiently track them down.

2. **Learn where they are.** Once you know the House Wren song, you have a powerful tool to see where they are in the environment. On

your walks, listen for House Wrens. What kinds of habitat do they like best? How close together are their territories—something you can tell by walking early in the morning and listening the whole way. House Wrens generally like edge or even field habitats, but if there are no nest boxes, they will need natural cavities to nest in.

3. **Put out nest boxes.** House Wrens nest in cavities. Put out a nest box with an opening between 1⅛ and 1½ inches in diameter that is 4 to 6 inches above the floor of the box. The floor should be about 4 inches square. Put the box 4 to 10 feet high, with some vegetation nearby and some shade for the box in the hot part of the day. Just do your best. I had to buy some big metal washers to keep squirrels from enlarging the entrance. You might want to put it on a stake with a metal baffle to deter snakes, particularly if you live in a rural area.

House Wrens are one of the best birds for birdhouses. If you want to make a study of nest box use, you could put out several of them, perhaps varying location or opening size, and see which the birds prefer. Sometimes males like to present more than one nest box to a female. Then see which they like and how they differ from the others.

4. **Join the Smithsonian's Neighborhood Nestwatch program.** This is only available in some cities, so check if yours is included. Then researchers will work with you to enhance your nest box observations. If you are not in a Neighborhood Nestwatch city, it is always worth recording your observations on eBird, noting in the comments section what you see the birds doing.

5. **Keep a diary of nest box activity.** You can watch the coming and going at a nest box, using binoculars to see what they are bringing

in. Keep track of how the brood develops and where the chicks go when they fledge. There are also cameras you can put in nest boxes to see exactly what is going on. Keep doing this over the years and see if their start dates change with temperature or rainfall.

6. **Teach others about House Wrens.** Once you have learned their song and where they nest, share your knowledge with others and encourage them to also put out nest boxes.

Dark–Eyed Junco

A Bird Worthy of a Lifetime of Study

When the first Dark-eyed Juncos show up in St. Louis, you know that winter has really come. Their white bellies look snow-brushed, their gray backs a warm shawl for the coldest nights. They twitter and hide, flashing their white outer tail feathers as they scurry into a pine tree or under the dead grasses. All winter they are common, so their absence is a sign of spring.

The last Dark-eyed Junco of the winter I saw at home on April 8. They had been here since October 24, and I saw them most days in between. I have a special fondness for these sweet birds, so often fluffed out to stay warm in the winter cold. Here we have the color variant called Slate-colored Junco. When I was a child in Michigan, our local bird was named the Slate-colored Junco, but now this is only one subspecies grouped under Dark-eyed Juncos. Dark-eyed Juncos branched off from Yellow-eyed Juncos, which occur mostly in Mexico, after the Last Glacial Maximum, when the glaciers of North America extended the farthest south, about eighteen thousand years ago. The junco split came as they flew north to different places, with those flying to Oregon to breed separating from those flying to Michigan, for example.[1]

In most of the United States, including St. Louis, we have Slate-colored Juncos only in winter. They nest in the cooler climates of Canada and the Northeast, extending down the Appalachian spine. The West has other subspecies, like Oregon Juncos, for much of the year.

Here in my winter garden, I watch the juncos jockey for position under the feeder for fallen seeds. I wonder what noise or sudden movement inspires them to run under the cover of the dead prairie grasses and flowers. I can see how fluffed out they are when it gets really cold. But I love to think of them on their breeding territories doing all the things that bring the next generation of juncos to the world.

When I think of Dark-eyed Juncos, one scientist comes to mind above all others—one scientist and her generations of students and collaborators. It is Ellen Ketterson of Indiana University in Bloomington. She is vivacious, determined, and an impassioned speaker at scientific meetings.

Ketterson was smart to do her Ph.D. research right at home, on the wintering Dark-eyed Juncos of Bloomington. She did not casually watch them as you or I might, with a cup of coffee as we look out a wintry window. Instead, Ketterson was scientific about it. She measured out a plot six feet by eight feet and kept it evenly covered with cracked corn and birdseed. She watched the plot carefully from six feet away.[2]

First Ketterson observed and counted the juncos, which started to come as soon as the food was put out. The most she saw coming to the seeded plot at a time was thirty birds, way more than I see beneath my feeder, but I don't put out grains so systematically.

Ketterson recorded the feeding behavior in her little rectangle. For a month, between January 24 and February 25, 1974, she observed the birds in thirty-nine periods of thirty minutes each. First she counted the number of birds in the feeding area once a minute. She also noted every time one bird displaced another. This is an aggressive interaction, because the bird that leaves loses access to food. She tallied these encounters for the thirty-minute period. Background data were time, temperature, cloud cover, wind, and snow on the ground.

Dark-eyed Juncos were most often on the plot early in the day or when it was extra cold or cloudy. They were also the most aggressive to each other at those times. Ketterson found that females displaced males only 14 percent of the time, always during snow and exceptional cold. I guess it is usually better for females to simply find an uncontested morsel.

Dominance is one of the most studied kinds of behaviors in animals. Exactly what causes some to defer to others is also well understood, as in the junco case, where females are lower in the hierarchy than males. If you come back to thinking about winter dominance after reading the rest of this chapter, you might wonder if testosterone is not involved, as it is in the breeding season interactions I'll tell you about soon. And indeed, this would be a reasonable guess, but it would be incorrect. As Rebecca Holberton, Kenneth Able, and John Wingfield showed, testosterone was not a factor in dominance among competing pairs of juncos in winter.[3] Instead, increased white in the tail feathers of males that made them look older than they were increased their rank. The testosterone story is a summer one, not one for winter juncos looking for seeds.

My daughter and her husband now live on the woodsy northern edge of Bloomington, where they are both professors at Indiana University, in sociology and geography, respectively. Someday I will buy some cracked corn and measure out a six-by-eight-foot square near their living room window and determine how many juncos come at a time. We can also look for displacements, seeing if there is dominance, though without banding we could not tell whether repeated displacements are by the same birds, only how often they occur. I wonder if there are still banded juncos in Bloomington from Ketterson's more recent studies. Of course I could also try the experiment at home in St. Louis.

Those winter birds have a surprise for us, for males and females, young and old, do not necessarily migrate to the same places. A quick think on migration might suggest larger, older males would go the farthest, and smaller, younger females the least far. After all, migrating is hard, isn't it?

Well, my guess as to which would migrate the farthest was exactly wrong. It is the females that go far. In winter there are only 20 percent females in northern states, compared with 75 percent females in Texas.[4] This pattern is true not only for Dark-eyed Juncos; it also holds for Tree Sparrows, Song Sparrows, Northern Mockingbirds,

Mourning Doves, and Yellow-bellied Sapsuckers. Further studies suggest the reason for this pattern.

For understanding migration, Ketterson did a more complicated study in Bloomington, one that looked at those dominance interactions in more detail. She looked at the young birds born that year, watching 191 interactions of known-age birds.[5] Then she watched 85 interactions in which an older bird interacted with a younger one and found that the older bird won 76 percent of the interactions.

So it might make sense for birds that lose dominance contests, the younger, smaller ones, which includes the females, to move farther south for food where they can escape the large, dominant males. Males might migrate less far, so they can claim a good breeding ground early.

Sufficient food can make the difference between starving and living, particularly over cold winter nights. Birds are always at the brink of starvation since the demands of flight prevent them from storing much fat. It is a tight balance. But they must always eat enough to survive the night if possible. It is worth determining exactly how much weight juncos lose overnight, something Ketterson and fellow animal behaviorist Val Nolan, who much later became her husband, decided to determine.[6]

With all the appropriate permits in place, they caught eighty-seven Dark-eyed Juncos between January 28 and March 1 in the late afternoon, around 4:30 p.m. They weighed the birds, brought them into the lab, weighed them again, measured their wing length, and determined their sex. The birds had mostly pooped before the lab weigh-in, as stressed birds often do, so that should not contribute to any overnight weight loss. Then they put the birds into paper bags in a dark room kept at 39 degrees Fahrenheit, the temperature of your refrigerator. They left the birds in the dark, cold, quiet until about 8:00 a.m.; so they had been in there an average of nearly thirteen hours, similar to the dark hours they would have experienced outside.

How much weight had they lost under these fairly ideal conditions, where it wasn't too cold and they couldn't waste energy by moving around? Overnight they lost about 7 percent of their total body weight. For a 160 pound person, that would be like losing a bit more than 11 pounds overnight!

But the juncos were fine the next morning when they were released. Other studies indicated that they can lose up to 30 percent of their body weight and not die. At the loss rate Ketterson and Nolan saw, juncos could fast for a bit over two days before dying. So let's hope they don't run into any big storms, for birds need to eat often!

At some point Ketterson hankered after seeing juncos on their breeding grounds. She had become captivated by work she read about on the hormonal control of behavior, mostly from John Wingfield's group, and wanted to see how hormones impacted juncos.

A subspecies of Dark-eyed Junco nests in the high Appalachians south into Virginia and North Carolina. A convenient place to study them is Mountain Lake Biological Station, maintained by the University of Virginia. It has housing and labs, perfect for field research. It is only four miles from the Wind Rock parking lot for the Appalachian Trail, where station visitors go for sunsets, since the biological station itself is nestled in a valley. Southwest from the station, a bit under two miles away, is Mountain Lake Lodge, where *Dirty Dancing*, the 1987 film with Jennifer Grey and Patrick Swayze, was filmed.

Ketterson was taking a big step from her winter work on juncos. But she was still interested in how animals behaved to benefit themselves. Now she extended that curiosity to explore the mechanisms underneath adaptive behavior. She had one mechanism in particular in mind: the role of hormones, especially the role of testosterone in achieving behavior that benefited the actor, typically the male, though females have testosterone too. Ellen Ketterson was inspired by the work of John Wingfield.[7] The challenge theory states that testosterone causes increased aggression in males only under certain circumstances, such as when males are competing for females or setting up their territories. Would this apply to Dark-eyed Juncos, Ketterson wondered?

Besides a question, Ketterson also had a technique in mind: experimental augmentation of testosterone.[8] This was done by catching males and surgically implanting a narrow three-quarter-inch-long tube, either packed with testosterone or, for the controls, left empty. It is important to do the surgery and implantation of an empty tube as a control to rule out the implantation procedure itself as the cause of any behavioral change. In the years they were studying testosterone, Ketterson and her team put the implants in under the left wing in late May to June, when nests either had eggs or young chicks, and removed them after July 15, after the chicks had fledged.

Ketterson wondered what might happen to male behavior at several levels. Would juncos match the results of other studies and show that with elevated testosterone, males became more aggressive, defended larger territories, and got more mates? And would there also be costs to testosterone treatment? Maybe such males would offer less paternal care and instead use their time to mate with females outside their pair bond.

Untreated Dark-eyed Junco males have testosterone peaks in early spring. The experimenters hastened and increased that peak with the testosterone implants. Besides the testosterone manipulation, Ketterson and her team took blood samples when they did the implantation and when the birds were recaptured between the end of May and the middle of July. These blood samples let them evaluate how much testosterone was in their blood and also do paternity studies to determine who fathered each of the chicks.

As they expected, the testosterone-implanted males had more testosterone in their blood when they were recaptured. Those males also weighed less and had less fat a month after implantation.

But what about the nesting behavior of the testosterone-treated males?[9, 10] The number of eggs laid by mates of testosterone-treated males was essentially identical to that of mates of control males (3.7 for testosterone fathers versus 3.6 for control fathers). However, from testosterone-treated males, 2.8 fledglings survived to leave the nest, while for untreated males 3.1 fledglings survived to leave the nest—not a big difference, but a statistically significant one. This might have been due to feeding differences.[11] They found that males treated with testosterone fed their young fewer times per hour, three times instead of four. But the chicks apparently did not suffer because the mothers compensated by feeding them more often, eight times an hour compared with five times, respectively. This was a result Ellen Ketterson told me she loved because it showed how attentive the females were to their chicks.

The biggest behavioral difference between treated and untreated males was early on when there were small nestlings in the nest. What were the testosterone-treated males doing with the time they saved by feeding less? Ketterson found that instead of feeding their young, testosterone-treated males sang more. In the early nestling stage, they sang about seventy songs an hour, while the males with the sham implant sang fewer than forty songs an hour. The patterns were similar later in the nesting cycle.

Does that extra singing actually bring in more females? To answer this question, they presented females a choice of males in an outside aviary.[12] The female was introduced to each male privately for thirty minutes. Then she was given the chance to choose between a control male and a testosterone-treated male in a cage with two dividers, where the female was in the central cage. As predicted, the female stayed closer to the male that sang more. In the wild this could mean she would be more likely to mate outside the pair bond with him, indicating testosterone treatments may have an advantage in mating outside the pair bond. That assumption could be looked at directly.

Wendy Reed and the Ketterson group did just this, exploring the overall effects of testosterone treatment and particularly whether it increased a male's ability to mate with females other than his social mate.[13] It turned out that all that singing by testosterone-treated males gave them the advantage they predicted. Reed found that males treated with testosterone fathered about 1.5 more young in nests that were not their own if the males were more than two years old. If the testosterone-treated males were under two years old, they gained only about 0.6 young. By contrast, untreated males had only 0.6 young in nests not their own if they were two or more years old, and only 0.2 extra young if they were under two years old.

Taken together, these results make me wonder why males don't evolve to have more testosterone. After all, the female makes up for the difference in feeding early, and the males pick it back up later in the season, when there are fewer females at the stage of egg laying. Testosterone did not seem to result in fewer independent young in the male's own nest. And treated males have success with neighboring females. This is a question Ketterson told me she has also spent a lot of time wondering about.

I suppose it is a trade-off, because there are also other costs to having high testosterone. An important function of males is to help defend the nest against predators like chipmunks. The testosterone-treated males were slower to defend the nest when the researchers introduced a stuffed chipmunk. But as far as the Ketterson team could measure, natural nests did not suffer more predation when the male was testosterone-treated, so this is unlikely to be the answer.

Testosterone-treated males used up their winter fat more quickly. They have higher corticosterone, the adrenal stress steroid, which could make them more vulnerable to disease. They may delay the pre-winter molt as they try to attract more females or care for late young. All told, testosterone-treated males survive the summer less well, with a 49 percent survival rate compared with a 65 percent survival rate of untreated males. Winter survival did not differ between the two treatments, though by winter Ketterson would have removed the testosterone tubes.

There is much more to tell about Dark-eyed Juncos. I could talk about the finding that males copy songs from neighbors, but those songs are of less value in attracting mates than a male's own invented songs.[14] Or I could tell of the study of Elise Ferree, who found that females with more white in their tail feathers had more sons.[15] Or I could tell you about something all birds have: the uropygial or preen oil gland.

Did you know that birds carry their own beauty oil with them at all times? When you see them working over their feathers with their beaks, they are applying this oil, which is secreted from the preen oil gland, located at the base of the tail, on the top.

Danielle Whittaker, also with the Ketterson group at the time, studied preen oil gland compounds and their impact on juncos beginning in the summer of 2008.[16] In that year she captured juncos from April 15 to May 15 and collected preen oil by rubbing a small capillary tube on their glands, which caused them to secrete the oil. Then Danielle analyzed the chemical compounds in the preen oil, particularly the volatile ones that other birds might smell.

Females preferred certain volatile compounds in the preen oil, causing the males that had them to be more attractive to females. Smells differed between males and females. Birds aren't generally thought of as animals that use odor much, especially compared with mammals, but this story has more to it.

The next thing that Whittaker found was that it was not the odor of the preen oil but of the bacteria that lived in the gland. The odors actually came from bacteria that specialized in eating the oils in the uropygial gland.[17] Whittaker found she could change the smell profile of a bird by treating it with antibiotics that killed the bacteria and the odor profile they generated. She also found that the bacteria that colonized the uropygial glands came from the environment. Since the mothers keep the chicks warm, they are in much closer contact with them. So, not surprisingly, the bacteria in the chicks' uropygial glands resemble their mothers' bacteria more than their fathers'. Likewise, when the researchers moved an egg from one nest to another, it grew up with a bacterial community like their foster mother's, not their genetic mother's. This is a kind of inheritance, but it is not genetic.

It is summer now, in the dog days, weeks past the solstice and before Sirius becomes visible in the eastern sky near Orion. The juncos are far north of me, caring for fledglings, perhaps tending to a second brood, with little thought of the coming migration south. Before that happens, the adults will undergo their autumn molt so they can fly south on strong wings and stay warm with fresh down.

The coming of winter marks a pause in the circle of life. Even at the beginning I'm impatient for spring to come again. But the sighting of the first Dark-eyed Junco is a moment of joy, a time when I slow down and prepare to appreciate the slower pace of winter.

DARK-EYED JUNCO ACTIVITIES
FOR SLOW BIRDERS

1. **Get to know the juncos.** If you are in the eastern part of the United States, you will have the slate-colored form and mostly see them only in winter, unless you are in the Northeast or down the Appalachian ridge. Males are more gray, and females are more brown on top. Learn their lovely trilling song and the way they fly low through the bushes, their white outer tail feathers flaring.

2. **Watch for dominance interactions.** Put some sunflower seeds down in an area you can watch, maybe three feet square, and see if the birds fight for the seeds. Do the males win in these interactions, moving onto areas and pushing away the females or juveniles? See

if you can keep track for ten minutes. See if you find different patterns at different times of day.

3. **Optimize foraging.** Juncos prefer to feed under shelter or farther away from the house. Put out several different patches of food, perhaps some close to the house, some farther away, and some under dead grass stems. Then count the number of juncos in each place. Do it several times, perhaps at fifteen-minute intervals. Another thing you could do is put out different food densities in the same habitat. Will the males congregate in the most dense patch? Where are there more dominance interactions? Count the birds at different times, or watch for interactions, always being careful to note their sex.

4. **Note predator avoidance.** Scatter food evenly over a really large area that might accommodate all the juncos there. They might then spread out so each can get all the food they want. But they probably won't, because there is safety in numbers. See if they clump together even when the food is scattered. Try to count the numbers in different clumps. What is the geometry of their distribution? If you scatter food all through some underbrush, do they clump less?

Flynn Park

My Neighborhood Patch

Maybe you have the perfect patch for birding near your home. It might be small but border a running creek. It could be a southern bayou or a swampy protected wetland. There might be a tangle of vegetation you have carved a narrow path into. It might be a place that attracts lots of birds.

Unfortunately my nearest park is nothing like that. I have a city park. The vegetation is mostly mowed lawn under scattered trees, with a few unkempt grassy areas. There are no shrubs, unless you count the sprouts from a fallen locust tree the city will soon remove.

It is called Flynn Park and is only a block and a half from my home in the little city adjacent to St. Louis proper. St. Louis is the kind of old city that did not expand as the population grew, so only the core of this citified area is really St. Louis. I live about half a mile from that core boundary.

University City, so called because it is on the northern side of Washington University, acquired the land for Flynn Park in 1923 when the subdivision was mostly built. It is a small urban park built in 1936 as part of Roosevelt's New Deal. Its 6.61 acres hold an elementary school, a playground, a little school vegetable garden, a small soccer pitch, five tennis courts, and trees scattered in a lawn with no bushy understory. I wish it were more wild.

I usually enter the park at the southeastern corner, pausing to turn on eBird, noting the temperature and whether it is sunny, cloudy, raining, or snowing. If it is very windy, I note that and do not expect to see many birds. I walk along the tennis courts to the pines at the last two of the five courts. In the winter a mixed flock of Golden-crowned Kinglets, Red-breasted Nuthatches, and Brown Creepers might reward me with a glimpse of them through the pines. My usual route then cuts into the park toward the playground, then west along the sidewalk bisecting the park to the pines at the intersection of Midvale and Kingsbury, where a plaster lion guards the steps. From there I wrap around the northern perimeter of the park, cutting back in at the sidewalk on its eastern edge. Just north of the school in the pines, about six Common Grackles have lately been breeding in the dense branches.

I have hundreds of checklists for this little park. Raptors are always highlights. I have seen Cooper's, Red-tailed, and Red-shouldered Hawks; Mississippi Kites; and occasionally a Peregrine Falcon, flying over from nesting on the nearby city of Clayton high-rises, where they were introduced. American Robins and European Starlings are most common on the meadows, and House Sparrows occupy the school building roof. Lately there have been Chipping Sparrows, American Goldfinches, Northern Cardinals, and Blue Jays, all common city birds. But on any given day there will be something more, so my lists for the not-quite-half-mile route is usually between nine and fifteen birds, rising even higher during migration.

People sometimes stop me to ask if I have seen anything exciting, which makes me hesitate. If I have not seen a goldfinch in a few days, then even that common bird is a sweet reward. The first Golden-crowned Kinglet of winter is also a treat. I hear only the owls, Great-horned, Barred, and Screech, at night. By far the commonest is the Great-horned Owl. The biggest treat is not any one bird but the slow changes, the flow of life over this green spot in an urban city. It might be the day I saw Snow Geese flying overhead, or the lone Mallard, or the crows that flew in singles or small groups east to west over the park if I got out early enough. Bird one small patch and keep track with eBird, and the species will surprise you. The changes in the season will be clear, from the doldrums of August to the excitement of April migration.

LOCAL PATCH ACTIVITIES
FOR SLOW BIRDERS

1. **Find a patch.** Your patch should be close to home. It might be a
   small city park like mine. If you are lucky, you may have a more
   wild patch like my sister has along Buffalo Bayou, right in the
   center of Houston. The important thing is that it should be somewhere you can bird often, ideally every day. If you have no parks or
   fragments of unmaintained vegetation nearby, a circuit of a few
   blocks, or even around the block, can do. What is important is that
   it be a place you can bird often and in the same way. If we became
   a nation of Slow Birders, methodically documenting the birds we
   find in our local patches, that information, put together, would tell
   us what is happening to our environment, at least from the birds'
   perspective.

2. **Walk your patch as often as you can.** I try to walk my patch
   every morning. This may sound like a lot of discipline, but it is
   not, because I have a small dog who needs his morning walk. I
   usually, but not always, take the same route through my patch.
   My walk in the park is just under half a mile. I wish it were a
   little longer. I am not organized enough to arrive at the same
   time every day, but I do notice that the earlier I get there, the
   better, particularly for seeing egrets or crows flying overhead. The
   saying is that the early bird gets the worm, but foraging is not
   mostly what birds do early. Birds such as crows and egrets fly
   from their nighttime roosts out to foraging areas. But most of all,
   there is the dawn chorus, when the songbirds advertise their talents. It is why bird classes often start at 5:00 a.m. Just compare
   the birds you hear at first light with those a couple of hours later
   and you will hear the power of the dawn chorus, particularly in
   springtime.

3. **Listen as you bird your patch.** It is a challenge to learn the birds by
   ear, but a rewarding one. I listen as I walk my patch, hearing many
   more birds than I see, though my eyes are always searching the sky
   and the branches. One of the things I really try to do is realize
   when I hear something new. Often it is a sound that a bird I know
   makes only rarely. But sometimes it is a new bird. I hone my listening skills with Larkwire. When in the patch, Merlin on the sound
   setting can tell you what it hears, though I hear more than Merlin
   does. The sister application, BirdNET, is a bit more refined and lets
   you highlight a specific sound on the sonogram for analysis.

4. **Use eBird Mobile as you walk your patch.** I turn on eBird at the
   corner of Pershing and Rossi, note the temperature and cloud
   cover, and pause to take a first listen. As I go, I enter the birds I
   encounter into eBird. A tap on the number adds one to the count.
   At the end, I hit submit, and my birds, counts, and notes become
   part of a permanent, accessible record. Of course it also works to
   write them down in a little notebook, which I sometimes do. I like
   to use pencil because it doesn't wash off. But the lists pile up fast
   for entering into eBird. Why do I love eBird so much and why are
   mentions of it littered throughout this book? The reasons are personal and environmental. Personally, it makes it really easy to see
   where I've been and what I saw. Environmentally, it adds to the
   worldwide dataset on what birds are where and how many.

5. **Stop and watch.** Your patch is close enough to home that you can
   bring a chair or find a park bench. Watch a bird for a while. What
   does it do? Does it interact with others? Where does it move and
   what determines the movement? Put yourself in the mind of a bird
   and try to predict where one will move next. Is it fighting over
   fruit? Is it flying to a nest of squalling young? Is it foraging in the
   grasses? How close is it to others?

Northern Flicker

Architects of Aspen Homes

Repeated high-pitched staccato shrieks—frantic poundings with no answer. Could this be a living horror show right in Flynn Park? No, it is a local Northern Flicker, but why so noisy?

I read that the Northern Flicker's long call is an unmistakable high-pitched staccato of about seven pulses per second, something like *kick, kick, kick, kick, kick, kick, kick.*[1] I hear this most days in the summer. Then I might hear their drumming against a dead snag, or against the metal chimney extensions on houses in my neighborhood. When flickers are noisy, they are usually up high so they can broadcast their presence to potential mates and rivals. But they are also often right down on the ground where the American Robins are. Food is the reason why, for Northern Flickers have a most unusual diet.

Ants. Flickers mostly eat ants. They eat *Camponotus*, the carpenter ants; *Crematogaster*, with heart-shaped abdomens; *Formica*, with their huge thatched colonies; *Pheidole*, which legendary ant biologist E. O. Wilson studied; *Solenopsis*, the fire ants; *Lasius*, which know no stranger; and all the rest of them.[2] Flickers find their ants on the ground, flicking their beak left to right in the short grass, or probing under a rock or log. How could a flicker, our second-largest wood-pecker after only the Pileated Woodpecker, survive on these tiny and inconspicuous creatures that mostly live underground? Even Ameri-can Robins, the other main ground forager in my neighborhood, eat much larger earthworms. How can ants sustain a 5.3-ounce bird?

Ants may be small, but they are numerous, far more numerous than any mammal. Taken as a whole, ants make up more biomass than any other group.[3, 4] Even in the forests and prairies of my region, there are more calories in ants than in mammals. This makes ants a great food if you can get at them. Ants live in hidden social groups, under-ground, under bark, in acorns, in hollow grass stems, everywhere ex-cept in the water. But they come out to forage on nectars from flowers and to hunt other insects. They are probably the most important pred-ators of the world.[5]

Ants defend their tiny hard bodies with bites and stings, which can be annoying or even fatal depending on who is being attacked. They also defend themselves with numbers. Even Northern Flickers will not venture onto the large mound of a *Formica* colony containing millions of ants. But flickers have no trouble picking off foragers as they leave or return to the nest. Northern Flickers also probe right into the nursery of a small colony, where the succulent larvae and unarmed pupae are.

We know what Northern Flickers eat because killing them used to be permitted. They were even viewed as the only savory woodpecker, hunted in particular after they had gorged on black cherries.[6] Foster Beal dissected the stomachs of 684 flickers he studied, collected across the eastern United States and Canada. He found 61 percent animal and 39 percent vegetable matter. They also had sand and soil, presum-ably ingested along with the ants. Ants made up half of all food in the 684 stomachs. Ninety-eight stomachs contained only ants. Beal counted the tiny ants carefully in three of them, and in one arrived at

5,040 *Crematogaster* ants and 100 ant pupae. The other two had over 3,000 ants.

These days, a careful researcher can collect flicker feces since they often excrete upon capture.[7] The top four ants in Northern Flicker dung were *Formica fusca*, *Tapinoma sessile*, *Lasius* species, and *Myrmica* species. And these made up nearly 90 percent of the diet for both male and female flickers. So if you don't like ants, Northern Flickers are your friend, though the converse is not true, since it is possible to like both. I do.

Flickers do not spend all their time eating ants. They need to find mates, build and defend nest cavities, and care for their young. We can watch all these activities. In my neighborhood one day, it began with a fight for a nesting cavity right in front of my home. It happened on a high snag in the silver maple across the street. These twigs have a view of the street and the neighboring trees, making them a favorite lookout. I have seen Cedar Waxwings, Common Grackles, American Robins, Fish Crows, Mourning Doves, House Finches, tiny Ruby-throated Hummingbirds, and above all European Starlings survey the world from this perch. It is the starlings that are the problem for Northern Flickers. European Starlings are introduced and quite invasive and are not a species Northern Flickers have evolved to overcome, or at least not for very long. You see, lower down on that same tree is a cavity. Starlings claimed it.

On April 19, a pair of Northern Flickers tried to usurp the cavity and oust the sharp-beaked starling. Or, for all I know, the flickers had it first and it was the starlings who were the invaders. I noticed the flickers first on the snag but then they flew down, and I crossed the street to see what was happening by the nest hole. Our dog Zeus and a visiting professor from Paris, Patrizia d'Ettorre, came along. First the flickers copulated, and then the male flew off. The female dropped down to the hole, staring down the starling. The starling did not move, hunkering lower in the cavity. I could see only her sharp yellow beak.

The flicker sat at the hole, but there was little hope. The other starling returned, fluttering a few feet above. The flicker stayed maybe twenty minutes, then moved up the trunk and to the side. I went in to dinner.

The next day, the starlings were still in the hole, and I heard the flickers down the block, where they had apparently found another cavity. I knew the starlings were still there because one sat on the high snag. Too bad our neighborhood doesn't have the big rat snakes that go after nestlings the way my daughter's more rural Indiana neighborhood has. At her home a five-foot rat snake she named Eloise first lounged on the deck rail and then ate the noisy baby starlings in her eaves just before dawn. Yes, my daughter has acquired my love of snakes.

About a month after the starling-flicker battle, I heard the flickers going crazy. On May 23, I woke up to a flicker racket. There were repeated calls given by more than one bird, presumably both parents. There were other sounds that I can't describe. They went on for about two days. And then stopped. These were the calls that so puzzled me. Were they fighting for another cavity? Had they been invaded?

It was time for me to learn more about Northern Flickers. They live on my block and in my neighborhood park. I see them in all kinds of places in my neighborhood. But what do I really know of flicker life? There was one person to ask: biology professor Karen Wiebe (pronounced Weeb), who had just retired from the University of Saskatchewan in Saskatoon, Canada, to go home to her beloved British Columbia.

I first met Karen on Facebook, on Doug Mock's Tuesday-night folk music with finger-picking guitar, back in the peak of the pandemic. We both happened on Doug on a night he was just testing his connection, but he ended up staying for us. Doug told me what a great scientist Karen is and that she studied Northern Flickers. I was interested.

First, I marveled at her study site, thirty-eight square miles in the general area of Riske Creek, about three hundred and fifty miles north of Vancouver. If you want to get a feel for this area, read the cowboy adventure books of Richmond P. Hobson Jr., like *Grass Beyond the Mountains*. They tell the story of the people who first settled along the Blackwater River. Ranching can't be good for wildlife, since the grasses grew on drained swamps, but the autobiographical story from the 1930s has strong descriptions of life in the cold forests and muskegs, along with the famous Panhandle Phillips. I hope I can visit someday, for it is also the area where Bruce Lyon and Daizaburo Shizuka work on American Coots, the subject of a later chapter.

By the time Karen worked there, the cattle ranches were part of the environment, but substantial forest remained. She said there were patches of quaking aspen (*Populus tremuloides*) and lodgepole pine (*Pinus contorta*) in the grasslands, with many lakes and ponds.[8] Farther north, Douglas fir (*Pseudotsuga menziesii*) and hybrid spruce (*Picea engelmannii x glauca*) became common, and the forest prevailed over grasslands. This mosaic environment created many edges between forest and grassland that were perfect for Northern Flickers. In most years from 1998 to 2013, Karen Wiebe and her team monitored between 100 and 150 active flicker nests. Karen climbed up the tree and sawed a little door close to the bottom of the cavity so that she could monitor the nest contents and weigh, band, and bleed the birds. Karen told me: "I did all the door-sawing to avoid risk to the students' lives. Standing on the top of a ladder against a jiggly dead snag, with a reciprocating saw slicing open the wood, just inches from my jugular . . . I figured my life was expendable, whereas I did not want to risk lawsuits from the parents of students." She also banded all the adults, but she let the students climb to the nests to monitor reproduction and band the docile nestlings. She bled the nestlings to get samples for DNA assessments of paternity. Some years she videotaped the nests to measure how often the parents fed the nestlings.[9]

At Riske Creek, flickers themselves carved nearly all their nests into aspen trees, even though they represented only a quarter of the trees in the region. Aspens are good for flicker nests not only because of their soft wood but also because they rot from the inside out. A half-dead aspen tree is likely to have a hollow core, perfect for a flicker nest. At Karen's study site, nearly half the aspens were dead or dying at a given time. But that was true only of individual trees. They are actually part of a huge interconnected clone. I like to think of them as a huge buried tree with each trunk acting as a twig on that subterranean tree. A clone with thousands of stems can live for centuries. Perhaps the largest living single organism is Pando, a magnificent aspen clone in the Fishlake National Forest in south-central Utah. Pando covers a bit over a hundred acres, weighs nearly seven thousand tons (about as much as fifty blue whales), and is several thousand years old.[10] So if we think of what looks like an individual aspen tree and think of it as a twig of an underground monster, then it is no wonder the trees we see are ephemeral, making soft wood where Northern Flickers chisel out their nests. Out of 160 trees chosen for nests in 1998 and 1999, only 1 was in a Douglas fir, 5 were in lodgepole pines, and 154 were in aspen.[11]

I was starting to form quite a cozy view of flicker life, but then I remembered the starlings across the street. If flickers pound out their own cavities, I would hope that they mostly get to keep them. But even in the natural forests of British Columbia, it does not seem to be the case. Karen Wiebe teamed up with Kathy Martin and Kathryn Aitken, and together they looked at the whole community of cavity nesters in the Cariboo-Chilcotin area of British Columbia.[12] During eight years, from 1995 to 2002, Wiebe and her team measured 1,692 cavities at twenty-eight sites. Nearly all, 95 percent, were in aspen, though aspens were only 15 percent of the trees in the entire area. The cavities were generally in dead or half-dead trees, accounting for 90 percent of all cavities, equally split between dead and half-dead trees. The birds that could dig out their nests occupied 30 percent of all cavities. These birds included Northern Flickers, Red-naped Sapsuckers, Hairy Woodpeckers, American Three-toed Woodpeckers, Pileated Woodpeckers, and Black-backed Woodpeckers. Of these, the Northern Flicker occupied 14 percent of all cavities.

The next category was the birds that could only poorly dig out cavities, for example by piercing an aspen that was mostly rotten underneath the bark. These occupied 13 percent of all cavities and included Downy Woodpeckers, Black-capped Chickadees, and Red-breasted Nuthatches.

The third category of birds that nested in cavities were those that do not make their own cavities at all but use those made by others or that naturally occur. These included Wood Ducks, Buffleheads, Barrow's Goldeneye, Hooded Mergansers, American Kestrels, Northern Hawk Owls, Northern Saw-whet Owls, Tree Swallows, Mountain Chickadees, Mountain Bluebirds, European Starlings, northern flying squirrels, bushy-tailed woodrats, red squirrels, chipmunks, short-tailed weasels, deer mice, and Brown Creepers, though this last one nests under bark. These made up 57 percent of all cavity nesters.

Because so many species are dependent on cavities made by others, Wiebe considers Northern Flickers to be a keystone species. She said, "Biodiversity would plummet if flickers did not create cavities. I like to think of flickers as ecologically the most important bird in the forest ecosystem." No wonder she risked her life to study them.

But what exactly is it like inside a flicker nest? If it had been me, peering down on those eggs, I would have been surprised in two ways. First, I would have been surprised to see so many eggs. The average number of eggs is eight, though females can lay as many as twelve eggs in a clutch. This seems like a huge number of young to take care of! My second surprise would have been how tiny those eggs are. Karen Wiebe found the average weight of an egg to be a quarter of an ounce, an eighth of the weight of an egg I buy in the supermarket. These small flicker eggs measure 1.1 inches long by 0.9 inches wide, on average.

Females lay only one egg a day, but they can keep laying if something happens to the eggs. There is a report of human egg thieves removing eggs, one a day.[13] The mother replaced the eggs, ultimately laying seventy-one eggs!

If I kept watching as the eggs hatched, after about eleven days I would see tiny naked chicks, tended carefully by their parents and kept warm at all times. The nest chamber would be fairly clean. The adults eat the hatchlings' feces until the chicks are about ten days old, prodding them to defecate by poking their cloacae. After that, the parents, mostly the father, pick up the fecal sac and fly off with it, dumping it far from the nest so that predators won't locate the activity from the odor of the droppings.[14] Karen Wiebe told me that Elizabeth Gow got more publicity and requests for interviews for this "poo paper" than for her scientifically more novel topics.

At about two weeks of age, the chicks leave the nest floor and cling to the interior walls of their home. At this point, when they defecate, the feces simply fall to the bottom of the cavity, so their once-cozy nest becomes their latrine. If any of them die at this stage, they simply fall down there and stay. The parents sometimes help the situation by chipping off bits of wood from the cavity interior to cover up the mess underneath. After about twenty-five days, the chicks are coaxed out of their nest by their shrieking parents.

Flicker nestlings need a lot of food. In 1910, Sherman figured out that parents feed newly hatched chicks about ten times a day, increasing to forty to fifty times a day later on.[15] Karen Wiebe found the fathers and mothers fed equally, about one visit each per hour.[16]

Because they eat ants, Northern Flickers are unusual among woodpeckers in not having a feeding territory that they defend against other flickers.[17] Candice Elchuk and Karen Wiebe studied flicker territoriality at their Riske Creek study site. In 1999 and 2000 they put radio transmitters on twenty-five males and twenty-seven females, attaching them to their tail feathers. They wanted to see how much the flickers overlapped on their feeding grounds. They counted the flickers as sharing a foraging area if they were within 150 feet of each other. Then they took recordings and watched intensively until they had 368 separate foraging observations from which they could draw foraging areas for each flicker with a radio transmitter. They found that they overlapped with other flickers 29 percent of the time. As they hunted for ants, the flickers pretty much ignored other hunting flickers.

This lack of competition for food makes sense to me because they are mostly taking worker ants or grubs if they can get into the nest. This is a resource that is quickly renewed as the ants produce more ants. It is also very scattered. So if you see two flickers feeding in the same lawn, you cannot assume they are in any way related. They might as well be completely unrelated people in line at the neighborhood taco truck.

Flicker parents leave the nest area with their fledglings soon after they emerge. Maybe the best areas for ants are farther from the nesting hole. Maybe the parents deplete the ant colonies near the nest when they have chicks to feed. But the fledglings are not fed long, not by mom. Dad sticks around, feeding the fledglings an average of sixteen days, compared with the mother's twelve days.[18] And then those new flickers are on their own. By the next year they will have chiseled out nests, have found mates, and be rearing flickerlings of their own.

I would like to think that the flickers that nested this year across the street will be there next year, rearing a new set of young. I would like to think that like our money bird Blue Jay, who was with us for years, my flicker friends will also stick around. It seems only natural that our second-largest woodpecker would have a long life. But that is not the case. Northern Flickers usually do not live for more than a year or two. Once flickers reach a year old and are breeding adults, nearly half of them die each year. Karen Wiebe and her colleague found that in British Columbia, annual male survival was 42 percent and annual female survival was 44 percent, lower than that of many other woodpeckers.[19]

Young flickers do not generally return to the area they were born. In sixteen years the Wiebe crew banded 8,272 Northern Flicker fledglings, of which only 138 males and 105 females returned to nest locally, only 3 percent overall.[20] Those that returned tended to have hatched earlier and to be in good condition. When they nested close to their natal nests, they tended to do well, with earlier hatch dates and better nest success. It is surprising more do not return home given these successes. They tended to do so in years of warmer springs during migration and times of denser populations.

But once the flickers choose a nesting location, they stick to it year after year as long as they live. In Karen's population, depending on the year, between a quarter and close to a half of breeding adults had been banded in the location in a previous year.[21]

Why should a big bird like a Northern Flicker have such a short life span? It seems like they have evolved for it because they lay lots of small eggs. It is the opposite of a bird like a Bald Eagle that lays just two eggs and rears a single chick. White Egrets, Blue Jays, and many other birds live a lot longer than flickers. Is it hawks that kill them? Sharp-shinned Hawks, Cooper's Hawks, Broad-winged Hawks, Red-shouldered Hawks, and Northern Harrier are all reported to kill flickers. Karen Wiebe and her collaborators could document that 9 percent of the Northern Flickers that they had fitted out with a radio collar were killed by birds during the summer.[22] These predators are probably the reason Northern Flickers like to forage in grasses that are close to the forest edge instead of farther out in the open. Migration may also take its toll, something other woodpeckers do not do.

Another thing I wondered about Northern Flickers is whether they mate outside the social pair bond. Karen teamed up with the Belgian Bart Kempenaers from the Max Planck Institute for Ornithology in Seewiesen, Germany, southwest of Munich, to answer this question.[23] Bart is an expert in using variable DNA markers called microsatellites to determine family structures in birds. Wiebe collected a tiny glass tube of blood from each chick and parent she studied for parentage studies. Out of 326 nestlings from 41 broods with a single mom and dad, there was not one case that indicated mom had mated with another male.[24]

A few of the females were polyandrous, meaning they had two nests each tended by a different male. Bart and Karen checked forty-one nestlings from seven such broods and again found that the father tending the chicks was the genetic father. But in one case one chick was from the female's other mate. There were only four days between the start of egg laying at one nest and the end of it at the other, so the female probably had sperm in her reproductive system left over from the first male.

A male that mates with a female that is not his social mate can pass on his genes without doing all the work. This doesn't happen in flickers, but something else does. Once a female has laid all the eggs in her nest, she sometimes looks around for a neighbor's nest and sneaks in a few eggs. Bart and Karen could figure this out because these chicks did not match either parent.[25]

There is one thing about Northern Flickers that every birder knows and that I haven't discussed yet. It is that there are two different colors of flickers, called yellow-shafted and red-shafted. This refers to the color under the wings and under the tail. In St. Louis we have Yellow-shafted Flickers. They were once considered to be two species with a large hybrid zone just east of the Rockies and extending into British Columbia. In fact, this was the case when I first started birding. Most of the flickers Karen Wiebe studies are hybrids that can have a lot of different variations on the red and yellow underside theme.

The hybrid zone is not moving. It seems to have been stable for over 150 years.[26] What keeps the two colors separate? The answer may come from much earlier work.[27] The differences between yellow and red flickers arose during isolations in long-ago glaciations in the West. Then, as the glaciers retreated, the birds came together. This could have been in the Pinedale or Wisconsin glaciers in the Rocky Mountains ten thousand to thirteen thousand years ago. A more recent reason could be that the two kinds of flickers migrate south to different sides of the Rockies, as Karen Wiebe explained to me.

As I walk about in my neighborhood or elsewhere in my circle, I listen for Northern Flickers, distinguishing their frantic cadence with the slightly slower one of the Pileated Woodpeckers. And in late May or early June, I listen for parents coaxing their young to let go of their home and come out. And I look for those tender flickerlings just learning to hunt ants.

NORTHERN FLICKER ACTIVITIES
FOR SLOW BIRDERS

1. **Learn to recognize Northern Flickers.** All too often I see a Northern Flicker flying low away from me, showing its conspicuous white rump. It was foraging for ants in the grasses close to me, and I intruded. If I am more attentive, I can watch them. Learn everything about how they look and also their calls, both the frantic one and the single notes. Sometimes I hear one doing one call and the other answering with the other. Once you know when flickers are about, you will see them often.

2. **Watch them foraging for ants.** Perhaps the most useful tool for a Slow Birder is a lightweight chair, easily carried. Then you can stop your walk, sit down, and watch. Sketch your surroundings and see where the flicker forages. Maybe you can even see its tongue come out to lap up ants. Sometimes they are in the grass, but other times

they concentrate along sidewalk edges or along rocks or logs. How long do the flickers stay in one place before moving? How far do they move? Do they go back to the earlier place? Make a chart of their progress. If more than one forages in the area, how do they divide it up? You could draw this in the notebook you always have with you.

3. **Watch a nest.** If you have flickers, in spring and summer you have nesting flickers. Try to find those nests, or to find one. It just takes a little attention. If you have aspens in the area, they are a good place to look. Once you find a nest, watch the hole as often as you can, setting up your trusty chair a little bit away. How often are the babies fed? If they are young, you might witness a fecal sac being carried away. Keep track of the nest and maybe you can observe the constant calling that coaxes the young to leave their smelly nest. Or that might even be the first indication of where the nest is, since the chicks are quiet until they're eighteen to twenty-five days old, when they are close to fledging.

4. **Try to identify the sex of the flickers you see and what they are doing (males have a kind of mustache extending away from the base of the bill; females do not).** If you see a flicker excavating a cavity, which sex is it? If you see two flickers waving their bills at each other in a funny and ritualized "wicka" dance in early spring, is it a male and a female or two individuals of the same sex? Maybe it is a trio with two birds of the same sex dueling and a bird of the opposite sex looking on. If you see an adult feeding recently fledged young, is it the mother or the father?

5. **Look for hybrids.** If you live along the hybrid zone out west, look to see which bird you have. Bird books have maps of these zones. Red-shafted males have a red mustache, while the yellow ones

have a black mustache. See what the colors under the wings and tails are. See if a mated pair matches the color forms.

6. **Leave your dead and dying trees standing.** A lot of animals use dead and dying trees, so leave them standing if they do not threaten your home. They will bring wildlife, possibly including Northern Flickers. I have a dead apple tree in my backyard.

Cooper's Hawk

Predator at Your Bird Feeder

On October 28, as I walked the half mile from my house to the nearest mailbox, I came across a pigeon wing on the sidewalk. Next to it was a foot and a bloody spine. These remains were in the same place I found a Blue-winged Teal wing a couple of weeks before. The sidewalk was whitewashed with bird droppings, indicating this area was a regular perch. I looked up, and right there on a sweetgum branch just twenty feet over my head was a Cooper's Hawk, still pulling flesh from a pigeon carcass. Bob Rosenfield, world expert on Cooper's Hawks, would call this a plucking perch, a place where prey gets processed. I would soon learn that this carcass would be used for more than food by the male bird that was dismembering it.

Plucking perches are not the only place to find Cooper's Hawks. If the songbirds suddenly lift up from your feeder and flee, look for a Cooper's Hawk. If you see feathers on the ground, look up for a Cooper's Hawk. If you hear a hoarse, throaty call, a *ka-ka-ka* or a *whaa* or even high whistles, try to find the Cooper's Hawk. This is the hawk of our times, one that has made our neighborhoods its home. Look carefully and you will see them often in most places at most times of the year.

Cooper's Hawks live all across our country, avoiding the farthest north in the winter and the farthest south during the breeding season. But just because we know where Cooper's Hawks are does not mean we know how many there are. Putting together numbers from territory sizes, Christmas Bird Counts, North American Breeding Bird Surveys, and counts at migration survey points like Bake Oven Knob on the Appalachian Trail, there were about eight hundred thousand Cooper's Hawks in 2016, a number that seems to be holding steady.

But it was not always so. We nearly hunted Cooper's Hawks to extinction, considering them undesirable predators on farmyard chickens or gamebirds like quail. Farmers even called them chicken hawks as they shot them.

Then something even more deadly reduced their numbers: the pesticide DDT, which came into heavy use in the United States around 1945. It killed insects at first, though they rapidly evolved a tolerance to DDT. But birds did not. A breakdown product of DDT called DDE hurt the ability of birds to absorb calcium, which led to problems like eggshells becoming so thin that a mother's soft weight would crush them. The problem was greatest in predatory birds because their bodies concentrated the chemicals they picked up from their prey. The tragedy of DDT's effects on birds is what caused Rachel Carson to write *Silent Spring* in 1962.[1] It is the book that launched the environmental movement, and it is worth reading today. DDT was finally banned only in 1972.

We know something of what DDT did to Cooper's Hawks. Noel Snyder and his team measured their eggs for damage due to DDT from 1969 to 1971. They found only five of fifty-one eggs had shells as thick as the pre-1946 eggs.[2] Five of the eggs Snyder sampled were already broken in the nest. He also presented data on population trends, showing a steep drop in Cooper's Hawk numbers corresponding to the 1946 introduction of DDT as a pesticide. The decline continued to the end of his study. By 1980, eight years after DDT was banned, research showed that eggs still contained DDT and its dangerous metabolite, DDE, but not at levels high enough to break eggshells.[3] The 1980 sample of eggs was no thinner than historic samples from before 1946. But the birds were still rare.

Cooper's Hawks were then so rare in Wisconsin that the Department of Natural Resources decided they should be listed in the conservation category of "threatened." To better understand this threatened bird, the Wisconsin Department of Natural Resources gave Raymond K. Anderson, then a professor at the University of

Wisconsin–Stevens Point, a call. Could he study them or find someone who could? Ray knew just the person to do that research, his undergraduate student Bob Rosenfield. If only he would stay at Stevens Point for a master's degree.

I was fortunate enough to talk with Bob Rosenfield on November 9, 2020. Bob told me that he firmly told his undergraduate advisor no to the idea of staying on. He was already packing to attend graduate school and planned to study other raptors at Frostburg State University in Maryland. But Ray was nothing if not persuasive, and with enough discussion, reframing of questions, and funding, Bob ultimately agreed to stay at Stevens Point. But there was one big problem.

Bob had never seen a Cooper's Hawk. They were that rare. How could he do a thesis on a bird that might not even exist anymore in Wisconsin? Furthermore, he had taken all the courses he cared to take at Stevens Point. He needed fresh perspectives for a possibly imaginary project. Bob was on his own for the first problem, but Ray helped with getting him fresh perspectives by introducing him to Frances Hamerstrom. She is famous for her work on raptors, particularly the Northern Harrier, and for saving the Greater Prairie Chicken. Hamerstrom had studied under Aldo Leopold and so was well versed in the politics of conservation. Bob Rosenfield knew he could learn a lot from her, especially because she was one of the first to study adult nesting raptors by banding them with leg bands. This was something he badly wanted to do should he ever find Cooper's Hawks.

So Rosenfield agreed to study the mystery bird and unpacked. Then he set out to see if he could find any. He searched the deepest, most pristine forests where Cooper's Hawks were thought to nest. He put out flyers and contacted falconry clubs to see if anyone had seen Cooper's Hawks.

To Rosenfield's amazement, answers began to flow in. In that first spring, he located an astonishing twenty-five Cooper's Hawk nests throughout Wisconsin. It turned out this was not a super rare bird anymore. But it was not nesting where he expected. Instead of deep, dark, mature forests, Cooper's Hawks nested anywhere there were a few trees. Instead of declining, the population was growing to numbers high enough for Bob to base a forty-year career on them and write an excellent book.[4]

Bob Rosenfield's discovery of Cooper's Hawks in 1980 documented a recovery that was repeating itself all over the country, including in my home of St. Louis. Now they are common, as Rosenfield's team discovered in two rural-to-urban locations in Wisconsin: Stevens Point and Oshkosh. These two towns had 38,000 and 66,200 inhabitants, respectively. Stevens Point is surrounded by extensive forest, except to the south, where there are crops. Oshkosh is much more agricultural, with no nearby forests.

First the team figured out where in the two towns Cooper's Hawks nested. They searched by foot and in their cars, driving all through Oshkosh in late March through April 2015, choosing a 3,100-hectare plot that included the city. They listened before dawn for calls of courting birds. They looked for feathers and white feces on the sidewalk, like the spot I saw on my block. They played tapes of females to stir up any local ones, something we enthusiasts should not do, because it disturbs the birds. They looked for nests before the trees leafed out. The Oshkosh work was mostly done by Larry Sobolik right from home. As a citizen scientist, Larry had contacted Bob Rosenfield and received guidance and help with things like banding the birds once the nests were sighted.

When they found nests, Bob Rosenfield climbed up to them to count the eggs and then later to put bands on the legs of the young. It is just as well that Cooper's Hawks nest close to the tree's trunk, since otherwise climbing to the nests would have been even riskier for Bob. They often choose to build nests on old squirrel nests or on old hawk nests. Rosenfield has climbed into trees after Cooper's Hawks more than 1,500 times! He told me he loves looking down from high in a tree even if there is an alarmed adult Cooper's Hawk flying below.

In Oshkosh they found thirteen Cooper's Hawk nests at a density of slightly fewer than one nest per square mile, and 92 percent of the nests produced young. In Stevens Point they found slightly more than one nest per square mile, and a 75 percent success rate.

If you are lucky enough to see a pair of Cooper's Hawks together, you will see that one bird is much bigger than the other. And the bigger bird is the female. In Wisconsin, females weigh 21 ounces on average while males weigh only 12 ounces. Other populations have different average weights, but the difference is large, with males only two-thirds to a half the weight of females.

Why should females be so much larger than males? It turns out that this is a bit of a mystery. Females fight other females for the right to be in a certain male's territory, a situation where large size helps.[5] But males establish those territories and also fight for them, so large size would benefit them too. But Lorenzo Pérez-Camacho and his team showed that being smaller is an advantage for hunting agile prey, so there was a trade-off, particularly for birds that hunt other birds. Another reason females might be larger than males is if males do more of the hunting while females defend the young from racoons and other nest predators, a situation that favors large size. In raptors, females are generally larger than males, so we should be looking for an explanation for size that applies to all the species.

It's not so easy to understand exactly what proportion of the Cooper's Hawk diet is made up of birds. To those of us with feeders, it would seem like birds is all they are interested in. Careful study supports that in general, but small mammals are also important.

Heinz Meng studied the Cooper's Hawks diet in detail near Ithaca, New York, from 1948 to 1958, before their numbers had crashed from DDT.[6] At that time, humans shot many Cooper's Hawks because they were thought to prey excessively on domestic chickens. Meng figured out what they were eating by collecting pellets and by frequent nest observations. Pellets are the vomited-up, indigestible and often bony remains of consumed animals. Meng identified remains of four mammal species and twenty-four bird species in his collection of 853 remains. Among them, he found 241 Starlings, 134 Northern Flickers, 118 Eastern Meadowlarks, 109 eastern chipmunks, and 79 American Robins. I bet in my neighborhood there would be more American Robins in the pool. Any hater of the imported European Starlings should be glad at how frequently Cooper's Hawks feast on them.

Meng also figured out what the hawks did with all that food. He found that it took sixty-six birds or mammals to raise a single chick to six weeks, not counting the food brought to the mother during the month she incubated the eggs.[7] On a daily basis, this is four meals a day in the first week, five a day during the second week, then varying between seven and nine prey a day during the remaining weeks. If you are wondering how there are any birds left when Cooper's Hawks are around, it is important to know that most of the birds they catch are the young of the year, not experienced adults.

If Meng painted the broad strokes of Cooper's Hawks' foraging and provisioning their young, Bob Rosenfield and his team watched incessantly enough to discover some shocking details. He began by watching forty-seven pairs of Cooper's Hawks in the springtime for several years.[8] These observations were intensive, from mid-March before nests were established until egg-laying in late April to early May. To capture every detail, they began around 4:00 a.m. each day. They found that females were present at the nest site for 99 percent of the time and males for 80 percent in spring. Males tended to leave later in the day, and when they returned, they brought the female something to eat.

Rosenfield was particularly interested in copulations for this study. He defined them as any time that the male climbed on the female. Mating in most birds is an act of about five seconds, with the male on top and the female moving her tail aside to touch their cloacae, the vent through which they excrete and mate. His protrudes a bit and hers dents in a bit, but it is nothing like the mating machinery of mammals. Actual sperm transfer is invisible to a human observer. All of the 120 copulations they observed involved vocalizations by one or both birds, a sound they denoted as *whaaa*. Every single time a male flew in and offered the female food, he mated with her. It is surprising that mating begins a month or more before egg-laying, long before any chick could be fathered. So perhaps the hawk I saw on the plucking perch was preparing a morsel to exchange for sex.

Putting all their observations together and taking into account the number of days it takes to complete a nest before egg-laying, Rosenfield figured that 372 copulations occurred per pair in the month before the last egg was laid! This number is based on his observation of 120 copulations among 37 pairs of birds and then extrapolating over the total time available.[9]

Moving on to the active part of the breeding season in April, females lay two to six eggs, about one every other day. Females lose their belly feathers so their bare skin can most efficiently warm the eggs. Since males lack such a bare brood patch, they are poor incubators, but they will sit on the eggs, warming them somewhat when the female is away from the nest.

Cooper's Hawk females begin incubating after the third egg is laid, so if there are more than three chicks, the eggs laid later will produce smaller chicks. After the thirty-five-day egg incubation, the female continues to warm the chicks until they are about two weeks old, because these babies thermoregulate poorly. She also shields them from rain or direct sunlight with outstretched wings. The male continues to bring the female food all through the incubation and early brooding period. About a month after hatching, they leave the nest. But they come back and hang out in the nest or on the limbs adjoining it. In this they are quite different from songbirds, who flee the nest as soon as they can to hide individually in bushes. Cooper's Hawk young are fed for another seven weeks after they leave the nest. Toward the end of that time, adults simply put whole prey at the nest or nearby, and the young grab the food. The siblings stick together and might even hunt together, though they do not cooperatively share their robins and pigeons.

It is a lot of work to rear a brood of Cooper's Hawk chicks. The males are dedicated to the task. But are they the fathers of the chicks they rear? Do they demand a mating with each morsel they bring back to ensure their paternity? Or are these males also rearing broods with other males' chicks, as is the case with so many songbirds?

Previous work in hawks indicated that these majestic birds were above the shenanigans of the songbirds. Merlins and American Kestrels, for example, showed little or no extra-pair young. But what about Cooper's Hawks? Rosenfield asked that question with his team by looking at birds in Milwaukee, Wisconsin, in 2003, 2004, and 2007.[10] They used the usual techniques of banding the adults with aluminum bands with numbers and colored bands they could see, and climbing to the nests of young that they could reach and taking blood samples. In all, they examined forty-four nests with 140 young and found that nearly 20 percent of those young were fathered by males other than the one tending the nest. These foreign chicks were in a third of all nests. Larger broods tended to be more likely to have young from other males. The all-important genetic work for this study was done by one of Bob's former undergraduates, Sarah Sonsthagen, now with a population genetics lab in Alaska that focuses on fish but also has time for hawks. So Cooper's Hawks are not so faithful to their mates.

Who do the females find to mate with outside their pair bond? The most likely suspect is the guy next door. But that turned out not to be the case for Cooper's Hawk females, since the chick DNA not matching dad did not match that of the neighbor males either.

Instead, Bob Rosenfield surmises, she is mating with one of the year-old males who has not yet established a territory. These males are hard to follow, so this will be difficult to affirm given that those males are challenging to catch.

Making one's living off birds has its challenges, since birds can fly away so easily from a predator. But certain traits make snatching a bird out of the sky easier. The story begins with the craziest title ever for a scientific paper: "Do British Columbia Cooper's Hawks Have Big Feet?"[11] According to Bob Rosenfield, it all began with his care in taking data. He measured the middle toe of every bird he caught at first simply because that is what his advisor did. He did not wait to have a specific question, but it was part of the morphological data that was easy to get when the bird was in hand for banding and blood collection. Later he measured the big toe, the one that points backward, also called the hallux.

Next, it makes sense to talk about overall body size, remembering that smaller size goes along with greater agility—more important for catching birds than mammals. It turns out that Cooper's Hawks in British Columbia are smaller than those in Wisconsin. As predicted, the British Columbia birds get 85 percent of their food from birds like House Sparrows, American Robins, and European Starlings. By contrast, the Wisconsin birds get only 43 percent of their food from birds.[12] The remainder of the diet in both cases is small mammals like chipmunks. As Rosenfield expected, the British Columbia birds have longer middle toes relative to their body size. The researchers argued that Cooper's Hawks use their longer toes to claw songbirds right out of the sky.

Cooper's Hawks are one of my favorites because they are top predators who have made our neighborhoods their home. It makes me feel that all is not unnatural in our cities, since the Cooper's Hawks have come back from the DDT brink to flourish. I feel a thrill when one flies into view or is spotted clutching an unlucky robin. I am glad when I figure out where a plucking perch is or find a nest. We may have lost most of the mammalian predators of the Great Plains, but in our neighborhoods we still have this aerial predator, a natural part of the ecosystem.

COOPER'S HAWK ACTIVITIES FOR SLOW BIRDERS

1. **Get to know Cooper's Hawks.** This is the hawk most likely to be swooping up from your feeder. After all, Cooper's Hawks are all through our neighborhoods, all across the country. One challenge with rural Cooper's Hawks is distinguishing them from the similar Sharp-shinned Hawks, though these are far less common in urban areas. The larger heads of Cooper's Hawks might be the best thing to look for. Their heads look more like those of squirrels, and Sharp-shinned Hawk heads look more like those of rats.

2. **Look for nests in spring.** They may be piled on top of old squirrel nests, near the trunk of a tree about two-thirds of the way up. Cooper's Hawks pick fresh twigs that are still green, making their nests look different from squirrel nests, which are characterized by dead leaves. Listen to recordings of their courting calls on your bird app and try to find them early on springtime mornings. They begin calling about half an hour before dawn. There will be a nest only about every square mile. If you find a nest, pull up a chair and settle in for a good watch. How often does the male bring in food? Can you witness one of their brief copulations, the exchange for every starling or chipmunk?

3. **Look for plucking perches.** These are places where the hawks process, eat, and sometimes cache their catch. It is usually within fifty

yards of the nest, so if you find one, you are close to a nest. Next spring I'll try to find the nest, since the plucking perches tend to be used year after year. If you find one, see if you can figure out what prey species they are eating.

4. **Stop and watch when you spot a Cooper's Hawk.** How long does it stay perched? Where exactly is it? Where does it swoop? Does it have something in its talons?

Cedar Waxwing

Evanescent Berry Pickers

Cedar Waxwings are like thoughts that arise unbidden in meditation. Try to focus on your breath, on the pattern of light, color, and dark right in front of you. And yet thoughts wisp in like bits of smoke, to-do lists, something left astray, or a worrying conversation. Let them all go and focus on your breath, my meditation guide tells me. Still, thoughts float in unbidden, just as Cedar Waxwings arrive unpredictably from on high, their sweet whistles in the morning sky too high-pitched for some to hear. I could not take you to see Cedar Waxwings, but I could tell you when they are suddenly here. These enigmatic birds present a mystery I would love to solve.

Cedar Waxwings are an improbable bird, from the black mask outlined in white to the feathery crest, or the tail dipped in yellow the color of yolk. Best of all are the little waxy tips of crimson on the ends of some wing feathers. Their other colors are more subtle, a yellow wash on the belly, chestnut on the head and neck fading to gray across the back and then intensifying to black on the tail. They look as if painted by one of the great Japanese artists of long ago, delicate yet strong, subtle yet stunning.

I see Cedar Waxwings sporadically in Flynn Park, two blocks from my home. In autumn, they twist around in the Sargent cherry trees as they eat small fruits, not competing for fruit with one another but sometimes chasing a robin away from a cherry-filled branch. Cedar Waxwings are always in groups, so when I see one, I know to look for others. But I never know exactly when I will encounter them. First, I hear their thin whistles. It is a pitch so high that my husband cannot hear it.

Cedar Waxwings breed in the northern half of the United States and the southern half of mainland Canada, south of the boreal forest in open woods and old fields. They move out of the northernmost parts of their breeding range to winter along the southern fifty miles of Canada and then all the way south to Nicaragua. In St. Louis, we have Cedar Waxwings year-round according to eBird. I like to think of Cedar Waxwings wintering in Mexico, country of my early childhood. Perhaps they are in the eucalyptus groves of Chapultepec Park, where I once played. But even there they do not stay in one place long, as I will discuss later.

Cedar Waxwings are true frugivores. From October through April they survive almost entirely on fruit.[1] Jean McPherson did a thorough study of their diet during the winters of 1983 to 1985 on the University of Oklahoma campus in Norman.[2] She rode her bike frequently through campus, documenting the amount of fruit on trees and the Cedar Waxwings that fed on them from early December to mid-May. She rode her 7.5-mile route eighty-three times, stopping whenever she heard or saw Cedar Waxwings.

I guess Cedar Waxwings were not so hard for her to find once they came to campus. But that could vary a lot from year to year. There were none in 1985 until late January, for example. But then on February 27, 1985, she saw a record 673 birds!

McPherson found that Cedar Waxwings favored the sticky white fruits of mistletoe, stripping these berries entirely before trying other fruits. Their second favorite fruit was hackberry, followed by yaupon and deciduous holly berries, but really any fruit would do.

Next, McPherson looked at food preference in aviaries, where she could control what the birds were fed. She wanted to study individual birds and their personal choices, but when she put a Cedar Waxwing in a cage by itself, it sat there and refused to eat.[3] This is a bird so social, it will die when alone rather than eat.

McPherson found that in groups of eight birds, they ate the fruit readily, allowing her to do her study and conclude that Cedar Waxwings like small, red fruit best and do not seem to take into account nutritional aspects like protein content. But that does not explain their love of white mistletoe fruits.

It takes a special physiology to live on a diet of so much fruit. Margaret Morse Nice temporarily adopted a fledgling Cedar Waxwing to see how it digested fruit.[4] She fed it fruit first thing in the morning, then waited for the fruit to work its way through the bird's digestive system. Since fruit has so little protein, she reasoned that the Cedar Waxwings would digest it quickly. And so they did. Margaret found that blueberries took twenty-eight minutes from entry to exit, chokecherries forty minutes, and black cherries twenty minutes. Her lone Cedar Waxwing fed readily, but it was not truly alone because it was in a room with two Song Sparrows that the youngster took to be his own kind, begging readily from them.

Because they are so dependent on ripe fruit, Cedar Waxwings reproduce later in summer than other birds. The first fruits they eat in the spring are often berries left over from the previous year.

Perhaps the best way to determine what a bird eats and when it eats it is to simply shoot it and see what is in its stomach. We do not do this anymore, but there was a time when it was normal to shoot birds for study. The US Bureau of Biological Survey, now the US Fish and Wildlife Service, shot thousands of birds and documented what was in their stomachs between 1885 and 1950. Mark Witmer went to those records and reported on the stomach contents of 283 Cedar Waxwings.[5] From November to April, their stomachs were half full of red cedar berries. Other common fruits in their stomachs included apples, crab apples, black haw, American pokeweed, riverbank grapes, blackberries, mulberries, service berries, and black cherries. In all, Witmer found the diet of these birds was 84 percent fruit, even more than that of American Robins, at 57 percent fruit, the next highest.

If I followed the appearance of fruit on trees, I might more regularly find Cedar Waxwings. Maybe this is what Alan Monroy-Ojeda and his team had in mind when they banded birds including Cedar Waxwings in the lush Ethnobotanical Garden in Oaxaca, Mexico.[6] Though it is only five acres, the garden's grounds and water supply make it a natural refuge for migrants. Monroy-Ojeda trapped birds with mist nets on the last Sunday of each month between December 2001 and April 2010. His crew identified, banded, and measured them before letting them go. The most common migrants they caught were Cedar Waxwings, Warbling Vireos, Nashville Warblers, Yellow-rumped Warblers (the Audubon's subspecies), Western Tanagers, and Orchard Orioles. In all, they caught 1,565 birds. If the birds did not already have a band, they banded them with an aluminum band embossed with a traceable number. A fifth of them had already been caught before, either the same winter or a previous winter.

But they never recaptured a Cedar Waxwing. Even on these wintering grounds, Cedar Waxwings are evanescent and social, tracking the fruit trees and neither staying long enough to be recaptured in one place nor necessarily returning the next year.

I don't know if the migrants I see in the spring come all the way from Oaxaca. They are here in number by May. To be exact, last spring I heard them at home for the first time on May 11, when three flew overhead then perched on a dead snag high in a maple tree across the street. That spring I last saw them on June 1, when twenty individuals flew overhead, pausing in two separate groups in the high tops of sweetgums and oaks. I saw them nearly every day between May 11 and June 1, 2020, for a total of 199 birds, all likely to have been different individuals given how they move around. They were probably heading north, perhaps to my home state of Michigan. I have not figured out where to find Cedar Waxwings breeding near my home, though my *Missouri Breeding Bird Atlas* says they are here.[7] I did not see them again until October 3, as they moved through flying southward.

The one time Cedar Waxwings need to stay put is when they are nesting. This is also the one time they collect insects, though even the young manage to flourish mainly on fruits after their first two days of life. This is also the time a biologist might best conduct a thorough study of this small but important stage in a bird's life. As in all the other stages of Cedar Waxwings' lives, their nests tend to be in a kind of exploded aggregation, not clustered together yet not far apart. For example, Loren S. Putnam, discussed in more detail below, measured distances between nests at Franz Theodore Stone Laboratory on South Bass Island near Put-in-Bay during that optimistic long-ago summer of 1946, with the war ended and the baby boom on the horizon. Between the lodging and the laboratory, there were six nests in a hundred-foot-square area, with another one just outside that square. Three of the nests were in the same large maple tree.

For careful details, it is great to find someone who has spent a lot of time with the birds. Putnam watched Cedar Waxwings for his Ph.D. thesis during most of World War II. He published it in *The Wilson Bulletin* shortly after he got his Ph.D. from the Ohio State University in 1947.[8] He took the old-fashioned approach to a study: simply discover everything he could about his bird. This is one of my favorite kinds of publications, a focus on a bird in a treatise that is not concerned with just one key story.

Putnam put colored bands in addition to the aluminum Fish and Wildlife bands on the birds' legs so he could tell them apart. He used a nest trap and a drop trap to catch and band Cedar Waxwings, baiting the trap with soft nesting material. The nest trap was a tube with an open trap door pointing in the direction the birds came toward the nest. He put an open trap on a nest when the chicks were five to eight days old, then activated the door so it would shut when a bird came in. He preferred to trap the female first and never trapped both parents on the same day.

At Putnam's study site, Cedar Waxwings arrived in the second half of May and began nesting in the second week of June. Most of the adults were new to the site, something he knew because he sighted only 2 of 54 banded adults from a previous year. He never again saw any of the 174 young that he had banded. These birds were just as nomadic as those Monroy-Ojeda banded in Oaxaca.

On South Bass Island, the birds followed fruits, beginning in May with fruit from the previous year on the cedars and hackberries, but then turning to ripening tart cherries, then mulberries. The birds also visited fruit trees on Gibraltar Island, a few hundred feet away, feeding there on cedar and hackberry fruit, then on roundleaf serviceberry and chokecherry and ending with elderberries, the only one of these plants I also have growing in my yard, though I've never seen Cedar Waxwings eating my elderberries.

Putnam identified the trees in which the birds nested: 28 percent in maple, 27 percent in cedar, 14 percent in apple, 10 percent in pear, 6 percent in hackberry, and 5 percent in plum. The waxwings placed their nests five to twenty feet above the ground. They built their nests of grass, twigs, and plant stems, then lined the bowls with cobwebs, moss, and soft grasses. The nests are loose and bulky and take only five days to build, but those are busy days. Each nest contained about 2,327 pieces of plant material.

Once the nest is built, the female lays an egg every day until her clutch is complete. The female begins to warm the pale eggs with her bare belly, her brood patch, when there is only one egg in the nest, though she spends only about a third of the day on the first egg. By the time she has laid all the eggs, she spends nearly all her time keeping the eggs warm. The male does not have a featherless brood patch on his belly, so he is not much use at incubating. The eggs are usually laid over four or five days but hatch within two days of each other, so the last-laid egg gets fewer hours of incubation, about 83 percent of the 353 hours that the first-laid egg gets.

Putnam easily answered a question that at first puzzled Scott Johnson for cavity-nesting House Wrens: How does the male know when the first egg has hatched? In Cedar Waxwings, the female let him see by simply rising up from the nest so he could see the naked chicks for himself. Both gazed down at the first newborn chick for a few minutes, and then the male flew off. On the male's next visit a dramatic change transpired. Instead of mulberries or wild cherries, he brought back something Putnam called a soft white material, which he surmised was a mass of small caterpillars. This fatty, proteinaceous food was just what the young chicks needed to thrive. His visits more than doubled in frequency to every fifteen to twenty minutes. I just love the image of the two birds peering down in amazement at their newborn chicks and then getting to work.

By the third day of life, the chicks' diet turns mostly to the fruits that sustain their parents. They are in the nest for about sixteen days and then fed by the parents away from the nest for another six to ten days. After that these juvenile Cedar Waxwings take off on their own, forming small groups with nearby chicks in neighboring trees, where they eat fruit and catch insects on the wing. Their parents may be renesting, an effort begun by the female while the male tends the fledged chicks. By the end of August, breeding done, the parents join the groups of first-year young. Ultimately most seek fruit trees far away and never return to Put-in-Bay on South Bass Island.

I would be remiss not to mention a danger to Cedar Waxwings that strikes them at their most vulnerable, when they are nesting. The threat came out of the Great Plains after Europeans invaded the continent and cut the forests, creating prairie-like terrain. The threat is the Brown-headed Cowbird, the brood parasite that sneaks its eggs into the nests of others. How much of a risk are cowbirds to Cedar Waxwings? Steve Rothstein answered this early in his long career of studying cowbirds. He began at the University of Michigan Biological Station (UMBS) near Pellston, Michigan. This is the same place where I learned to be a biologist in the summer of 1972 and the winter, spring, and summer of 1973. You can look up this remarkable field station and see that it dates back to 1909 and now has ten thousand acres covering about a third of the shore of Douglas Lake and continuing south to cover some of the shore of Burt Lake. It is an international biosphere reserve. The part of the station on Burt Lake includes part of the ancestral home of the Burt Lake Band of Ottawa and Chippewa, though UMBS only acquired these lands in the 1990s.[9]

When I was at Bug Camp, as we called it, there was a leafy over-story of red oaks, big-toothed aspen, birches, and a dozen or so other tree species. American Redstarts sang from the trees. But it had not always been that way. It was clear-cut by loggers up to 1880, then burned repeatedly until about 1923. I learned of this from the director, David Gates, when I was there. He was director from 1972 to 1976 but had visited the station from its earliest infancy, since his father taught botany there. David marveled at the lushness of the forests now, saying when he first came it was burned stumps on which the hot summer sun shone.

Rothstein, working at UMBS in 1968 and 1969, three years before my own studies there, chose a 2.3-acre white pine plantation of young trees only ten to twenty-five feet high. What surprised him about the Cedar Waxwings nesting in this plantation was how close together the nests were. At both the north and south ends of the plantation were groups of nests, 8.7 nests per acre, with some as close as twenty feet apart. Rothstein felt this clearly extended David Lack's classification of Cedar Waxwings as loosely colonial.[10]

Rothstein then went on to look at how the Cedar Waxwings behaved toward Brown-headed Cowbirds. Rothstein classified Cedar Waxwings as rejectors of cowbird eggs because they force out real or artificial cowbird eggs, particularly during the egg-laying period and the first few days of incubation. Cedar Waxwings get rid of the cowbird eggs by stabbing them, burying them in the nest, or simply abandoning the nest.[11, 12] The small size and small bills of Cedar Waxwings mean they cannot just roll Brown-headed Cowbird eggs out of the nest.

For more detail on the frequency of cowbird eggs being laid in Cedar Waxwing nests, Rothstein got unpublished studies from the

UMBS files, along with published studies and his own work. He found 25 nests that were naturally parasitized out of 334 nests in total, for a parasitization rate of only 7.5 percent.[13] When there is a cowbird chick in the nest, the waxwing chicks gain less weight. But the cowbirds cannot survive on a fruit diet and ultimately perish.

So cowbirds in waxwing nests are a mistake for both parties. If 90 percent are rejected by the waxwings, why do the cowbirds parasitize them? It turns out that Cedar Waxwings were the most abundant bird in Cheboygan and Emmet Counties in Michigan, where UMBS is located, especially in edge areas. This means cowbirds are making a lot of mistakes by exploiting the most common nests.

Rothstein compared the fate of his beloved cowbirds in Cedar Waxwing nests with that of cowbirds in Chipping Sparrow nests. Chipping Sparrows were the second most common bird and readily accepted cowbird eggs.[14] In 1968 and 1969, Rothstein found 118 Cedar Waxwing and 83 Chipping Sparrow nests. There were European Cowbird eggs in 36 percent of the Chipping Sparrow nests. By contrast, there were cowbird eggs in only 7 percent of the Cedar Waxwing nests. So you could say the cowbirds wasted one egg in a waxwing nest for every four in Chipping Sparrow nests. But from the Cedar Waxwing's perspective, Brown-headed Cowbirds are not a big problem.[15]

Cedar Waxwings flit in and out of my life since I never know when I will see them. There is no lifetime researcher of Cedar Waxwings the way there is for House Wrens, Dark-eyed Juncos, Northern Flickers, or Cooper's Hawks. Maybe it is too discouraging to study a bird that you band and come to love only to never see it another season. But many of us love them anyway.

Scott Johnson, whom I know from House Wrens, told me in an interview on October 9, 2020, that Cedar Waxwings are one of his favorites. I expected him to share the reason I love them, their unexpected arrival, high trills, and elegant, formal suit. But Scott had another reason. When he was eleven and first started birding at home in Minnesota, the Cedar Waxwing was the hundredth bird he saw.

One mystery I do not know the answer to is who fathers Cedar Waxwing chicks? Is it the diligent male that brings in the food? Or is it the bird next door? Are they like American Robins or House Wrens with a fair amount of cuckoldry, or are they faithful like Northern Flickers? The answer awaits work by future researchers.

In the meantime, I will simply enjoy Cedar Waxwings. They are not rare but are hard to predict, so when I hear them, I enjoy them, more than those unbidden thoughts in a meditation session. May your life be favored with their unexpected visits.

CEDAR WAXWING ACTIVITIES
FOR SLOW BIRDERS

1. **Check the size of the flocks.** If there is one Cedar Waxwing, there will be more. See if you can count the flock size. It might be easiest as they fly away from a fruit tree, for when one leaves, they all tend to leave. What do flock sizes relate to? Are flocks in trees with copious fruits larger? Are they larger at the beginning or end of the season?

2. **Watch Cedar Waxwings in a fruit tree.** If you have fruiting trees nearby, Cedar Waxwings are likely to find them. Pick out one bird and watch it eat. Can you count the berries it swallows per minute? With their short guts and fast digestion, they defecate often. See if you can observe that too. What are their techniques for getting berries? Do they shake the branches to get them to fall? Maybe their techniques vary when there are a lot of birds nearby. Do the Cedar Waxwings eat all the fruit or leave before it is gone? Can you quantify this? What would you count?

3. **Watch a nest.** If you are lucky enough to find a nest, perhaps near a stream, take some time to watch it. See who comes and who goes and for how long. Maybe you will be there when the babies leave the nest and can watch their early attempts at flight. You won't be able to capture one and watch it the way Margaret Morse Nice did, but wild watching is just as rewarding. See if you can watch the young birds land, as they have trouble with that long after they succeed in flying.

Forest Park

City Habitat for 220 Bird Species

One of the great American city parks is only a mile from my home. It is called Forest Park, a bit of a misnomer because only a few corners of it are heavily wooded. According to the St. Louis Parks Division literature, the park opened on June 24, 1876, and is 1,300 acres, larger than Central Park in New York City. Over twelve million people visit it every year.

It seems as if there is a stream running through Forest Park, beginning near the northeastern edge, wending east through a glorious basin at the bottom of Art Hill, looking down from the St. Louis Art Museum, then continuing past the Muny outdoor theater before turning south to Jefferson Lake, just past the skating rink. Off this stream are multiple smaller lakes and ponds. Great Egrets, Green Herons, Mallards, and sandpipers make this waterway seem real. But it is not. It is entirely artificial, with its flow controlled, its channels formed, and its banks sculpted.

A river runs under the park, the River des Peres, but it is forced into a thirty-two-foot-high tunnel underground, right around the corner of Harvard and Dartmouth Avenues near Olive Boulevard, ten blocks north of my home. The river is allowed out of its confining concrete only half a mile south of the southeast corner of the park between Manchester Avenue, also known as the historic Route 66, and Interstate 44, south of the railroad tracks and industrial Barron Avenue. Apparently the natural waters were too unruly and often flooded the park before they were banished. The Sunday fishermen around Jefferson Lake do not seem to mind that their lake is not natural and neither do the wetland animals, so I suppose I should stop worrying about the river running underneath.

I checked what I have logged in eBird for Forest Park, and it is seventy-five species for Forest Park and fifty-eight species for the Kennedy Woods section of the park, where we go mostly for spring warblers. I am not much of a lister, but I do like to remember places by their birds. There were thirteen bird species we saw only in Kennedy Woods, though they are likely to be in the rest of the park. They were Barred Owl, Brown Creeper, Eastern Towhee, Golden and Ruby-crowned Kinglets, Scarlet Tanager, Swainson's and Wood Thrush, and five warblers: Black and White Warbler, Black-throated Green Warbler, Chestnut-sided Warbler, Northern Parula, and Ovenbird. This leaves thirty bird species we saw only in the rest of the park, too many to list here.

Others have listed 220 species on 4,069 checklists for Forest Park and 163 species on 622 checklists for Forest Park–Kennedy Woods. Before I go, I like to see what others have seen. Just looking now on this late August day, I can see that the warblers are migrating south, fleeing the winter that still seems far off. Someone saw five species of warblers a couple days ago.

Forest Park is big enough for many kinds of birds. If I spent more time there, no doubt I would see more of them. It is a park where it is easy to bring a chair and sit somewhere there are interesting birds. I might choose to sit by a bridge that has Barn Swallows nesting underneath and watch how they come and go, ever successfully avoiding collisions. I might have parked myself by the Baltimore Oriole nest hanging so low from a sycamore branch over the water, looking almost tropical. Or I might have simply stopped in the middle of a grassy field and watched the robins foraging.

The birds I chose for Forest Park are very common ones: European Starling, House Sparrow, and Northern Cardinal. The first two are not even native to the United States. All three are easy to watch in Forest Park. I see the House Sparrows under the eaves of the visitor center where we often park. Along the path on the side of the waterway is a place where it goes through a wet area. In that area is a long-dead tree, the bark fallen from its branches. European Starlings have chosen its cavities for nests, so I often see a few of them sitting high on the bald limbs. Northern Cardinals I see most often in low trees or bushes, often with a red berry in their beaks. Any of them could be easily watched here in a habitat as native as can be expected in the middle of the city.

I always say that a natural area in the middle of a city has a story behind its preservation, a fight to keep it. But I don't think that is true for Forest Park. It was designed so long ago, before St. Louis had grown around it. Then its role in the 1904 World's Fair cemented its affection in the hearts of St. Louisans. It declined in the 1980s, but then Forest Park Forever was founded in 1986, and people generated the funds to renovate and preserve this central St. Louis park for the people.

On any given walk I might spend an hour or so in Forest Park, often while my husband runs about four miles. The birds I most see are common ones, but each has their particular place. Mallards rest on the shore or paddle in the water. Mourning Doves roost on snags high above the wetter areas. Chimney Swifts soar overhead chattering. If I see an American Kestrel, it will usually be only one, perched up high. It is August, and the European Starlings are gathering. I saw seventy-eight of them on a snag. Starlings are much more common than the Northern Mockingbirds I saw fly onto a lamppost behind the Muny theater. American Robins, American Goldfinches, Song Sparrows, Northern Cardinals, and Carolina Wrens can generally be seen on any Forest Park visit. It is a place all St. Louis goes to when they want to get outside.

CITY PARK ACTIVITIES
FOR SLOW BIRDERS

1. **Identify and get to know your local city parks.** It is hard to miss Forest Park, but there are also smaller city parks worth getting to

know. Once in the park, explore its corners, the regions without trails, the rougher vegetation.

2. **Check for your park on eBird.** If it is not listed there as a hot spot, make it one. You can do this as you submit your checklist. How to do it is clear on the eBird website; I haven't seen a link on the mobile app. The suggestion will go to the local compiler, who should accept it as long as it is a public place. Forest Park was already a hot spot, but I had to suggest making my neighborhood park one. EBird lists will tell you what you can expect to see in your park. The summaries can tell you what season different birds are there.

3. **Walk the same pathways over and over again, birding with eBird.** When you look back over your records through the seasons, you will be able to see how the birds change in their activities.

4. **Look for nests in the spring and summer, particularly close to any lakes, streams, ponds, or swampy areas.** I find nests more common or more easily seen in the wetter parts of the park. If there is a forested area, it will have different birds from the fields. Forest nests are harder to spot but rewarding to discover.

5. **Bring a chair, binoculars, and a notebook and arrive early in the day.** Find a place to watch and see what birds you find and what they are doing. Use the techniques mentioned on page 47—ad lib, scan sampling, and focal animal observation—to record what you see. Try sketching the scene and the birds.

6. **Join a bird walk.** Forest Park frequently has beginner bird walks given by the St. Louis Audubon Society. See if you can find something similar in your park. If not, see if you can share what you learn with the curious. Merlin is a great help for identifying birds.

7. **Listen from one place.** What is the soundscape? Shut your eyes and see how many different birds you can identify. Can you draw sound using a pleasing pattern of your own design?

8. **Join your park society, if there is one, supporting it as you can.** We have the Friends of Forest Park, which was crucial a few decades ago when the park was losing its soul and becoming perceived as a dangerous place to go, rather than the heart of the city that it is.

European Starling

How Bad Are 200 Million?

Hardly anyone likes a European Starling in America. Their yellow beaks stab so viciously at the Yellow-shafted Flicker or the Red-bellied Woodpecker as they try to claim the cavity the woodpecker chiseled. But European Starlings are in America because we brought them here. They have thrived only because of the American landscape we have altered.

The European Starling is the only member of its family, the Sturnidae, to occur north of Spain. This family of about a hundred species is native to South Asia and Africa.[1] In Europe they found cold weather, but also the kind of variable habitat they love, one that was largely created by humans. Exactly how starlings first came into Europe is not well known. But how they came to the United States is.

As a member of the American Acclimatization Society, Eugene Schieffelin thought that New York needed European birds, especially the birds of Shakespeare. One of them was the European Starling.[2] In 1890 he released sixty European Starlings in Central Park in New York City. He then released another forty birds in the same place the following year. Now there are more than 200 million European Starlings in the United States. Like the House Sparrow, they are at home with us, nesting in our eaves and eating our garbage.

But unlike the House Sparrow, they also thrive far from humans. And this makes European Starlings much more of a threat to our most treasured native birds than House Sparrows are. One of my earliest birding memories is of watching a starling oust a woodpecker from her nest. The woodpecker looked bigger to me. It was probably a Red-bellied Woodpecker, but it was too long ago for me to be sure. The woodpecker protested with much fighting and calling. Yet nothing could counter that implacable yellow bill, thrusting and insisting, and the starling won the cavity after several days of battle. This battle made me think this iridescent bird was pure evil, an invasion of nature. I worried that the woodpeckers would not survive. That yellow beak haunted me.

I am not the only one to be concerned about European Starlings. The Invasive Species Specialist Group of the International Union for Conservation of Nature has nominated it to its list of the 100 World's Worst Invaders, along with only two other birds, the Common Myna and the Red-vented Bulbul.[3] Take note, the Common Myna is also in the starling family. To get on the list, a species has to have had a serious impact on biological diversity or human activities.

Invasion impacts life and its diversity in many different ways. After all, how does one compare the starling that steals a woodpecker's cavity with avian malaria that steals a bird's life, or fire ants that scour the landscape of food that otherwise would feed all manner of other animals?

If European Starlings were not so successful, we might look at their iridescence and listen to their funny scratchy voices and triangular wings and not worry about them. They could be a curiosity like the Monk Parakeets in Houston. So the first thing I wondered was what makes a European Starling thrive in North America? At its most basic, success for animals simply means that each pair produces two young for the next generation. Any more than that and the population will grow.

The first thing we might want to know is how long individual European Starlings live, because that will tell us how many times they breed. Individual European Starlings have survived nearly to voting age in North America, but these records do not tell us much about what happens to the average bird or how that impacts how often they breed.[4] Researchers measured death rates in New England and found that about half of all European Starlings die each year. In other areas, between one-third and three-quarters of all starlings die annually, so New England is in the middle. Death is somewhat more common in young starlings, in females, and in winter. So this means that most of the birds squawking on the ledge under my neighbor's eave are probably not the adults that were there last year.

How can a species with such high annual mortality rates reach numbers surpassing 200 million on our continent? Maybe those that survive are unusually healthy. But starlings carry heavy parasite loads that might make them sick. Virtually all of them have internal parasites, particularly helminth worms, as Elizabeth Boyd discovered upon dissecting three hundred European starlings.[5] She also found they had nematodes, acanthocephalans, and cestodes, and one even had liver flukes. Many also had parasites in the respiratory tract. Externally, she found they had lice of various kinds and mites, both bloodsucking and feather eating. Boyd found so many different types of parasites that she thought starlings would be good for a course on parasitology. But she could not say how these parasites might have affected starling longevity, since her birds were part of a collection that had been shot.

If half the adults die each year, the only possibility to expanding their numbers is great success in reproduction, something made more likely by their cavity-nesting habit. In those cavity nests, starlings lay about five eggs. The eggs are incubated for eleven to fourteen days by both parents, then cared for for twenty-one days in the nest and another ten after fledging, for a total of about four weeks of care. If the parents finish early enough in the season, they will rear another brood.

Typically well over half of all nests succeed in fledging at least one and often more chicks, according to Brina Kessel.[6] She planned to get her Ph.D. with the famous naturalist, political activist, and author Aldo Leopold at the University of Wisconsin, but he died fighting a fire in 1948, a year after she got there. Furthermore, she discovered that Wisconsin did not let women get Ph.D.s in its wildlife management program at that time, so she went back to Cornell and got her Ph.D. there for work on European Starlings in 1951.

From 1945 to 1951, Kessel studied European Starlings in nesting boxes along roads bordering a rectangle 1.4 miles long and 0.8 miles wide. She put out about one hundred boxes at least 230 feet apart in the area of pastures with the occasional tree and untended hedgerows, perfect starling habitat. Kessel studied 532 nests, which were presumably tended by double that number of adults, 1,064, though some males might have mated with multiple females. There was an average of five chicks in each nest, and 85 percent of them survived to leave the nest.

But that is not all the death that chicks might find, since even after fledging, danger lurks. These dangers take many forms, from predation on just-fledged chicks to winter mortality. Kessel went through her data carefully and concluded that the chance of a fledgling surviving to reproduce is only about 20 percent, a number similar to that of American Robins or Song Sparrows.

According to *Birds of the World* and Breeding Bird Surveys, it seems that US starling populations have stabilized after growing and nearly doubling in many areas through the 1970s. In the fifty or so years since European Starlings reached Kessel's study site in Ithaca, New York, they had already expanded their numbers so much that they had reached a fairly constant population size.

One reason for starling success is that they seemingly eat just about anything. Starlings love insects of all kinds, snails, millipedes, and spiders. They also eat many kinds of fruits and nuts, including acorns. But there is something they do not eat—table sugar.[7] It turns out that European Starlings, like a number of other bird species, lack the enzyme sucrase and so cannot digest sucrose. When Carlos Martinez del Rio and Bruce Stevens offered starlings sucrose, or glucose and fructose, they found that the starlings preferred the glucose-fructose mixture at any concentration.[8] In fact, they hardly touched high concentrations of sucrose. In their next experiment, they forced either the sucrose or glucose-fructose mixture down their throats and then took small blood samples. The sucrose did not increase their blood sugar levels. They could not digest it. So starlings may peck at the remnants of your burger and your french fries, but they will not go for your candy bar.

The broad diet of European Starlings may be part of the reason they are more common than Northern Flickers, who eat only ants for protein. But a broad diet is not likely to be the only reason for starling success. One thing European Starlings share with Northern Flickers is safe nest sites protected from many predators: tree cavities. But the flickers create the cavities while the starlings steal them. Karen Wiebe showed at her Riske Creek, British Columbia, study site that starlings took as many as 7 percent of the cavities that flickers had excavated.[9] Riske Creek is an area the starlings did not reach until the 1950s. Starlings and flickers arrive at Wiebe's study site at about the same time each spring, around April 20. But the starlings start nesting earlier, nearly a week before the flickers. The difference in nesting time made Wiebe wonder if flickers could avoid starlings by nesting later, but this did not seem to be a strategy that made flickers more successful in this population. Once the flickers lost their nest to a starling, they were more likely to reuse old nest cavities instead of excavating new ones. These old nests tended to be infested with parasites, which made them less desirable.

Can we quantify the overall harm that European Starlings do to woodpeckers? Have they caused recent declines in woodpeckers, such as that of the Red-headed Woodpecker, which declined from 1966 to 2015 across its range in the eastern United States? The Red-headed Woodpecker is strikingly colored, with an entire red head and cape, a black back and tail, a white belly, and wings that flash with black as they fly. My old friend Walter Koenig and his team investigated whether starlings caused woodpeckers' decline.[10] They used data from the Breeding Bird Survey and the Christmas Bird Counts.

Koenig and team grouped the data by decade and found that

Red-headed Woodpecker numbers declined in both Breeding Bird Surveys and Christmas Bird Counts. By contrast, Red-bellied Woodpeckers, European Starlings, and American Kestrels all increased. Then they did a comprehensive analysis of each survey separately. In the Breeding Bird Survey, Red-headed Woodpecker numbers and European Starling numbers increased together. By contrast, Red-headed Woodpecker numbers decreased with increasing accipiters, which include Cooper's Hawk, Sharp-shinned Hawk, and Northern Goshawk. The Christmas Bird Count showed similar patterns, though the negative effect of accipiters was even stronger, and the positive effect of starlings was weaker.

The researchers surmised that starlings are not actually helping the woodpeckers, but that they may both be impacted by the same factors, like the quality of the forests. When Koenig and his team looked at forest cover directly, its increase was the only significant effect reducing numbers of Red-headed Woodpeckers in the Breeding Bird Survey, while for the Christmas Bird Count, the only significant factor was the number of accipiters. These predators also increased with decreasing forestation. So while we may witness a starling driving a woodpecker from its nest, this does not mean that they are driving out the woodpeckers at the population level. We are doing that with habitat changes. By the way, if I were doing this study today, I would use eBird as the best source of data and not these once-a-year counts.

In an earlier study, Danny Ingold looked more directly at competition for nesting holes among Red-bellied Woodpeckers, Red-headed Woodpeckers, and European Starlings around Mississippi State University in Starkville.[11, 12] It is a place I visited once to give a talk. I was impressed by the number of catfish ponds I saw in the area as the plane descended. Danny Ingold watched 96 Red-bellied and 105 Red-headed Woodpecker nests from 1985 to 1987 and found that starlings usurped 52 percent of the nests of the former species and

7 percent of the nests of the latter. Ingold attributed the difference to the later nesting of the Red-headed Woodpeckers. Pairs of Red-bellied Woodpeckers that lost their cavities to starlings had lower reproductive success, so starlings did have a negative impact on them, but the pattern was weaker for the rarer Red-headed Woodpeckers.

Earlier I talked about starling breeding to understand what accounts for their numbers, but there are other things that go on in their family lives. The males help incubate the eggs and even have a mostly featherless brood patch to put their warm breasts right on the eggs, something most male songbirds lack. It is an indication that males care for the eggs more than other male songbirds. But does this mean that the males are the fathers of the eggs they tend? In many songbirds, this is not the case for all the eggs, so what about European Starlings? Rianne Pinxten and her team studied this near Antwerp, Belgium, using genetic markers.[13]

Pinxten and her team looked at DNA from sixty-two chicks from fourteen nests and found that 10 percent of the young from 29 percent of nests had chicks whose genetic fathers were not the male tending them. So young of different males are common but not overwhelming. In contrast, in this population, eggs that did not come from the mother of the nest were rare—detected only once.

In another population, many nests had eggs laid by a female not the one tending the nest. Peter Evans found that between 11 and 37 percent of clutches had extra eggs in a study of nest boxes in Surrey and Aberdeen, UK.[14] Since egg dumping (as parasitism by females is vividly called) increases when there are fewer free nest boxes, it seems that females mostly lay eggs in others' nests when they cannot acquire a nest of their own. The female parasites have to lay their eggs after the host has started laying her own eggs, because the nest-owning females always rid the nest of any egg that is there before they themselves start laying.

It is easy to think that an egg from a stranger in the nest and the need to raise the subsequent needy chick is simply bad luck for parents that worked hard to build the nest for their own young. But if it happens often enough, it is something that is a fairly normal part of the landscape, something that could impact the evolved behavior of the caring parent.

If it were true that your daughter often brought home a friend from school for dinner, you might start planning for it, perhaps cooking a little extra in case this was a day an extra person showed up at the dinner table. And so it is with starlings.

Harry Power and his team at Rutgers University reasoned that if parasitism were common enough, the mother would lay fewer eggs herself so the pair would not be overburdened with chicks to care for.[15] They worked from 1983 to 1986 on the Kilmer Campus of Rutgers (now called the Livingston Campus) in Piscataway, New Jersey, putting up new nest boxes along a path that had long been used for starling research. They marked the eggs as they were laid so they could see if an extra egg popped into a nest. Starlings, like all birds, lay only one egg a day.

They were also able to do something that would not be allowed on a migratory songbird. They collected and killed female starlings after their nests had not received any eggs for a few days. Then they compared the number of postovulatory follicles in their ovaries to eggs in their nests. These follicles are the places in the ovaries that used to have eggs in them. By counting the follicles they could tell how many eggs the females had laid. If there were more follicles in the ovaries than eggs in the nest, something happened to the missing eggs. Either the females laid those eggs elsewhere, or the eggs were pushed out of the nest, perhaps by parasitic females.

With their study, Power and his team found that a third of nests in their population had at least one egg that could not have been laid by the nest mother because two eggs appeared in one day. To make up for the likelihood of receiving such an egg, they reasoned that the starlings typically produced clutches of five eggs, even though they could easily and successfully raise six chicks. By laying only five eggs, they could, even if a sixth egg showed up, still raise all the young without undue strain.

Perhaps hearing the travails of starling life has softened you toward these birds a bit. After all, they are far less invasive than we are. In the United States there may be 200 million starlings, but there are more than 300 million of us, and we are much bigger. Also, we take much more than cavities from other animals. While European Starlings rob woodpeckers of their cavities, rigorous studies of their impact on woodpecker populations indicate that habitat change caused by humans has the bigger impact. So if you love your fellow human beings in all their imperfection, perhaps there is a space in your heart for starlings.

Another reason to admire starlings is to consider their relatives. European Starlings are part of an ancient Asian and African group. Starlings as a family include groups from South Asia, Eurasia, and Africa, more than a hundred species in all. These thriving birds are often social, eat a wide variety of foods, and may even be ancestrally associated with large mammals, as their sister birds, the oxpeckers, are.

Some of the tropical species are spectacular. Consider the Superb Starling. This gorgeous bird has white eyes that gaze intelligently out of a mane of glossy black feathers. Its belly is robin red, its back a glossy dark turquoise. Modest white divides the red belly from the black bib and reappears under the tail. This stunning bird is native to East Africa, including the Mpala reserve in Kenya, where Dustin Rubenstein and his team work.[16] Besides being brilliantly colorful, the Superb Starling is noisy and lives in groups averaging twenty-six birds, including several breeders. The nonbreeders sometimes help provision the young and defend them against predators. Superb Starlings are one of thirty-four species of African Starlings.[17]

But we do not need to go to Africa to find mystery in starlings. If I wanted you to love European Starlings, I would start with murmurations, those mesmerizing movements of thousands of birds soaring, turning, turning again, then weaving around a forest, only to soar as if one again. The term "murmuration" comes from the sound of thousands of wings beating together, soft, low, and profound. It is best heard with eyes shut. The cloud of birds can include as many as 750,000 individuals and forms spheres, planes, and waves. Though they are in constant motion, they do not go anywhere, instead swirling around a roosting point on the ground to which they will all drop at sunset. It is wonderful to be close to a murmuration of starlings, those pre-roosting evening rivers of life.

In 2016 I witnessed murmurations on Otmoor Reserve, outside of Oxford, England. I took a cab out to the wet moor, requesting that the driver return for me in an hour and a half. I walked about a mile out along paths between wet meadows and impoundments to the place the Royal Society for the Protection of Birds had placed a few blinds. Others were already waiting there, and I hoped one of them would return me to Oxford if my taxi didn't make it back.

We waited in the darkening light. And then we saw them moving as if one above the tree line. There were thousands of birds, but not tens of thousands. They rose, they turned, they dropped, catching the evening sun more on some turns than on others. If they were ribbons of schooling fish, they might flow around me, shimmering between my fingers, but these were birds in the air, each moving on their own but together. Afterward I found my loyal taxi driver had waited for me, not wanting to risk leaving me in the dark.

Murmurations are displays that delight biologists and physicists alike, the former asking why they do it, the latter asking how they do it. Anne Goodenough and her team of biologists considered two hypotheses: that starlings avoided predators by flying in these huge flocks or that they did so to attract smaller groups to the roost, which would make them warmer.[18] She called these the "safer together" and "warmer together" hypotheses. The anti-predation hypothesis she broke into several sub-hypotheses, that larger groups diluted the risk of predation for any one bird, that larger groups would detect predators more quickly, and that larger groups would make it hard for a predator to track any one bird while flying.

Goodenough put out a survey on websites of the Royal Society of Biology and the University of Gloucestershire. The investigators publicized the survey in the UK on TV, in newspapers, magazines, and blog posts, and on Facebook and Twitter. The volunteer citizen scientists recorded date, time, location, temperature, whether it was urban, suburban, or rural, and what the underlying vegetation was. Then they estimated the number of birds in the murmuration, how long it lasted, and what happened when it ended. They also recorded the presence of any possibly predatory birds and what they were doing.

In all, Goodenough received data from 3,211 murmurations from twenty-three countries. Most of the reports were from the UK, but the United States and Canada reported a hundred events. The analyses focused on the 2,427 murmurations in the UK that had at least five hundred birds, so were bona fide murmuration-sized groups. Of those, the end was witnessed in 1,066 cases, with all birds descending simultaneously onto the roost.

They found that the average murmuration included more than thirty thousand starlings and lasted twenty-six minutes. As the winter progressed, murmuration sizes increased, reaching a climax in early February. They were shortest at the winter solstice.

The predators near murmurations in the UK were Sparrowhawks, Buzzards, Marsh Harriers, Hen Harriers, and Peregrine Falcons, in that order, and were found at 30 percent of observations. More predators meant more birds in the murmuration. When predators were present, the starlings also settled synchronously onto the roosting site, supporting the predation hypothesis.

Physicist Michele Ballerini and his team study winter starlings with a multi-camera setup at Rome's main Termini train station to understand how starlings manage the coordinated flight typical of murmurations.[19, 20] They have found that the stunning behavior comes from each starling simply keeping track of six or seven near neighbors. With this number, the starlings can turn and bend optimally, particularly after one sights a predator. Using their multiple cameras, Ballerini and team could also determine that the starlings flew more closely together on the edges of the group than in the center, just what one would predict if predators were the cause. After all, a predator will hit an edge bird first.

I guess I'll live with a double attitude toward starlings. I don't like it at all when they steal woodpecker cavities, but they are beautiful in their own right, and affection is a much more pleasant feeling than disgust.

I know it is autumn not just because the maple leaves turn red and orange but also because the gangs of young starlings gather on the Flynn Park grasses. These birds are duller than their glossy parents, at least for now. The flocks sometimes number more than twenty birds, and I wonder what their teenage conversations are about. They make a buzzing sound, almost like a soft leaf blower. These teenagers sleep together in hollows, then awaken and forage on the ground. It would be fun to watch them come out of their nighttime shelters.

Starlings are our birds. We brought them here, and our mangling of the environment causes them to thrive. The least we can do is try to understand them. Removing them is impossible at this point. And remember, they do less damage to native birds than we do with habitat destruction.

EUROPEAN STARLING ACTIVITIES
FOR SLOW BIRDERS

1. **Find European Starlings.** It won't be hard for a Slow Birder to find starlings. I recognize them easily when they're flying because their wings form a clear triangle on each side of the body. They nest in our eaves and forage in the grass, so they are easy to find. See if you can get a sense for how many pairs live around your home.

2. **Find nests.** Starlings often nest in home eaves, but they are also in tree cavities. Get in the habit of looking more closely at trees for hollows, particularly in the spring nesting season. If there is a nest in a tree, a male may sing from higher up, as one did last year from the snag in the maple across the street from my home. Make a map of the starlings around your home.

3. **Observe European Starlings eating.** Starlings eat everything. Are they in the grass digging up insects? See if you can detect them separating the plants by opening their bill and revealing what is underneath. Watch one starling on the ground for ten minutes, keeping track of exactly what it does.

4. **Guess the starlings' ages.** In late summer there will be flocks of teenage starlings with comparatively dull colors. The adults will also be duller earlier because they lose the tan tips to their feathers as they age. Once they molt, their feathers will be bright again. Pay attention to the feathers.

5. **Watch a starling nest.** If you find a nest in your nest box, you could check it often, perhaps installing a nest box camera. You could number the eggs as they are laid to see if more than one egg ever appears on the same day, indicating an egg-dumping female. See

how many eggs are laid and watch the succession from young to fledglings. However, European Starlings do not have the legal protection that migratory native birds have, so it is permitted to simply remove a starling nest and wait for a native bird.

6. **Study group behavior and vigilance.** In late summer and early fall, starlings gather in flocks. See if you can count the size of these flocks. As they forage on the ground, watch how they move. Do individual birds consistently move to the center of the group, forcing those already there out a bit in a never-ending motion? Do some stay vigilant, looking around while others feed? Are the groups different sizes on different days?

7. **Find a murmuration.** Few natural acts are as exciting as a starling murmuration, that flying flock of hundreds to thousands of birds, seething together, then spinning and moving in a new direction. Look for a video of one online. If you are lucky enough to find a murmuration in the fall or winter, watch it. Try to describe the pattern. Count the birds by estimating and see if they settle all at once at a roost. Look for a predator and see how the predator shapes the flood of birds.

8. **Census starlings.** Compare the numbers and places you see European Starlings in your neighborhood with those at a state park or in the country. Walk for ten minutes and compare the different habitats while looking and listening for starlings at each stop.

House Sparrow

Universal Human Commensal

Who doesn't love House Sparrows? Their cheerfully monotonous cheeps are among the first bird sounds a human baby hears, since they so often nest under house eaves. Because we are so familiar with their cheeps, it is easy to think that House Sparrow song is the basic template for all bird speech. When one hears the clear notes of an American Robin or the repetition of a Northern Cardinal, they seem special and unusual. But of course House Sparrow notes are only their own.

No other wild bird is as tied to us as the House Sparrow, a species found on all continents except Antarctica. To despise House Sparrows may be to despise ourselves. What then does it mean that in their native European habitats, House Sparrows are declining to worrying levels? In Great Britain, House Sparrows are declining so much that they are on the UK Red List of birds in need of urgent action. This is not true for the House Sparrows in America. But before we worry about their decline, it can be interesting to consider how they became so ubiquitous in the first place.

These highly adaptable birds have diverged across the planet, beginning in Palaearctic and eastern Oriental zoogeographic ancestral lands. The House Sparrow subspecies are divided into two geographic and morphological groups: *Passer domesticus domesticus* in more northern areas and *Passer domesticus indicus* in the Sinai Peninsula and through all of India. There are also a handful of other subspecies in northern Africa and between the *domesticus* and *indicus* populations. Of these, one is of particular interest, the *bactrianus* subspecies. *Passer domesticus bactrianus*, as it is formally called, does not associate with humans, instead preferring grasslands, particularly along rivers and lakes. Furthermore, it is migratory, wintering on the Indian subcontinent and then migrating north to breed right up to the Himalayas, along the Hindu Kush, along the eastern shore of the Caspian Sea, and up to the Aral Sea. Since all the other subspecies prefer to live among humans, the question is, did this trait evolve twice in the two main groups, or did it evolve once in their common ancestor? And what is closest to that common ancestor anyway?

To figure this out, Glenn-Peter Sætre and his colleagues at Norway's University of Oslo, Iran's Ferdowsi University of Mashhad, and Sweden's University of Gothenburg collected 181 samples of House Sparrow subspecies.[1] These included the subspecies that came to America—a story familiar to many, and one I'll tell next. The researchers took the most samples in an area where *domesticus* and *indicus* meet along with *bactrianus*, along the southern edge of the Caspian Sea and down to the Persian Gulf. These are the samples that should answer their question about whether House Sparrows acclimated to humans once or twice.

Once Sætre and his colleagues had the samples, they extracted DNA and sequenced several highly variable regions, some from the mitochondria, some from the sex-determining Z-linked gene, and some genes expressed in the brain. They wanted to find genes that were evolving quite rapidly, as they expected the diversification to have occurred as the House Sparrows spread out since the last glaciation of the Younger Dryas, about 11,500 years ago.

They found that there was only one genetic group of House Sparrows; the birds did not differentiate into two different groups. They also found evidence for an expansion that they could roughly date to between 3,000 and 7,500 years ago, when human agriculture was expanding around 10,000 years ago. We know the date for agricultural expansion from work on the first grains that Quentin Atkinson and colleagues conducted with a DNA analysis similar to that done on the House Sparrows.[2] So Sætre and his colleagues argued that House Sparrows cozied up to humans only once, when agriculture began some 10,000 years ago in the Middle East.

There are strong arguments for this relationship to have begun in the Middle East. Somewhat astonishingly, the oldest House Sparrow fossil comes from nowhere other than the ancient city of Bethlehem! This fossil is estimated to be 400,000 years old, long before human agriculture began. Furthermore, all the other House Sparrow fossils older than 10,000 years are also from the Middle East, one of the places where agriculture is thought to have begun. So, most House Sparrows, right from the beginning, benefited from the availability of grains stored by agriculturalists for food, and from nooks in houses and animal sheds for their nests.

But Sætre's team was not finished with this story. Much more recently, they did a project headed by Mark Ravinet to take it one step further.[3] First, they verified that the House Sparrow we see under our eaves and in our backyards really did split a single time from the *bactrianus* subspecies that still lives wild in the Middle East and Central Asian steppes east of the Caspian Sea. With that split, the House Sparrow tied its fate with ours. When we abandon towns, the House Sparrow does too. To further affirm this, Ravinet and team sequenced the entire genomes of forty-six House Sparrows and nineteen Bactrianus House Sparrows, along with a couple other close relatives from Spain and Italy that are not part of the story I am telling here. They found the Bactrianus House Sparrow indeed split from the House Sparrow around eleven thousand years ago, when humans were just beginning agriculture in what they call the Neolithic revolution.

Since they sequenced the whole genomes, they could ask questions about what genes were most different between the human-associated House Sparrow and the still-wild Bactrianus House Sparrow. Essentially they were using the latter as an indicator of what the pre-human-associated sparrow would be like. They found evidence of evolution in two very interesting genes. One, called *COL11A*, had to do with increased bill and skull thickness in the human-associated House Sparrows. The other, *AMY2A*, had to do with amylase genes, which are important in starch digestion. Both make sense. When the House Sparrows became affiliated with humans, those that evolved stronger bills were better able to eat the larger seeds and grains humans cultivate and then digest the larger amounts of starch in these larger seeds.

As humans and their agriculture spread, so did House Sparrows. Perhaps their zenith was before the Industrial Revolution, when horses were our means of transportation. Sparrows ate the seeds in the hay horses ate. They could nest in number in barns and houses. But as machinery replaced animals, particularly in the 1920s, when cars replaced horses, House Sparrow numbers plummeted. Denis Summers-Smith describes this decline in Britain.[4] In London's Kensington Gardens, for example, there were more than five thousand House Sparrows around 1920. The numbers declined abruptly in the years leading to 1930, then slowly to 1990, when there were fewer than one thousand in the park. By 2000, there were fewer than ten. There were similar declines in other areas.

On my morning walks in fall 2016, when I was a visiting scholar at Magdalen College, Oxford, I saw House Sparrows only occasionally, and it was not in the wilder areas of Christ Church meadow. It was along the back edge of the meadow where some apartments had bird feeders.

Summers-Smith attributes the general decline since 1990 to changes in agricultural practices. Crops are increasingly planted in the fall, not the spring. Instead of letting grasses mature to hay in the field, they are cut for silage before setting seed. Silage is fermented grass, something we usually see wrapped in huge bales of white plastic.

Increased use of herbicides and pesticides may also contribute to House Sparrow decline. Other issues include predation by cats and lack of sufficient insects to feed the young. House Sparrows are social birds and like to nest in colonies of at least ten pairs. They do not thrive as rare birds, only in groups.

I always think that when an organism that is tightly associated with us declines, we had better start considering what we are doing to our environment. After all, even in North America House Sparrow numbers declined by 84 percent between 1966 and 2015, according to the North American Breeding Bird Survey. But they are not going extinct.

House Sparrows may be tightly associated with humans, but they are not even supposed to be in the United States. Or in Australia, New Zealand, South Africa, or even Kenya. In all these places, they were introduced. What, we wonder, would be in their place had they not been loosed into our world? Who has suffered the most? The Eastern Bluebirds and Tree Swallows that arrive later on their breeding grounds only to find that the cavities they need for nesting have already been occupied by resident House Sparrows? People may save their nest boxes for native species by blocking their entrances early on when there are only House Sparrows around. People may choose to put out boxes with small entrances, reinforced with metal washers to keep the boxes for House Wrens and Chickadees. Or they may even pull House Sparrow nests and their contents out of the boxes, for as an invasive species, they are not protected by the Migratory Bird Treaty Act.

But how exactly did House Sparrows arrive in our country? I would have thought that such an important story would be clear, but it is not, as Michael Moulton and his collaborators from the University of Florida have shown with a bit of historical sleuthing.[5] According to the Moulton team, Walter Bradford Barrows reported that House Sparrows were first brought to the United States "in the fall of 1850, when the Hon. Nicolas Pike and other directors of the Brooklyn Institute imported eight pairs into Brooklyn, N.Y."[6] Barrows based his information on the results of a request by the US Department of Agriculture. In 1886 the USDA sent out 5,000 copies of a circular asking for information about the presence of the House Sparrow.[7] It received more than 3,300 answers and found that two-thirds of the respondents said there were House Sparrows at their location. Those answering that they did not have House Sparrows were mostly US mail postmasters, so the sampling of House Sparrow absence was probably not as complete as that of House Sparrow presence.

Was the first introduction by Nicholas Pike actually successful? We will never know for sure. Pike says that they did not release the eight first pairs until spring 1851. He does not say exactly where they were released, but he says that they did not thrive. Moulton suggests this might simply mean that they were not visible but were still present.

There were many subsequent introductions: one in the spring of 1853, when fifty House Sparrows were released in the Narrows between Staten Island and Brooklyn and another set was released at Greenwood Cemetery in Brooklyn. Other releases escalated the invasion, including those in Portland, Maine, and Boston and Quebec City. In 1867 House Sparrows were released in New Haven, Connecticut, and Galveston, Texas. Among the many other releases, perhaps the most notable were in San Francisco and Salt Lake City. People then coddled and moved House Sparrows to new places in ways unimaginable today. They fed them. They sheltered them. They loved them. They brought them everywhere. They became so expensive in the

United States that people imported them on their own directly from England and Germany. Was it really that these birds simply reminded them of home, of the cozy landscape they left for the sparsely settled New World? Or had it simply become a status-based fad?

Whatever had inspired the mania for House Sparrows in the first place, by 1880 people realized that House Sparrows had spread across the country. They were no longer so loved. Ultimately the USDA realized it had a problem and commissioned the Barrows report mentioned above. They found people were already viewing House Sparrows as a problem. Protective laws were repealed. Michigan even paid a bounty of a penny a head on these flourishing birds, who ravaged granaries and built messy nests wherever they could tuck them.

The Barrows report goes on for four hundred pages, documenting the early days of the House Sparrow. They were shot by the thousands, sold in markets for a dollar per hundred, and considered delicious in pot pies. People began to realize House Sparrows were regarded as destructive and worthless in their native England. Problems they caused make up the headings of sections of the Barrows report and include "injury to buds, blossoms, and foliage"; "injury by filth"; "injury to fruits, garden seeds and vegetables"; and "injury to grain." The report includes a table of the birds House Sparrows were found to harm. Eastern Bluebirds, American Robins, House Wrens, Mockingbirds, Purple Martins, Chipping Sparrows, and unspecified wren, swallow, and martin species were each mentioned by 50 to 377 people answering the flyers. Cavity nesters suffered the most harm. I won't tell you anything more from this report, but it is a fascinating glimpse into the lives of birds and people in the 1880s. And it is free to download.[8]

I don't know if House Sparrows would eventually have found their way here without help, perhaps from nests aboard a ship that had been too long in a British or European harbor. But once they arrived, as long as there were people, they flourished. Now they are part of our landscape, so ornithologists can study them to understand basic questions like how their families operate.

Patricia Schwagmeyer and Douglas Mock have delved into House Sparrow lives in detail, embarking on this joint project after decades of separate research, hers on thirteen-lined ground squirrels and his on egrets and herons. They wanted a common and local bird good for experiments and for involving their students, as they tell in the essay they wrote when they received the Wilson Ornithological Society's Margaret Morse Nice Medal, the society's highest honor.[9] They tie the success of their research first to putting colored bands on birds' legs to tell them apart, ultimately banding thousands. Margaret Morse Nice was the first to do this by putting a pink band on a Song Sparrow on March 26, 1928.

The second source of success for Schwagmeyer and Mock was their deep understanding of the theory in animal behavior. Another particularly satisfying connection of the Schwagmeyer-Mock team to Margaret Morse Nice is that they were at the University of Oklahoma, in Norman, where the Nices once lived, beginning in 1913. The Nice home was at 445 College Avenue, just a block from the Schwagmeyer-Mock abode.

The House Sparrows that Trish and Doug studied were in nest boxes near the university's Animal Behavior Laboratory, formerly a WWII naval air station. They coaxed the sparrows nesting under the building eaves into a row of nest boxes equipped with perches and protected them from Loggerhead Shrike predation with a four-inch-long hardware-cloth entry tube.

Schwagmeyer and Mock quickly began to appreciate the House Sparrows' intelligence. They needed many tricks to catch the House Sparrows so they could band them. They then weighed, measured, collected a blood sample, and banded the birds in a car. They then took them away from their own vehicle before releasing them because otherwise the sparrows would learn to recognize their vehicle and scold it instead of behaving naturally.

There was a big question that inspired Schwagmeyer and Mock to do all this work. It concerned the puzzle of monogamy. What monogamy means to biologists is the social pairing of one male with one female and joint care of the young. As a mating system, this is very rare in animals and pretty much unheard of in microbes, plants, and the like. Though monogamy occurs in some arthropods like isopods, burying beetles, and snapping shrimp, and in a few mammals like prairie voles, white-toothed shrews, Kirk's dik-dik, gibbons, and golden jackals, it is in the birds that monogamy triumphs, with 92 percent sticking with their mate at least for the season. House Sparrows, by contrast, just might be that ideal system for understanding monogamy.

Monogamy really has two challenges. The first has to do with mating, and the second has to do with caring for the young. These challenges are different for males and females. So progress on the monogamy question can be made only by considering the separate interests of males and females.

The male and the female have evolved to strive to be genetic parents of the young they tend and also to leave to their partner as much of the work of rearing the chicks as possible. So a male guards a female against mating with another while he himself might try to mate outside the pair bond. That he might actually succeed in mating outside the pair bond was first shown for House Sparrows in 1987 by Terry Burke and Michael Bruford.[10] Using DNA probes first used on humans, they identified a single House Sparrow chick that did not come from the putative father. This began an explosion of research that transformed our view of birds. Instead of faithful partners dutifully rearing their chicks, they were indeed dutifully rearing chicks but also trying to find mating opportunities elsewhere, and those chicks the males reared might not be their own.[11]

Both parents guard against another female sneaking eggs into the nest, though the father will do so less if there is a chance he mated with that other female. So even though there may be social monogamy, both parents may carry genes that push them to mate outside the pair bond, the female to get a father for her chicks with better genes or that allows her access to his territory, and the male to have young he does not have to care for. But if these efforts at mating outside the pair bond get in the way of caring for the chicks, they will not be favored. This is the great trade-off. The solution is complex in House Sparrows because nearly a fifth of the young are sired by males other than the one that cares for them. Not quite half of all nests have one or more of these unrelated chicks.

The female starts out with a greater stake in her nest of eggs, since an egg makes up a much greater share of her body weight than does sperm for the male. This greater interest is relevant because of its replacement cost. It will be harder for a female to lay a new nest of eggs at the limiting rate of one egg per day than it will be for a male to produce more sperm if he can find a willing mate. But after that, baby birds are as easily cared for by the male as by the female, a sharp contrast with, say, a baby skunk whose mother, like all mammals, is uniquely equipped to nourish the young with her milk. If caring for these young is the best option for leaving more individuals in the next generation, then that is what the parents will do.

That one-egg-a-day limit for a female will encourage the male to stick close to her during the laying period of five or so days so he can mate with her each day and be the father of those four or five chicks. In House Sparrows, incubation starts after all but one egg has been laid and continues for about eleven days. The female is the only one that develops a brood patch, so she can sit skin-to-egg and warm them optimally, but males also incubate the eggs, though less efficiently. This might be the time when the males try to seek other mating opportunities without the burden of paternal care. It turns out that they are quite effective in finding other females to mate with at this time. As the eggs get closer to hatching, they become more valuable because they have survived the early dangers. Accordingly, the male increases his share of egg brooding from about a sixth of the time early on to nearly half the time just before hatching.

Once the chicks hatch, their needs are tremendous for the next two weeks. After all, it takes between three and four thousand insects to bring a chick to fledging. Which is two hundred to three hundred trips a day. And that doesn't even count their need for warmth, defense from predators, and nest hygiene. The cost to a male's reproduction if he did not care for them is high enough that he spends much time feeding the chicks in the nest and for about a week afterward. But exactly how much he cares, how much she cares, who mates outside the pair bond, and what explains it, are the great questions Doug and Trish address with an elegant combination of observations and experiments.

Mock and Schwagmeyer are famous for completely exhaustive approaches to fieldwork—also discussed for Mock in the chapter on Great Egrets. It was no different with these House Sparrows. To understand the best way of measuring exactly how much food went to the chicks and whether the male or the female brought it, they watched five nests from dawn to dusk on alternate days for the two weeks the chicks were in the nest.[12] Each nest thus had thirty to thirty-six hours of observation. They then analyzed their observations to see if there was a specific period of the day that was most representative of the whole day and could capture how feeding patterns changed with time and among nests. On these nests, food delivery varied from six to seventeen times per hour, so there was a lot of variation to explain. By picking the right time, five hours per nest at the right time of day was as valuable for testing hypotheses as thirty hours per nest. They found that the two-hour period most representative of the whole day was what they called T3 and corresponded to

late morning, about 10:00 a.m. to noon. Good to know. This doesn't
mean parents are at their peak in feeding; that is first thing in the
morning, when the chicks have had a foodless night to recover from.
It means that this is the time that gives the best picture of the
whole day.

Schwagmeyer and Mock made another discovery important in
assessing what parents did for their chicks. It had to do with what it
takes to produce successful offspring.[13] Many researchers simply
count the number of young at hatching and then see how many have
survived to fledge and what they weigh as a measure of successful
parental investment. More careful researchers might ask questions
about foraging and count the number of trips each parent makes to
the nest with food. But each trip is not the same, since some trips
bring tiny insects while others bring comparatively huge grasshoppers
or caterpillars, nearly an inch long. And it turned out that numbers
of these huge food items, or "enormous" as they called them, were the
most important in predicting offspring success, even though they
were provided on only 14 percent of all foraging trips. So, to measure
what a given parent does for the young, don't look at total times they
feed the babies but instead look at the number of huge prey items they
provide.

Another important feature of this study was that they did not just
look at nestling survival to the time the young left the nest, or even
survival to the end of parental care. Instead they continued to observe
the young into adulthood, when the young sparrows joined the breeding population. This they could measure because of the sedentary
nature of House Sparrows, so the survivors were still in the same
population. Some of them might have been a bit farther away and so
missed, but a lot of them were in the same population taking advantage of the perfect nest boxes. It is a rare study indeed that goes all
the way from a grasshopper offered as food to a nestling to whether
that baby makes it to join the adult population the following year.

Now that I've explained how carefully Schwagmeyer and Mock considered reproductive success in House Sparrows, it is time to return to the original question of the tension between parents for each producing as many babies as possible with the best possible partners, though the social parent at the nest and the genetic one may not be the same.

Once settled with a partner, female and male will prefer that the other do more of the work. How this gets resolved is one of the great questions in animal behavior. Is there a kind of daily negotiation played out between House Sparrow parents as to who broods, defends, and brings in the all-important enormous prey to the chicks? Does the male hold back, causing the female to increase her care? Is it a never-ending series of adjustments as to who does what, or is it a kind of sealed bid where the partners forge a deal at the beginning of the nesting season and then do not change their behavior?

To figure this out, Schwagmeyer and Mock did a really clever experiment.[14] They changed the cost of foraging by clamping 0.07-ounce split-shot fishing weights to the base of the tail feathers of either the male or the female of experimental pairs. These weights increase the cost to the birds by disrupting their balance and making flight more effortful.

They observed how much the parents fed the chicks from about three days after hatching until the tenth day after hatching, taking care to observe in that late-morning time that is most indicative of the whole day and to note the size of the prey the parents carried. They then compared the days immediately before and after the weights had been applied with the changes in food deliveries that occurred at control nests, and found that males brought in only about 40 percent as much food when they had to deal with the balance-disrupting weight. Weighted females, on the other hand, reduced their food delivery only very slightly. But the differences lasted only a day or so. After that both sexes seem to have adjusted to the weights and brought their foraging back to prior levels, perhaps at a personal cost to their longevity. But what did the females do about the short time when weighted males brought less food to the chicks? It turns out that females increased their feeding rate, but only slightly, and kept up that higher rate when the males returned to normal foraging levels. When females were weighted, males increased their own food deliveries and kept up the higher level of feeding after the females recovered. This is surprising because females never did reduce their feeding levels much.

Schwagmeyer and Mock then took another approach to experimentally reducing male parental care. They did it by implanting timed-release testosterone tubes in males, with the control being implanting empty tubes in other males.[15] They needed this control to be sure that just surgically inserting the tubes beneath the skin was not causing any behavioral changes. Higher testosterone is well known in birds to reduce male parental care and to increase male aggression. It also makes him more likely to sing more to attract other females, just as it did in Dark-eyed Juncos, discussed in their chapter.

The researchers implanted testosterone or empty tubes in males at the beginning of courtship in March for three years, 2001 to 2003. They implanted about ten males with testosterone and ten males with an empty tube each of the three seasons. Then they measured how much the males took care of the eggs and chicks and to what extent females compensated for the expected reduced care. Male House Sparrows implanted with testosterone spent on average only five minutes per hour incubating eggs, while control males spent thirteen minutes per hour, a huge difference. Females incubated more minutes per hour to make up for males. So females do respond to a change in male behavior when it comes to incubating.

The researchers next wondered if the testosterone-treated males also reduced feeding when the chicks were hungry. They found that the testosterone-treated males brought food to their chicks 62 percent less often than control males. The females did not compensate for reduced feeding by testosterone-treated males.

This study, along with the earlier one with weights, indicates that females do not compensate for slacking males during feeding even though they do during incubation. It could be that less food per hour simply means it takes chicks longer to mature, while less incubation, particularly during cold spells, could be fatal. Or it could be that females have better information about incubation since they can detect egg temperature changes through their brood patches. Of course every day in the nest box increases the danger of predation, so not compensating for reduced male feeding also has its risks.

In their next study, Mock and Schwagmeyer did something that had very surprising results. They reduced parental burdens by hand feeding the nestlings themselves with baby bird food twice a day, giving them about a quarter of their normal daily intake.[16] Then they watched the nests and recorded parental feeding behavior for about fifteen hours at each of the twenty-three nests where they were feeding the chicks. What would the parents do with chicks that were not as hungry as before? And would it change the balance between male and female feeding?

It turned out that the parents at first were not responsive to the extra food the chicks got. They kept feeding them as before. Females increased feeding when the chicks were five days old, as they usually do, but the surprise was that the males also increased their feeding, topping the control male's feeding by 25 percent! So when the chicks were supplemented, the male matched the female by increasing feeding in the second period of life, when the chicks were five to ten days old, as compared with the earlier period, when they were three to four days old.

How to explain this surprising result? Mock and Schwagmeyer

suggested that it might be that the father gave the chicks more food because he perceived them to be higher quality, more likely to survive to reproduce and so particularly worthy of extra attention. The chicks could have encouraged that perspective by their louder begging.

Another way of understanding this result requires that we return to some basic House Sparrow biology. Sparrow parents are not like you and me. They have not read the Bible and know nothing of the prodigal son. Instead they have evolved to give the most to those that already have. When the male observes he has a brood of chicks doing particularly well, he increases his efforts because these may be his best bet for genetic immortality.

This behavior may seem counter to maximizing the numbers of chicks he sees to adulthood. After all, in unsupplemented broods, why not give those chicks the same extra he was giving to these extra-strong-looking chicks? Perhaps the answer is that the extra work costs him. A parent could completely deplete itself, giving everything to the young with no thought to self. Such a parent would be unlikely to live to the next season. But a mother bird is not like the European black lace-weaver spider who encourages her young to consume her. A mother's own interests extend past the current brood. A House Sparrow typically has more than one brood a season and can live for several seasons. So males and females feed this batch of young but still take care of themselves, balancing their future reproductive possibilities against the current efforts.

There is something else that parents do to be sure to feed their babies sufficiently while still surviving themselves in the face of unpredictable insect availability. After all, those enormous insects so vital to nestling prosperity are highly variable in their availability from one season to the other and also within seasons. So how can parents realistically decide how many young to rear in each brood? House Sparrows have an age-old solution. It has to do with creating a "loser" chick, which they do by beginning to incubate the eggs before the last one is laid.

Since they typically lay four or five eggs in a nest, the chick that hatches last will have three or four siblings to compete with for food. And the weaker ones are likely to be given less food since parents preferentially feed chicks with bright mouths, as then graduate student Matthew Dugas found by experimentally painting the mouth edges of some House Sparrow chicks.[17]

Since food availability is highly variable between years, it is hard to predict how many chicks the parents can rear in any given year, so they make an extra. If they did not begin incubating before the last egg was laid, or did not prefer to feed stronger chicks, this would not be so. But do the weaker, last-laid chicks actually die? In a huge study over thirteen years, Mock, Schwagmeyer, and Dugas found that 42 percent of a thousand nests lost a chick. These were not cases of predation, for those took the whole brood. They were cases where one chick simply did not get enough food. After the chick died, the parents kept up their same feeding rate so the remaining chicks got more food and thrived.

Why not simply lay fewer eggs so these 420 chicks did not have to die? It is because the parents that do that leave fewer copies of their genes in the population. Such a behavior is simply not favored by evolution. Start more chicks and more than half the time it will pay off. At this population level, it would be 580 extra chicks born because parents took the risk of laying a number of eggs that they might not be able to raise.

There is another factor that might be hard for us to comprehend. It is the amazing trajectory of chick development, true for most songbirds and based on the hazards of being a young bird in a nest, vulnerable to all kinds of predators. And that is that growth and development are blindingly fast. As Mock and his team put it, these baby sparrows convert their food into growth at the phenomenally efficient rate of 28 percent in the first five days. Then, as they start providing their own body heat, depending on the adults less for warmth, that rate halves to 14 percent. These babies are digesting their food and turning it into baby sparrow extremely quickly. They might die with even a slight reduction in food, particularly if the reduction occurs before age eight days. And getting more food later does not change this. They cannot make up for the earlier loss.

Even tiny amounts of food matter. Schwagmeyer and Mock found that the amount of food that made a difference to a chick's survival was 2 grams. I put this in grams because its ounce equivalent is the unwieldy 0.0705. Specifically, what they found was that parents would have more surviving offspring if losing one chick meant the remaining chicks each gained 2 grams from the extra food they got when they did not have to share with the chick that died. A chick does so much better if it can get to 26 grams at fledging. What is that amount like? An AA battery weighs 24 grams, a good comparison.

House Sparrows have flourished wherever we have flourished. From their Middle Eastern origins, they have spread on their own across the lands and, with our help, across the oceans. They stick to us, living where we live, avoiding places we have left alone. This habit might make them an ideal invader. But because they are with us, we see them often as a constant reminder of human folly. I bet Doug Mock and Trish Schwagmeyer grew to love their House Sparrows as they spent twenty years teasing out the most intricate details of their family life and its strife.

I'll look at the House Sparrows nesting under the eaves at Flynn Park Elementary and in the buildings in Forest Park with a little more respect. They may displace native birds, but only in the human-constructed landscape. And we have learned so much about behavior from them.

HOUSE SPARROW ACTIVITIES
FOR SLOW BIRDERS

1. **Watch where House Sparrows nest.** It may seem House Sparrows are everywhere, but what if they are nowhere we are not? What if where we see them is simply a reflection of where we ourselves are? Make a map of where you see them and note how much it is restricted to human buildings. Log the nests or even just the birds themselves. You could even do a transect, walking away from a building, perhaps one like I see in Forest Park. If you are a hundred yards from a building, do you see House Sparrows?

2. **Listen to House Sparrows.** Who is singing? Can you record their different syllables? With a careful listen, maybe you can appreciate that even their simple notes have a lot of variety.

3. **Look at the bibs on the males.** The darkness of male bibs is a trait that has been much studied for what it may mean about dominance. But the results are not so clear. Maybe you can find a place House Sparrows are foraging and see if males with bigger bibs displace males with smaller bibs.

4. **Look carefully at male bills.** See if you can detect color changes with the seasons.

5. **Watch a nest.** If a House Sparrow nests in your bird box or somewhere else you can watch it, see if you can time the feedings. Look for those enormous prey that are so important to nestling success.

6. **Watch flocks.** The young of the year in late summer and fall will tend to move about in groups. If you see one of these groups, try to

watch what they do to stay together. If one flies, do they all fly? What exactly do they do?

Take advantage of the tameness of House Sparrows for a close look. And remember, not only did we bring them to this continent, but our activities are what give them food and shelter.

Northern Cardinal

Find Me Anywhere

St. Louis is Cardinal country. We wear our iconic bird on our caps and our T-shirts. It bands us together, for the favorite sport of St. Louis is baseball, and our team is the St. Louis Cardinals. I like to think a thief intent on my backpack might pause if I had a Cardinals baseball cap on, showing we are on the same team.

Northern Cardinals have nothing to do with religion, but the name we give them comes from the brilliant scarlet costume of Roman Catholic cardinals. Male Northern Cardinals are nearly the same color as the Catholic cardinals' vestments, a brilliant red tending toward tomato. They also have a jaunty crest and a black mask and chin flanking a serious bill, which bird-banders watch carefully— better they clamp down on one's entire thumb than on the delicate webbing between one's fingers.

To me, female Northern Cardinals, with their tan and russet, are just as beautiful as male Northern Cardinals, yet they share with the male a bright red beak, tail, and wing undersides. Both sexes also have a crest pointing to the sky. I like to think the male is what a five-year-old would draw with bold red strokes, while the female shows the sophistication and doubts of a teenage artist trying to be subtle. It makes sense that in the south, where cardinals are common, they are simply called "redbirds."

Some people seem to be in a stupor so deep that they do not notice the birds around them. When they come to and look with amazement at the natural world, the Northern Cardinal is often the first bird they notice. From new birders I often hear surprise at the intense red of the male Northern Cardinal, along with the joy at his unmistakable song. This new awareness may be happening today, March 1, somewhere in St. Louis as cardinals sing from the leafless treetops, anticipating spring.

It is no wonder that the Northern Cardinal is the official state bird for seven contiguous central-eastern states: Illinois, Indiana, Ohio, Kentucky, West Virginia, Virginia, and North Carolina. No other bird claims as many states. Northern Cardinals may be the most chosen state bird because they are among the most conspicuous birds in the human landscape. We can therefore ask if the human landscape has helped or hurt them. How do they meet their needs in the built environment? We can start to find the answer in our own gardens, where cardinals are very common.

The 2020 Great Backyard Bird Count, an interorganizational effort between the Cornell Lab of Ornithology, National Audubon Society, and Birds Canada, ran from February 14 to 17, Friday to Monday. People, including me, counted and registered on eBird the birds they saw in their own garden, or a similar place they designated. There was one bird that appeared on the most North American checklists, 70,168 times in all. It was the Northern Cardinal. Next was the Dark-eyed Junco, on 59,318 checklists. Following those two were Mourning Doves, Downy Woodpeckers, Blue Jays, House Sparrows, House Finches, American Crows, Black-capped Chickadees, and Red-bellied Woodpeckers, in that order.

Apparently Northern Cardinals almost always top the list. They are good at suburbs, and that is where most birders' gardens are. There is a male right now sitting on the bare branches of a cherry tree at the back of my small garden, improbably red against the tree's dark, wet branches.

But Northern Cardinals do not occur all across our country. In some respects they have an unusual distribution. They are an eastern bird, barely ever pushing their way any farther west than Colorado or Wyoming. They are rare in Canada except for in southern Ontario. But Northern Cardinals also plunge south and west into Mexico, taking in all of Texas and over into southern New Mexico and Arizona, where they overlap with their paler relative, the Pyrrhuloxia.

Northern Cardinals seem so robust, so large for a suburban bird, that it is hard to imagine them ever suffering. But the Passenger Pigeon that could feather the sky with its millions also seemed invulnerable, so I always worry. I worry in part because of that high overlap with our gardens. I fear that cardinals have a different kind of challenge, the kind that comes not from outright enemies but from more intimate ties. Could we smother our beloved cardinals, not because we don't love them, but because they have become so dependent on our landscape, a landscape that might betray them? To answer this, it is worth exploring exactly why cardinals prosper so in the human landscape.

Cardinals like what we call edge habitat, neither forest nor prairie. In a way our gardens are all edge habitat, with their hedges, flower beds, and trees. Even in more rural areas, we have made more borders between field and forest, benefiting the cardinals. But we have increased edges not only by cutting down forests but also by introducing alien shrubs. Chief among these are Amur honeysuckle and multiflora rose. They seem to provide both the red fruit cardinals love and bushy vegetation for their nests. But is this dependence good for Northern Cardinals? Are nests in these bushes less likely to succeed than those in more native vegetation? This is just the question that Kathi Borgmann and Amanda Rodewald asked.[1]

Borgmann and Rodewald surveyed 143 Northern Cardinal nests on a transect along the Scioto River in Ohio. This river flows south, ultimately joining the Ohio River. The investigators concentrated on twelve riparian forest fragments near Columbus, Ohio, some in the city and some in the nearby countryside. They searched for active nests from May to early August from 2001 to 2003. They found that it was easiest to find nests by watching the birds as they carried nesting material or food to the nest. Once they found a nest, they checked it every couple of days. They categorized nests as having failed if they were destroyed, losing their eggs or young in the process, or if they were abandoned after incubation had clearly started, something that happened only after the nest had lost some of its eggs or chicks.

Borgmann and Rodewald were mainly interested in the impact of invasive honeysuckle and multiflora rose on nest success. They found that 24 percent of the nests were in the honeysuckle, 28 percent were in the multiflora rose, and 48 percent were in native trees and shrubs. The nests in native vegetation were 2.5 times higher above the ground than those in the invasive bushes. There was more predation on nests in native plants in the rural habitats, and less predation on nests in native plants in the more urban habitats.

In addition to studying natural nests, Borgmann's group placed seventy-nine experimental nests in invasive honeysuckle and multiflora rose and in native plants at a rural site. They used old nests of Northern Cardinals and American Robins and baited each with a single plasticine egg made to look like a cardinal egg. Predators attacked more fake eggs in the nests in rose and honeysuckle than in the native plants. Mammals seemed to be the main predators, based on the marks on the plasticine eggs. So, it seems that invasive plants are more dangerous for nesting cardinals.

Besides providing a place to nest, Amur honeysuckle and multiflora rose have red fruit, something that is very important for Northern Cardinals because the carotenoids in the fruit help them develop their red color, though they can also use non-red carotenoids to produce red plumage. Redness in males has been viewed as a signal of high quality that females may use when choosing their mate. This could be either because red berries are harder to get, or because only birds in excellent condition can metabolize the carotenoids in berries or seeds in ways that result in brighter colors.

Humans may have broken the link between male quality and male color by making red berries easy for males to get. If the important factor is availability, females would no longer be able to use this signal as a way of choosing the best male, something that might reduce their reproductive success. Amanda Rodewald and colleagues investigated this, focusing on Amur honeysuckle.[2] This imported plant is a good one to focus on because it is associated with humans, it has red berries with carotenoids, and its dense growth provides often-used, if poor, nesting habitat, as we saw earlier. The Rodewald team predicted that males depending on honeysuckle would produce brighter feathers, which might fool females into thinking they were better when they simply had depended on honeysuckle. Interestingly, they found different results between urban and rural areas. They were surprised to see that bright males produced fewer young in rural but not urban areas. Interestingly, redder males bred earlier in rural landscapes and later in urban ones. In those rural habitats, bright males had more honeysuckle in their territory.

One of the most significant ways a species can become more abundant is by expanding its range, finding a way to thrive in places it never did before. What might facilitate that spread?

According to *Birds of the World*, Northern Cardinals have spread north in the United States since at least the mid-1800s.[3] The first nest in Michigan was found in 1884 at the University of Michigan's George Reserve. Cardinals expanded into the Great Plains and into Arizona in the late 1800s. There were no cardinals in New England until 1940, with the first nest in Massachusetts in 1958, and the first nest farther north in Maine only in 1969.

What has caused all this expansion? Is it a warming climate? A change in food availability? A loss of predators? Part of the answer may be hanging in your garden. Bird feeders may seem like a personal choice, made so you can see birds in your back garden or on your balcony more easily. But in aggregate they have fundamentally changed the landscape for birds, particularly northern ones. How big an impact this is can be seen by the amount of money spent on seed, feeders, and the like: over five billion dollars in 2011 by 52 million Americans.[4, 5]

There is interesting research on the impact of feeders. Stacey Johansen and her team recruited 173 volunteers all across the United States and gave them each four squirrel-protected feeders.[6] The volunteers put the four feeders in a straight line with two yards between them. Each feeder got one kind of seed, either black-oil sunflower with intact shells, medium black-oil sunflower chips without hulls, fine black-oil sunflower chips without hulls, striped sunflower, cracked corn, nyjer thistle seeds, red milo (sorghum), safflower, white millet, or shelled peanuts split in half. Each volunteer got a predetermined seed rotation and monitored the feeders every other day by recording the birds at them every five minutes for forty-five minutes. Of all those seed types, Northern Cardinals preferred black-oil sunflower seeds. So if you want to attract cardinals, put black-oil sunflower seeds in your feeders. Habitat changes and feeders may help Northern Cardinals continue to move north.

Molly McDermott and Lucas DeGroote studied northern movement for twenty-one different songbirds in western Pennsylvania at Powdermill Nature Reserve near Pittsburgh.[7] This field station is directed by my old friend John Wenzel from my wasp days in the South American tropics. The banding operation at Powdermill is a big one, as birds are mist-netted and banded three to four days a week during the breeding season. The researchers aged the birds as hatch year or before hatch year and assessed how the date they started catching young birds had changed over the fifty-three years (1961–2014) that birds had been trapped, banded, and recorded at Powdermill.

For a little background, it is true that at Powdermill there was not a statistically significant increase in temperature or rainfall over the fifty-three years, though for both there were slightly positive trends.

But temperatures did increase statistically in early spring, and rainfall increased in May and June over that half century.

How did this affect Northern Cardinals? Females had brood patches earlier and had longer breeding seasons in warmer springs. This added up to increased numbers of young for each pair, on average. Increased spring rainfall resulted in later appearance of juvenile Northern Cardinals, while increased summer rainfall resulted in increased numbers of young. In their study Northern Cardinals were one of the few bird species that actually benefited from the warming climate, and this appeared to be because they often have more than one brood per year. The only other bird that also benefited was the Gray Catbird, while the other nineteen species that they studied did not benefit. However, many of the other species also have more than one brood per year, so we have more to learn about these patterns.

Thus far I've painted a complex picture of Northern Cardinals using the human-built environment, profiting from increased shrubbery and from the warming climate. *Birds of the World* says Northern Cardinal numbers have been increasing, and we can surmise that the cause is their ability to use human-altered landscapes.[8] There has been an increase in the number of cardinals in the Northeast over the last two hundred years. From 1970 to 2014 the increase was by about 17 percent in the United States and Canada, according to the Breeding Bird Surveys. The expansion was mostly first-year birds moving beyond the edge of the range as they tried to establish territories near where they were born but found they were already taken.[9] Such dispersal from their birthplace would have succeeded only if the unoccupied habitat was suitable. But there have also been regional decreases in the southeastern United States and the arid Southwest, so we cannot say cardinals are profiting from the warming climate without qualification.

Humans have had a great deal of influence on the lives of Northern Cardinals, but that influence is not the only story worth telling. I would also like to tell about song, for the clear notes of cardinals may be one of the first songs a beginning birder learns. They are clear, often rising or falling, and sung starting on warm days in January, often by a male high in a bare-branched tree or dense bush. But don't be fooled into thinking it is only the males that sing. Females of this remarkable bird sing too.

Listen to a Northern Cardinal singing on a spring morning. Its voice is unmistakable. And yet it varies. The most fundamental units of cardinal songs are *notes*: a note is a continuous sound. Robert Lemon, a researcher and professor at McGill University, was the expert on cardinal dialects and song matching.[10] His hearing was apparently so acute and discriminating that he could recognize father-son pairs in which the son had presumably learned its songs from its father. Bob Montgomerie verified this, saying that Lemon "lived and breathed birdsong."

Cardinals copy those they hear nearby. One example of this was provided by two young males that established territories in their first spring near an older male that had some unusual song characteristics. Before long, the young males were also singing that syllable. But they acquire new songs only when they are less than a year old. Northern Cardinals not only learn songs from their neighbors, but they also improvise on them as their songs develop, slightly modifying some notes and syllables. Lemon called this sort of improvisation "drift."

To really understand songs, Lemon looked at birds from different places and identified songs that differentiated dialects in different locations. He felt that the limited dispersal and lack of migration by Northern Cardinals help preserve dialect differences that develop in different locations, because it is rare for birds that sing new song variants to enter a population. Cardinal song is clear, frequent, and common, making their singing and song acquisition a good basis for understanding songs of other, less accessible birds in which Lemon found similar patterns.

Mary Anderson and Richard Conner listened to cardinals singing in East Texas in three different forest plots a bit over 2.5 miles apart.[11] Their goal was to determine whether songs varied even over this short distance, and if so, whether cardinals in the same plot had songs that were more similar than those of cardinals in different plots. If that was the case, they wanted to know whether the songs of males with adjacent territories were particularly similar, compared with songs of other males in the same plot. They also wanted to know whether the songs sung in different plots had different characteristics that particularly favored sound transmission in the plot in which they were sung. One site was a shortleaf pine sapling forest with a thick, shrubby understory, with trees about eighteen years old. The second study area was planted with loblolly and other pines and had a thin shrub understory. It was about forty-three years old. The third study area was about fifty-nine years old, mostly shortleaf pine with a midstory cover, which meant there was little understory.

The investigators gridded off the area and spent seventy days recording Northern Cardinals from March to July 1979. In all they recorded 2,611 songs from sixteen individual males. They recorded five or six cardinals in each of the three habitats. When they tracked the appearance of new syllable types in their recordings, they realized that they had to record about a hundred different songs to get all the different syllable types in the repertoire of a given Northern Cardinal.

In all, Anderson and Conner identified thirty-two different syllable types. Eleven syllable types were shared between all three of the forest plots, making up about half the syllable types recorded in each plot (twenty-three syllable types were recorded in the youngest plot, twenty-three in the middle plot, and twenty-one in the oldest plot). However, cardinals in the same plot shared an even higher percentage of syllable types than were shared between plots. Thus, songs did indeed vary across the short distances separating the plots.

Cardinals in more similar forest plots shared more syllable types: eighteen were shared between the middle-aged and oldest forest plots, fifteen were shared between the youngest and middle-aged forest plots, and only twelve were shared between the youngest and oldest plots. Syllable usage presented a slightly different picture, in which the youngest and middle plots were more similar to one another than to the oldest plot. On average, syllables used in the youngest plot had the most rapid changes in frequency, an acoustic characteristic that could transmit clearly when cardinals sang from the top of the young trees, but would not have transmitted as well when cardinals sang from below the canopy of the older trees in the other two plots. Cardinal populations were also densest in the youngest forest, with 0.42 pairs per acre, compared with 0.38 pairs per acre in the middle-aged forest and 0.36 pairs per acre in the oldest forest. Cardinals in the youngest forest also engaged in the most matched countersinging, in which birds direct songs to one another by using the same song types. Birds with song repertoires as large as those of cardinals are unlikely to sing the same song types by random chance, so we can confidently say they are matching the heard song. Increased competition for territories, with more matched countersinging with territorial rivals, would be expected to occur at higher levels in denser populations.

The low rumble of urban life can change what birds hear. Whether Northern Cardinal songs change to better transmit through urban noise was a question that Desiree Narango and colleagues tackled.[12] They found that in more urban landscapes, cardinals sang longer, faster songs, with higher frequency notes. Urban noise was the best predictor of pitch, while an increased number of other cardinals nearby was the best predictor of song length and speed.

Is it a surprise that female cardinals also sing? After all, they are apparently the ones to choose their mate, so they shouldn't have to sing to attract a mate. But song is their voice, and once they are mated, singing can tell the male when to bring in food. Sylvia Halkin studied female cardinal song in a nature reserve in Madison, Wisconsin, from 1981 to 1986.[13] She color-banded the birds and watched them. Only females incubate eggs, and they do so for eleven to thirteen days. Then nestlings remain in the nest for seven to thirteen days. For the first four to eight days of this time, the female broods the nestlings, warming them because they cannot yet maintain their own body temperature. The male brings food to the incubating female at the nest, and to both the female and the nestlings during the brooding period; later in the nestling period, both parents bring food to the nestlings.

So the question is, how does the male know how much food to bring when the female is sitting on the eggs or nestlings? I might answer that he should bring as much as possible, but there is a trade-off. The more a bird goes to and from the nest, particularly a bird as conspicuous as a bright red male cardinal, the better a predator might discover the nest.

Halkin found that females sang mainly when their mate had vocalized within forty feet of the nest, and mainly during the nestling period. Most females sang when the male was even closer, twenty to thirty feet away. The nests were hidden enough that the male and female could not see each other from these distances and so did not have a visual way of communicating. Exactly how these lovely birds talk to each other is a little complicated, though what they have to say is less so. The male wants to know if the female or the nestlings (if they have hatched) need food. She lets him know.

He can sing or he can give *chip* calls. Unlike their clear-toned songs, a cardinal *chip* call is a much simpler and shorter sound, like the sound of china clinking on china. During the nestling period, if a female sang after an approaching male gave *chip* calls, Halkin found that the male was more likely to come to the nest than if she remained silent. If the male's initial vocalizations included song, it seemed that the female could give two different signals. If she sang songs made up of different syllable types than the male's, the male was again more likely to come to the nest than if she remained silent. However, if she sang songs with syllable types that matched the male's, this seemed to be a "no, thanks" or "stay away" signal even stronger than her silence.

For this very interesting work, Sylvia Halkin received the coveted top student prize of the Animal Behavior Society, the Warder Clyde Allee Award, in 1987. When she replicated these studies at small numbers of nests in Minnesota and Connecticut, Halkin found that any female song from the nest, whether she matched the songs her nearby mate was singing or not, was associated with a higher rate of male visits to the nest, raising the possibility of geographic variation in this communication system.

Sometimes in animal behavior research new students despair that there are no new projects to do. It can feel like everything has been figured out and that all that is left are the crumbs. And so it might have seemed in Northern Cardinals after Halkin's excellent work on female singing behavior. But Joanna Vondrasek later found a new, perhaps more fundamental angle on female song as a means of maintaining a territory against others.[14]

Vondrasek banded and observed Northern Cardinals at Mason Farm Biological Reserve in Chapel Hill, North Carolina. The latitude there is 35.9° north, right on the northern edge of the subtropics, while Madison, Wisconsin, where Halkin did her work, is at latitude 43.1° north, in the middle of the temperate climatic zone. It is worth keeping possible differences associated with latitude in mind, as, for example, the breeding season will be longer in North Carolina.

Vondrasek put markers spaced about eighty feet apart to estimate bird locations to within a couple of yards as she observed them. When she had heard a male sing from ten different locations, she felt comfortable drawing the boundaries of his territory, and the female that associated closely with him was considered to be his mate. Vondrasek was interested in comparing the singing of newly formed pairs with that of established pairs. She could do this after the first year of her study by simply seeing if the birds were not banded, meaning they were new to the territory.

Vondrasek compared the singing of eight new and eight established pairs, listening to the birds before they were tending their eggs or nestlings, either before the breeding season or between nesting bouts. Females sing more before they begin incubating eggs. As Vondrasek had predicted, females from pairs that were together the previous year sang less and concentrated their singing to much earlier in the year than did females in new pairs. Established females sang from the end of April to the middle of May, while new females sang from the end of April to the first week of July. By contrast, there was no difference in the singing of males between new and established pairs.

Vondrasek concluded that females defend their territories with song and sing more on new territories. It could be that neighbors that know each other are less likely to intrude on each other's territory, known as the dear enemy phenomenon. Also, the females do most of their singing before they have serious parental duties with eggs or young.

A lot is known about Northern Cardinals since they are so common, nest within reach of researchers, and are large enough to find easily. But what makes them special is the way the redbird has adapted to the world as we have changed it, from modifying their songs to eating berries they never should have encountered. Sit back and enjoy this most conspicuous backyard bird.

NORTHERN CARDINAL ACTIVITIES FOR SLOW BIRDERS

1. **Watch them.** Northern Cardinals and American Robins may be the easiest two birds to watch because they are common, large,

and live right alongside us, often nesting quite low. Cardinals also stick to their territories for most of the year and eat from our feeders.

2. **Observe how they behave at feeders.** Put black-oil sunflower seeds in your feeder for your cardinals. Then just watch them. Males and females are easily distinguished and stick together through the year. See what they do. Do they go together to the feeder, or does one hang back in the bushes? Does the male bring a seed and feed it to the female? Watch a cardinal for a while to see where it goes. It probably won't go far. How close together are the male and female? My cardinals love the elderberry over the patio and seldom visit the feeder together.

3. **Listen to their song.** The male sings nearly all year, skipping only the most wintry months. I didn't fully appreciate cardinal song at first, thinking it all the same. But now I pay attention and see how wrong I was. Maybe you can record the song with your smartphone and see what the patterns are. You can get a few songs from your bird book app, or from Merlin. If you would like more songs and sounds to study, you can go to the Cornell Lab of Ornithology's Macaulay Library, https://www.macaulaylibrary.org/. Or you can look at xeno-canto, https://xeno-canto.org/.

4. **Find a singing female.** Listen early in the spring, or if you find a nest, maybe you can catch her singing to her male to call him in to feed her and the young. The nests are often so low and accessible that they can be easily observed from afar with binoculars. It is important not to disturb them. If the nest is deep in a bush so it cannot be seen, you can still tell what is happening by watching the parents fly in and listening to them sing to each other. If you can see the nest, you can record the timing of nest building, egg laying,

hatching, and fledging. Sadly, odds are a predator will take the eggs or chicks before they leave the nest. Then try to see where your cardinals nest next. If you aren't already friends with your neighbors, you might have to make friends with them so you can look in their backyards too. Remember, the more native bushes you have, the more likely you are to attract nesting birds. You could also do detailed watches, perhaps for half an hour every other day at the same time, just to see exactly what the birds do, how long eggs are incubated, how often the male brings the female food, and later, how often the chicks are fed. Just remember not to get too close or interfere.

5. **Compare rural to backyard birds.** Once you know your garden Northern Cardinals, it can be fun to watch more rural birds. Remember, they like edge habitat, the forested borders on open fields. Bring along a camping chair or a blanket on your next excursion and sit down near the forest edge. You might choose a spot where you have already seen a cardinal, or a spot where you expect one to settle. How do these country birds differ in their behavior from those in your backyard? Do they sing from higher in the trees? Are they visiting a hidden nest? How often do they fly out into the prairie or meadow? How do males and females interact? If it is autumn or winter, you might find a small flock of young birds born just the previous summer. How do they interact? Where do they go? Listen to the rural cardinals. Does their song sound different? Lower? Slower? Record them and look at the sonagram patterns when you get home.

6. **Observe their color closely in areas with different kinds of berries.** Cardinals are not all the same color. Look hard at them and consider their color—how red, how orange, how intense, what the contrasts are. It is controversial, but birds eating brighter berries on

nonnative shrubs might be brighter. Also, worn feathers can look faded.

7. **Join a group to get rid of honeysuckle and multiflora rose.** Cardinals more than many birds are hurt by nonnative plants. Honeysuckle and multiflora rose are common invasive plants that local governments and naturalists' clubs often organize volunteers to help remove from parks and natural areas. Participating in such a removal is a way to help cardinals. These plants resprout from the roots, so after cutting down the plant, the stump needs to be dug out or painted carefully with an herbicide.

Tyson
Research Center

Wilderness Nearby

Twenty miles from home is far enough for most of us to find a truly wild place, somewhere you do not hear road noise, somewhere an undammed stream may flow. It might be big enough for birds like Pileated Woodpeckers that need territories of more than 150 acres, about as big as Disney World's Magic Kingdom. I could get lost in such a place, or sit quietly waiting for life around me to resume. It is usually a solitary experience for me, one I so need as a break in a crowded week.

Just twenty miles from home, right on the edge of my circle, is Washington University's Tyson Research Center. It is about two thousand acres of Ozark forests that include streams, artificial ponds, and nutrient-poor glades that shelter rare plants. Common trees are eastern red cedar, chinkapin oaks, white oaks, and black oaks. In the bottomlands near the Meramec River are slippery elm and sycamore. Understory flowering dogwoods and red buds light up in springtime.

It is a place of important research, one of a string of field stations monitoring changes in forest composition and timing of springtime development, work done by dedicated teams of researchers, like the one Jonathan Myers runs. The director, Kim Medley, runs a great team that looks at everything from mosquito and tick abundance and impact to getting high school and college students out into the wild.

Also on the site is the Endangered Wolf Center, founded in 1971 and used to rear canidae, often for eventual release elsewhere. Most recently they fostered Mexican wolf pups, then introduced them into wild litters in New Mexico and Arizona.

Washington University acquired the land in 1963. Other parks around it include Lone Elk Park, West Tyson County Park, and, across the Meramec, Castlewood State Park. These preserves allow a large protected wild area close to St. Louis, places people can go if they do not have access to Tyson itself.

I go to Tyson for the solitude and, of course, the birds. The trails I follow are often old roads, for the area was heavily logged. It is a ridged landscape with steep slopes up to long flat tops along which the old logging roads run. Some are still roads to get to the various research sites, while others are now trails.

There are also abandoned buildings from previous research projects. My path wends from the headquarters building along a valley-bottom road, then up the side of a hill, across an often-running stream, and back to the valley floor. The birds I see are often expected. Carolina Chickadees, Blue-gray Gnatcatchers, Eastern Bluebirds, Pileated Woodpeckers, and others in the spring and fall migration. In winter the Dark-eyed Juncos and White-throated Sparrows scuttle through the drying grasses, first-year males making tentative notes of their songs. I might see the yellow flash of a Yellow-rumped Warbler long into the winter.

Solitude is not necessary for observing birds, but stillness is, and stillness often comes more easily with solitude. Wildness near home may not be on the scale of that in our national forests, but it is worth seeking out.

There are many birds whose stories I might have told for Tyson Research Center, but I chose only three: Northern Mockingbird, Yellow-rumped Warbler, and White-throated Sparrow. Since I am choosing common, well-studied birds, it is usually true that they are not particular to one of my sites, and so it is with these three.

Tyson Research Center once held the town of Mincke Hollow, along the largest valley. The families and their employees mined limestone until 1928, when their lease apparently expired. There was even a Tyson train station. The mining created a cave, Mincke Cave, which I went into when I first moved to St. Louis. But now it is off-limits to help keep the bats that nest there free of infection.

Long before, Native Americans including the Cahokia, Osage, and Shawnee visited the area, drawn to it because of the flint deposits, good for making tools and weapons.

At this point, twenty miles seems a long way to drive, but it brings me to this much more wild place, where the paths go on for miles and I have some hope of not hearing any artificial sounds, at least for a time. If I crave solitude, here I can get it, for I seldom run into anyone else on Tyson bird walks.

Tyson Research Center is a place I try to visit every week, for with weekly visits I can absorb both the changing seasons and the small variations. I can see when the Eastern Bluebirds checked out a nest box but then rejected it in favor of a cranny in a dead tree. I can wait for the afternoon Turkey Vultures to soar above the valley. I can listen for the squeaky chatter of Blue-gray Gnatcatchers. It is a wildness that I get only on the very edges of my twenty-mile circle, and I treasure it.

WILDERNESS ACTIVITIES
FOR SLOW BIRDERS

1. **Figure out a place near home that is wild.** It may be a park you know well, a wetland along a river, or somewhere you just discovered by exploring. Once you have found a place, commit to visiting it often and just observing. I have a friend who hid a chair under a tree well off the trail of his special place, where he would sit and listen to the forest.

2. **Walk the same path every time you visit, documenting the birds you see and hear.** I do this with eBird, but I also keep notes just for myself. In addition to this path, there are other areas I like to explore.

3. **See if you can document the seasonal changes for some of the more common birds you see.** When did the Eastern Phoebe return in the spring? When did you last hear or see the White-throated Sparrow?

4. **Look for nests.** Most birds use nests for a very short time, so if you want to follow one, visits will have to be frequent. But even empty nests can tell you where birds like to nest.

5. **Notice if some of the birds you see often in town are absent.** I seldom see House Sparrows at Tyson, for example.

6. **Sketch.** I have my grandfather's teenage sketchbooks, which show me what an important skill it was for him as he grew up in Berlin before World War I. I wish I worked harder earlier on my drawing and hope to do it now. I find I see more clearly when I try to capture what I see.

Northern Mockingbird

Mimus polyglottos, Our Best Singer

Are mockingbirds most known around the world from their title mention in Harper Lee's famous book, *To Kill a Mockingbird*? After all, in 2006 British librarians ranked it as the top book to read before you die, just ahead of the Bible and two ahead of Tolkien's the Lord of the Rings trilogy.[1]

Harper Lee used mockingbirds to signify innocence, with Atticus telling eight-year-old Scout that it was a sin to kill them, something Scout verified with her neighbor Maudie, who added that all they do is sing and never hurt anyone. Sadly, Blue Jays seemed to be fair game for Scout's new air rifle.

Harper Lee was not the only one to treasure mockingbird song. Song nearly wiped out mockingbirds in St. Louis and Philadelphia in the late 1800s, when they were captured and caged. Older birds were prized for their repertoire, while younger ones had fewer songs but were tamer.[2] Fortunately, in 1918 the Migratory Bird Treaty Act protected Northern Mockingbirds and more than a thousand other species, so the numbers in St. Louis have recovered somewhat. It is still an uncommon bird.

The glorious song of uncaged Northern Mockingbirds is something for all of us to enjoy. It is no wonder that five states chose the mockingbird as their state bird: Arkansas, Florida, Mississippi, Tennessee, and Texas. These are all southern states where mockingbirds are common, but Northern Mockingbirds can actually be found all over the country, delighting us with their song and their saucy behavior toward one another. It may seem odd that this southern bird is called the Northern Mockingbird, but it just depends on one's reference. There is the Tropical Mockingbird even farther south in the states of Chiapas and Yucatán in southern Mexico.

The Tropical Mockingbird also extends into South America, where there are yet other species of mockingbirds.

Mockingbirds have an important place in the history of thought, for it is with mockingbirds, not finches, that Darwin began to think that species were not fixed but instead evolved and diverged from common ancestors.[3] He had three species of what he called mocking-thrushes and noted they came from different islands, leading him to think they had diverged from a single common ancestor from the mainland. Today it is possible to go to the Galápagos and see these very mockingbirds. But that is far outside my St. Louis circle.

The parks near my home seem ideal for urban mockingbirds, but mockingbirds are not terribly common in St. Louis. My walks in Forest Park or at Tyson Research Center include only the occasional Northern Mockingbird. I saw many more when I lived in Houston, where the landscape is entirely divided up into Northern Mockingbird territories. I know this best for the Rice University campus, where my former graduate student Debbie Morález DeLoach did her Ph.D. research on mockingbirds.

Recently I reread Debbie DeLoach's Ph.D. thesis.[4] One thing about a thesis is that it tells the story in a more complete way than any research paper would do. The first thing that struck me was that Debbie had daily scheduled walks along her mockingbird route for five to six months during the breeding seasons of 1991 to 1993. This on-campus route covered 170 acres that contained about thirty-five Northern Mockingbird territories in various configurations over the three years. She skipped the walk only on rainy days, because those are days that the birds shelter and are hard to see. She went every day. I let that sink in—six months with breaks only when it rained. At the time I did not realize how relentlessly she worked.

I remember often seeing her tall, slim form standing outside, clipboard in hand. She took ten-minute observations on each active territory, looked in nests a couple times a week, and banded the young once they were eight days old. Sometimes she had to call on Juan Alejandro, who operated the campus cherry picker, to get to the higher nests. Debbie looked directly into low nests, used an automotive mirror taped to a stick for higher ones, or stood on either a six-foot ladder or the top of a van, or—I hate to think of it—balanced on top of the ladder on top of the van. She was dedicated and did not ask me, her advisor, in advance if that was all right.

Debbie really wanted to know everything possible about Northern Mockingbirds—what they looked for in territories, why they sang so much and so variably, how they chose their mates, whether they were faithful to them, and how they cared for their young. The first thing she had to do was just what any teacher would do: take roll. To do this, Debbie put recognizable colored bands on the birds' legs. Then she could watch them to see who was where. But before she could put color bands on their delicate legs, she needed to catch the birds, with the proper permits in hand, of course.

There are lots of ways to catch a mockingbird. The one that worked best for Debbie was something called a potter trap with a top door. Debbie baited it with red grapes. When she wasn't using the trap, she put red grapes on top to attract birds without trapping them so that they would get used to its presence. A lot of animals, including birds, fear anything new, so it was important to familiarize the mockingbirds with the traps.

With eight traps Debbie was able to catch and band all the birds in her territories in about two weeks. While Debbie had the birds in hand, she weighed and measured them. She also took a tiny amount of blood for DNA work in order to tie nestlings to their actual parents, using techniques that are the same as those used for humans. She put another drop of blood on a slide to look for blood parasites. Occasionally the bird pooped as she handled it, and she collected that, too, and inspected it for parasites.

Once the birds were banded, Debbie could map their territory boundaries by observing where they were. This takes a lot of work because the birds spend most of their time in a small part of their territory but defend a larger area. She had a gridded map of the campus with the scale of each inch on paper equaling about fifty feet on the ground. On this grid she drew in buildings, trees, shrubs, hedges, signs, lampposts, sidewalks, fences, exterior furniture, trash bins, sculptures, fountains, tennis courts, and greenhouses, giving each a unique code indicating the map section and type of object. Over that map, Debbie put a sheet of acetate to mark her behavioral observations, using a different sheet for each individual and different colors for males and females and for different ages of young.

The result of all these daily observations is a lot of dots, some circled many times to indicate that the bird was at that place multiple times. In her thesis she gives one example for a male and one for a female. The female spent most of her time right at or near her nest.

The male Debbie used as an example in her thesis was very active near the nest but also sang from twelve different places. He had aggressive interactions in ten places, all concentrated along one side of the territory where he probably had a rival. Similar calculations could be made for all the birds of the study.

The twenty-three mated males DeLoach observed had territories that averaged 3.5 acres, or almost two soccer fields. Each territory contained enough shrubs for the fledglings to shelter in while they learned to fly. Most of the shrubs were in the form of hedges. The twenty-three males that nested successfully had on average 512 linear feet of hedge. The eight unmated males had an average of only 404 linear feet of hedge, apparently not enough to attract a female.

Overall, mockingbirds are monogamous, with one male mating with one female. Rarely, a male will attract two females to his territory and care for young at both nests.

Mockingbirds usually succeed in keeping their territories from one year to the next, though in the fall and winter they defend only the core area. DeLoach found that 86 percent of fifty-six males and 70 percent of fifty females stayed in their same territory as the year before. If they moved, it was usually just to an adjacent territory.

Females are making a different choice for territories than males, since they are also getting the male that comes with the territory. DeLoach found that when the birds leave the territory of the previous year, it is usually not voluntary.

Sometimes the numbers don't do justice to the stories behind claiming and keeping a territory. Some females choose a male and territory next to a favored male, and then challenge his mate later, trying to move over to where they really want to be. The most intense fight that Debbie saw was between an unmated female and a female with a mate. This fight happened early in the breeding season. The two birds flew at each other, chased each other, and grappled. At one point they were both bleeding from the fighting. And then the challenger flew away, over a three-story building. But it turned out she had not left for good. The male's territory extended over that building, so the second female took up nesting there, out of sight of the first female. It seems surprising to me that a mockingbird territory would go over both sides of such a big building, but it did. The intervening building allowed this male to become a bigamist.

Overall, the Rice University mockingbirds were quite successful in producing independent chicks. It takes about twelve days of incubation by the mother for the eggs to hatch. Then they are cared for by both parents for another twelve days in the nest. The female continues to be the one to brood the young, keeping them warm and protected from rain and wind. Once the young have left the nest, both parents care for them for another two or three weeks. A male might pause in these duties to build another nest for a new brood with the same female. The pair can rear two or three different broods in the same season, but never from the same nest. In Debbie's study, if we consider only the birds that successfully paired up, 80 percent of them produced at least one chick that made it to independence.

So what makes a male more likely to attract a mate and produce young? We already talked about the importance of enough bushes in his territory. Mated males had longer wings and were seen on their territory a month before the unmated males. For example, in 1992 the first sighting of males on their territories was February 12 for thirty-one mated males and March 12 for five unmated males. After their arrivals, males that eventually attracted a mate began singing a week after arrival, while unmated males took a bit over two weeks in their territories to begin singing for females.

The form song takes is also important for male reproductive success. Males with more versatile songs, measured both by song versatility and transition versatility, had more broods and reared more independent offspring. DeLoach measured versatility as the number of different song types per fifty contiguous songs, multiplied by how often the bird switched between different song types during those fifty songs. The advantage of this measure is that you have to record only fifty continuous songs, not try to capture the entire repertoire. The number of days males sing is not a good measure of their singing talents because once a male has attracted a female, he sings much less, particularly after the eggs are laid. Now that I know this, I like to listen for the changes from one song to another.

It seems likely that a bird that has already had a breeding season would do better than a youngster in its first year. This was true for both males and females. Experienced males and females had more young that survived to independence than did novice parents in their first year—about two to three times more. At least female novices have the advantage of always being able to find a mate, unlike young males.

Here I have been discussing breeding success as measured by the number of chicks in the nests of their caregivers. But what if some of those chicks were actually fathered by another male? What if the female found a neighbor to mate with, then returned to her nest, laid eggs, and let her partner help rear chicks he was unrelated to?

DeLoach teamed up with Colin Hughes, then of the University of North Dakota. He had been my very first graduate student and so knew the Rice University mockingbirds well. He is also a fantastic birder. Colin developed variable DNA markers that could be used to see who the parents of each egg were.[5] This was the reason Debbie had collected blood from the adults and the eight-day-old chicks. She expected there to be a good amount of philandering, because song is such an extravagant trait that it seemed a waste to devote it all to attracting and keeping a single female.

But it turned out that mockingbird song did not seem to function to attract mistresses. DeLoach genotyped 324 chicks in all from 1991 to 1993 on a total of 105 territories. Only 10 out of 324 young, 3 percent, were fathered by a male that was not partner to the mother that laid the eggs. These 10 were in nine different broods across the three years, so only one nest contained more than one chick fathered by another. Unlike many other songbirds, Northern Mockingbirds were quite faithful to their partners, at least in our Houston population.

DeLoach recorded one other kind of parasitism on the effort of chick rearing by parents, something that is called egg dumping. This happens when a female finds someone else's nest and manages to lay an egg in it. DeLoach discovered four chicks in two nests that did not match the female. In both nests, the attending male was the genetic father of the chicks, so he had allowed a female he had mated with to come to his nest and lay eggs while his actual mate was elsewhere.

Music is what sets Northern Mockingbirds apart. A mockingbird's song lifts into the air, notes following one another in a melody Mozart might envy. The songs repeat and then change but always build on what went before, like a Philip Glass piece. Mockingbirds can go on and on, ever varying their performance. Biologists dissect this magic into notes, songs, and bouts. A bout can have anywhere from two to twenty or more repeats of the same song, where a song is just a few notes.[6] Songs in bouts that are close together tend to be similar.[7] Myriad bouts make up the singing work of a morning for a male mockingbird.

How many different songs might a single Northern Mockingbird sing? To answer this, Kim Derrickson listened to four Northern Mockingbirds at Tyler Arboretum in Lima, Pennsylvania, in 1980.[8] He recorded their vocalizations so he could visualize the songs with spectrograms, song frequency plotted over time, just like what you can see when you record songs you hear with Cornell's Merlin app. In all, Derrickson analyzed more than 10,000 bouts of songs. His top singer was a male that sang 412 different song types out of 2,698 bouts. Of those songs, 31 percent occurred only once. This large number of singleton songs suggests that had Derrickson recorded even more songs, the total number would have increased. The male with the fewest song types sang 102 different songs out of 168 studied. Of those, 57 percent were unique, so even his actual repertoire must have been a lot higher.

The melodies in those songs have to come from somewhere. Many birds sing the songs their father sang. But mockingbirds get their melodies from everywhere, giving them ownership of their mocking name. Most of the songs Northern Mockingbird males mimic are those of other birds, but you might also have heard a mockingbird do a passable imitation of a backing-up truck or an ambulance siren.

It turns out mockingbirds also mimic frogs and toads of coexisting species with the right quality of song. David Gammon and Anna Corsiglia of Elon University in North Carolina found that mockingbirds mimic twelve different species of frogs and toads.[9, 10] The way they did this is worth reporting as an example of really careful science. This was not an easy study to do. First, Gammon and Corsiglia collected more than forty hours of song from 370 different mockingbirds from twenty-two different states. They found these songs mostly on xeno-canto, the Macaulay Library, and eBird. Then they figured out what singing frogs and toads (*anurans*) co-occurred with the songs from sources like the International Union for Conservation of Nature's Red List.

Gammon and Corsiglia ended up with seventy-one frogs and toads that overlapped geographically with their song samples of Northern Mockingbirds. They expected the songs that would be copied would be in the bandwidth that mockingbirds use, 750 to 7000 hertz. They focused on common frogs and toads, avoiding rare or elusive species like spadefoot toads. In particular they looked for repetitive songs that might be attractive to mockingbirds. Corsiglia became a frog song expert first, passing quizzes by Gammon and those from the US Geological Survey (https://www.pwrc.usgs.gov/frogquiz). Once she knew these songs, she was ready to listen to mockingbirds and look for frog or toad songs. Out of more than ten thousand mimetic songs in 370 birds for which they had song recordings, they were able to identify all that mimicked frogs or toads.

Corsiglia first identified twenty-six mockingbird songs she felt sure came from frog or toad mimicry, along with seven additional possibilities. Gammon independently scored the songs, matching her assessments twenty-eight times, for an interobserver agreement of an impressive 85 percent. Then they discussed their differences, listening carefully many times. Corsiglia changed her mind twice, and Gammon changed his three times after comparing and relistening. They also eliminated another seven questionable songs, leaving twenty-four frog or toad songs from twelve species that mockingbirds mimicked, species that overlapped the ranges of those mockingbirds. These species included the Northern Pacific treefrog, Cope's gray treefrog, Woodhouse's toad, and the red-spotted toad. In these cases the spectrograms of frog or toad songs were uncanny matches for the mimetic mockingbird song.

Another question that intrigued Gammon is whether mocking-birds can keep learning new songs their whole lives.[11] It might make sense that they can, since they are able to mimic so many different sounds. If they do, that would explain why older males sing more vari-able songs than younger ones. So if a female wanted an older male for a mate, all she would have to do is listen.

Gammon dug into this question by recording fifteen wild, banded Northern Mockingbirds on the Elon University campus between 2009 and 2013 early in the morning.[12, 13] He recorded them in one year and then again in a later year to see if they had added songs to their repertoire.

Gammon considered only songs that mimicked other species, like the Carolina Wren and the Purple Martin, because he figured that mimicry would be the source of new songs. He figured that the songs learned from other mockingbirds, including their own fathers, were either learned when they were young or could not be distinguished from those they learned when they were young. And, to be frank, he told me that it would be extremely difficult and time-consuming to categorize all the songs from their own species.

Gammon scored the songs blind. This means that when he was analyzing the audio recordings and sonograms, using software named Audacity and Syrinx, he did not know if it was an early or late song. This avoids inadvertent bias, something even scientists need to worry about. He used personal experience and listened to recorded songs from the *Birds of North America* series to determine whether songs were mimetic and what they mimicked. He included four hundred mimetic songs for each bird at each time period, totaling over eleven thousand mimetic songs for the fifteen birds in the two periods. These songs were of ninety-seven types from forty-five different bird species. The birds the mockingbirds copied the most, slightly over 50 percent of the copied songs, were the Carolina Wren, Tufted Titmouse, Northern Cardinal, Blue Jay, and Eastern Bluebird, in order of frequency.

I suppose the results were disappointing to Gammon, for though he found more mimicked songs when the birds were at least a year older, it was not by much, averaging forty-six songs per bird in the early sample and forty-eight songs in the later sample. It was only when he focused on two common types of song, the Eastern Bluebird loud song and the Blue Jay "pump handle" song, that he found significantly more variants in the later year than in the earlier year. Based on this, Gammon considered that Northern Mockingbirds do learn new songs after adulthood. It seems to be a simple question, so it is surprising the answer was so hard to come by.

One of the things about science these days is that we are learning how often females are ignored and how they are different from males, true even in human medical drug trials. This is also true for mockingbirds. When I asked David Gammon about female song, he said that, yes, females do sing, but he had heard them only twice.

Besides singing, Northern Mockingbirds spend a lot of time foraging. Watch a mockingbird as it hops along the ground. When mockingbirds do this, they are looking for food, insects, or other creatures that have settled on the grass or among the roots. One of my students once tried to calculate the angle between a mockingbird's head and the location of the prey when it pounced. If they pounced from too far away, they might miss the prey. If they pounced from too close, the prey might see them and escape. He drew triangles from his drawing of the bird's eyes to the location of prey from successful and failed capture attempts and found the perfect distance to pounce. But there was a complication.

Sometimes the mockingbirds quickly open and shut their wings, flashing white wing patches. Do they do this to startle insects, making them more visible and easier to catch? Francis Allen reported on the significance of wing flashing in 1947, when scientific articles were written in a more vivid style.[14] In his article, Allen quotes Mrs. Harriet Mann Miller, who apparently wrote under the male pen name Olive

Thorne Miller: "At the end of a run he lifts his wings, opening them wide, displaying their whole breadth, which makes him look like a gigantic butterfly, then instantly lowers his head and runs again, generally picking up something as he stops."[15] Allen further noted that wing flashing occurs when the young are in the nest or just fledged and needing insect food, further supporting the tie to catching insects.

Jack Hailman also studied white wing flashing in June to August 1958 and April to July 1959.[16] Hailman gives a more austere definition of wing flashing as "the bird stands on the ground with body held in normal position (spinal column at an angle of about 35 degrees with the ground), and with its head forward, begins the wing motions . . . The wings are opened simultaneously in a series of distinct motions, or hitches." He goes on to say that when the wings are opened, the white sections appear to flash.

Hailman found that wing flashing was followed by foraging. In 1959 he measured the actual strikes on prey and found 191 strikes versus 67 non-strikes. But he also found wing flashes when the birds were disturbed. This study only compared flashing with no flashing. In another species with white spots, Ron Mumme did a controlled study.

In his case, the bird was the Hooded Warbler. The idea was that adults flashed white spots in their tails to increase insect capture.[17] Mumme showed the importance of the white spots by comparing the success in insect capture of birds with natural white spots and of those whose white spots had been colored over by the experimenters. The former caught more insects.

We see mockingbirds so much because they overlap with humans. This overlap is no accident. It turns out that nest predators of small birds, smaller than mockingbirds, are more common in urban areas. These nest predators proliferate in urban areas because there are no true top predators there. The predators include Fish Crows, American Crows, Common Grackles, Blue Jays, and Red-shouldered Hawks.

So the birds we have around us are either larger, like Northern Mockingbirds, Northern Cardinals, Blue Jays, and Mourning Doves, or smaller ones that nest in defensible cavities, like Carolina Chickadees and House Wrens. The only small birds that nest in open cups that thrive in cities tuck their nests away in thick scrub or in human artifacts to escape predators, like House Finches.[18]

Mockingbirds that live in the human environment have other challenges. We threaten them, causing them to flee, even when our intentions are good. We make a lot of noise. We cover much of the environment with concrete and buildings. But mockingbirds are smart and can protect themselves as long as there is still habitat for them to nest and feed. They can even tell one human from another and mob one known to have approached their nest too closely.

Douglas Levey and his team discovered this by studying human recognition on the University of Florida campus in Gainesville during the breeding season, when the birds were incubating eggs, so they had something important to defend.[19] The campus was in session during the study, which meant that hundreds of students passed some of his mockingbird nests per hour. The more people who walked past the nest, the more tolerant the birds were of human proximity overall.

The experiment had to do with recognition of individual humans not disguised in any way. The intruder walked straight up to the nest, standing within three feet of it for fifteen seconds and then putting their hand gently on the rim of the nest and leaving it there for another fifteen seconds. They did this for four days in a row, and then on the fifth day a different person approached the nest similarly.

Another researcher hidden nearby watched everything and recorded when the bird left the nest, how many alarm calls she gave, and whether she attacked the human intruder. All measures of alarm went up over the four days of intruders, with the bird attacking from farther and farther away as the threat became clear. She also gave more alarm calls and more actual attacks on the end days. On the fifth day, when the different person approached the nest in exactly the same way, this person did not get increased flushing distance, alarm calls, or attacks. This person got treated no differently from the first person on the first day. They did the experiment on twenty-four nests. The Levey group has a remarkable video of a mockingbird picking the person out of a group of students and attacking.

Human disturbance distracts mockingbirds from the important business of rearing their young, but this is probably not the most pernicious thing humans do to mockingbirds. Loss of habitat is the biggest problem.

Another way in which humans change the environment for mockingbirds is that they change the sound environment. Artificial sounds in the human environment tend to be low frequency. Think of the noise as automobiles drive down the highway, the low grinding of garbage trucks, and, indeed, most mechanical sound tends to be low. So if a mockingbird male wants to attract a female or defend his territory, he should sing in a way that distinguishes his song from background noise.

Mitchell Walters and his team looked into mockingbird song in urban environments.[20] They compared birds in areas with high traffic, over a thousand vehicles passing per day, with those in residential areas with low traffic. Then they recorded a five-minute sample of song from about fifteen yards away. These samples contained between 31 and 155 different songs. Right before the song recording, they recorded the background noise using special equipment. They recorded thirty-three males in residential areas and forty-nine along roads with high traffic. As expected, there was more background noise along the high-traffic areas. Mockingbirds in the high-traffic areas sang higher-pitched songs. The louder the low-frequency traffic, the higher the songs. These examples show mockingbirds change their behavior to manage in human environments.

If I had a favorite bird, it might be the mockingbird. If I were still in Houston, it certainly would be the mockingbird, but here in St. Louis I don't see them often enough for them to be my favorite. For that I like a more common bird. I might see a mockingbird out at Tyson or even in the alley behind my home. But Northern Mockingbirds most often surprise me in town, perhaps singing from an electrical wire as one did when I was waiting to order some dry pasta and wine at Parker's Table early in the pandemic, when we had to queue outside to place our orders.

I guess this is what it is like when a bird is on the edge of its range. But it is not on the edge of its range. EBird shows mockingbirds right up into Canada, though they are not common here or in Canada. They do not divide all of St. Louis into their territories. Instead they are a special delight, uncommon but not rare. I watch for mockingbirds, thinking that while Harper Lee's book is marvelous, even more so is the actual bird.

NORTHERN MOCKINGBIRD ACTIVITIES FOR SLOW BIRDERS

1. **Observe where mockingbirds sing.** Mockingbird song is mesmerizing and exhilarating. Listen for a moment to a male singing from up high. The longer he goes on, the greater the chance he has not yet attracted a mate. If he sings on your regular birding route, maybe you will notice the day when he sings less or even stops. Then it might be time to see if you can find the nest, but remember not to get too close. Maybe the first thing to do is to categorize the places mockingbirds sing from, their nature and their height.

2. **Consider the song itself.** First just listen. Become a mockingbird song expert. Then use BirdNET or Merlin to record the song and look at its makeup. Ornithologists call the short syllables of notes

a song. Repeated songs are organized into bouts. A new bout will have a different melody. See if you can tell how many notes make up a song. How often is one song repeated before the bird moves on to a new song? Is the new one similar to the previous one? See if you can count all the songs a bird sings in a given amount of time. I love to listen and tally the numbers of songs I hear and their repetitions. I particularly like the differences in pauses between the songs depending on the melody. One bout might have comparatively long pauses while another has practically no pause.

3. **Female song.** Most of the song is from males, but early in the season females sometimes sing from their nest, a simple song that is nevertheless recognizable as a mockingbird song. See if you can hear a song that might come from a female. This is hard to tell since the females and males look the same. You might succeed simply by paying attention to the quieter partner on a territory.

4. **Register the other sounds.** Besides songs, Northern Mockingbirds make other sounds. There are calls of various sorts. One is short and hoarse, then there is a short high call, and there is another high call that can be longer. How would you describe all the songs and calls you hear and what causes them? When there are young in the nest, singing is unusual. Maybe you can also hear a soft peep from the adults when they are feeding the young.[21]

5. **Look for a territorial display.** Mockingbirds are highly territorial, so if you live in an area where they are common, you might see a territorial dance. It is a hopping competition along the edges of a territory. You could watch this and try to make a map of the territories around the area you usually watch birds. Whatever you do, pause and watch when you find a mockingbird. They will reward you.

6. **Watch juvenile mockingbird behavior.** Feeding behavior worth watching for is that of young birds just starting out. You can recognize the juveniles by the dark spotting on their breast and sides, something they have until they molt in late summer, August to September. How does their behavior differ from that of adults? Actually, juveniles bear watching wherever they are and whatever they are doing. Just take notes.

7. **Watch berry eating.** I also like to watch how birds eat berries. What makes them choose one over another? Has the rejected berry already started to ferment, or is it not yet ripe enough? How long do the birds stay on one branch before moving to another place? How long do they stay in one tree? How much do they fight over seemingly plentiful berries? Sit and watch with a tape recorder or your field notebook and see what you find and if birds act similarly or have different tactics.

8. **Watch a nest.** If you find a nest, sit and watch it from a distance, far enough away that you need binoculars to not frighten the parents. Does one bird perch nearby before approaching the nest while the other flies straight in? Maybe you can estimate how high those perches are and how far they are from the nest. There are cell phone tree-height applications you could try. See if you can hear that special call that males give before approaching. Just watch from a distance. If a predator like a hawk or a cat is nearby, see what happens and how the bird changes its behavior. See how long there is between visits to the nest. See if you can tell what the parents bring to the nestlings. Fruit is more likely to be part of the diet as the nestlings age.[22]

9. **Watch a mockingbird forage.** There is more to a Northern Mockingbird than sound. Take ten minutes and just watch. You might

have spotted the mockingbird on the ground as it hops about foraging. You might have spotted it in a fruit tree eating berries. You might have spotted it stealthily headed to its nest or doing a territory line dance with its neighbor. If the mockingbird is on the ground, watch what it does. How many hops does it take before plunging its beak in after an insect or a worm? Does it flash the white in its wings? Can you watch long enough to see if flashing the white in its wings makes it more likely to catch an insect? After all, some people think the wing flashing is to startle insects and thereby reveal themselves, while others think it is a predator defense. See what your observations say. It is also likely that wing flashes work best with larger insects you could see with binoculars. You can use the mockingbird's beak length as a size standard for prey, determining if prey are larger or smaller than the beak. Look also for swallowing by the mockingbird. I bet you can see it. Take notes, keeping track of where you were to identify the mockingbird.

Yellow–Rumped Warbler

The Wax-Eating Northerners

If you were to play the "I'm thinking of a bird" game with a birdy friend and had to give her only one word to guess Yellow-rumped Warbler, that word would be "common."

Bird-watchers call them "butter butts" and move on to more unusual species, unless they are on a Christmas count and therefore compelled to say exactly how many there are. But I like to watch the butter butts flitting among leaves, cruising up tree trunks, or even flying out from a perch to hawk insects like a flycatcher. Somehow they give me the illusion that all is right with the world.

You would think that such a common warbler would be easily identifiable, with their brilliant yellow rumps and yellow side patches where the wing joins the body. But Yellow-rumped Warblers do have an identity problem. Apparently three or even four species are lumped together as the Yellow-rumped Warbler.[1] At one time the eastern birds were called Myrtle Warbler, while out West they were Audubon's

Warbler. Going farther south into the Sierra Madre in Mexico there is the nonmigratory Black-fronted Warbler, and in Guatemala the Goldman's Warbler. So why should they be lumped together as a single species now called the Yellow-rumped Warbler? After all, they look quite different, as any bird guide will show.

Furthermore, these four birds are not thought of as the same species by the birding community. I carelessly logged a Yellow-rumped Warbler as a Myrtle Warbler on eBird when I was in Tucson visiting the University of Arizona. This is what we call it in St. Louis and I was on autopilot. Within a day the local eBird recorder challenged me and I realized my mistake. It was an Audubon's Warbler that I had seen, a male, with its yellow throat and distinct song. Embarrassed, I corrected it on eBird and will never forget that desert sighting.

So why are they considered the same species? Don't birds or any organism of the same species show it by being able to mate with one another and produce healthy offspring, so documenting successful reproduction is essential? This view of species is called the biological species concept and was most clearly explained by the German evolutionary biologist Ernst Mayr in a landmark book written in 1942 entitled *Systematics and the Origin of Species*.[2]

Since Mayr wrote that book, what exactly a species is has gotten a little more complicated, because it turns out that it is easier to see the history of those interactions in their DNA than to actually watch who mates with whom. Now we can look at whole genomes and see the genetic history of all those matings written in their DNA. This is a different species concept from the biological species concept and is called the species concept. Ideally, they should match, but behavioral changes are likely to precede changes in the whole genomes. Among scientists, there is lots of discussion (and some disagreement) about what makes a species, whether it is the behavior of mating or the underlying genes.[3] Both play into our understanding of speciation in the Yellow-rumped Warblers.

Slow Birders will be able to see the behavior especially if they are in an area where multiple forms occur, but they can only read about the DNA. Audubon's and Myrtle Warblers overlap along a drooping west–east line across the northern third of British Columbia, and then down along the border of British Columbia and Alberta, not quite as far as Montana.[4] Myrtle Warblers are generally east and north. Audubon's Warblers are more western, as any field guide should show.

The answer to the speciation question is along that line where they overlap. Can they reproduce together? But we could ask why there is a line of demarcation there at all. Why would they not have merged long ago? The answer to this question is both general and particular. The general answer is that any boundary between kinds of birds in that area is new. Quite new. Newer than 18,000 years, because until 18,000 years ago the Laurentide Ice Sheet covered all of Canada, hugging the US border, then dipping down into Minnesota and the Dakotas, extending well south of Chicago to part of Missouri, and extending east to just north of Philadelphia. The Laurentide Ice Sheet wasn't new. It first formed about 2.6 million years ago in the Pleistocene. The ice sheet was two miles thick in some places, and as it melted away, it left moraines, eskers, drumlins, and glacial till, as well as the Great Lakes. For something as long-lasting as a species, this was basically yesterday.

This means that the land where the Myrtle Warbler now breeds was buried under two miles of ice at a time that is not so long ago for evolution. Where the Audubon's Warbler now resides was at least partly ice-free during the Pleistocene. So the two forms could have diverged in the south in places free of ice, the Audubon's west of the ice and the Myrtle east and south. Then they could have come back together after the ice melted. That would have given them a few thousand years to meet and mate.[5]

What other examples of evolution can we compare this to for perspective? Lineages of humans and chimps diverged from each other 5 to 7 million years ago.[6] But for the much more similar chimps and bonobos, the divergence was only 2 million years ago. You know bonobos, right? That smaller chimp that solves social conflicts with a little sexual love, including face-to-face mating? We might adjust these time estimates for age at breeding, which is 1 year in warblers, roughly 10 years for chimps and bonobos, and perhaps double that for humans. That would be the equivalent of the warblers being diverged for 120,000 years, or ten times the actual period. That is still seventeen times less time than the chimps and bonobos had to diverge.

So, the Audubon's and Myrtle Warblers may have been together for a relatively short time evolutionarily. But still, they have different throat colors, and their geographic ranges have a narrow contact zone. Do they mate with each other? I could not find any behavioral information from someone who simply watched them. But Gordon Alexander found hybrids.[7] And at Rocky Mountain National Park, on May 2, 1940, Packard found a male singing the Myrtle Warbler song but with the yellow throat of an Audubon's Warbler.[8] It being the 1940s, he thought nothing of simply collecting the bird, probably with a shotgun, then putting its skin in the park's collection, along with several other similar birds. These birds were in flocks of mostly Myrtle Warblers. Alexander, on the other hand, did not hear song but collected males with throats containing both yellow and white feathers.

A tight, long-lasting contact zone between Audubon's and Myrtle Warblers indicates they are likely to be two species and that hybrids have some sort of disadvantage that keeps those two species from merging fully. David Toews and his team took a genomic approach to looking for differences in what they call the Yellow-rumped Warbler species complex.[9] They sampled the DNA of ninety-four birds, including eighteen Myrtle, fifty-seven Audubon's, fourteen Black-fronted, and five Goldman's Warblers. Because they were working between 2001 and 2006 and not half a century earlier, killing the birds was not necessary. Instead, they took a tiny sample of blood from the brachial vein in the wing.

What they were looking for was something called a single nucleotide polymorphism, or SNP (pronounced "snip"). A SNP is a place in the genome where some birds have a different code from others. Remember there are four bases that make up the genetic code of all living things: A, C, G, and T. If at one place two birds differ in the letter, that is called a SNP. Map thousands of those to see how similar they are, and you get a good idea about species borders.

These researchers did such an analysis and found 37,518 SNPs. That seems like a lot! Then they used a technique called principal components analysis to make a graph summarizing all this variation on a simple plot. Each bird got a dot on this graph. If all the dots from Myrtle Warblers and Audubon's Warblers were in the same region of the graph, then we would infer they are the same species.

But it did not turn out that way. Instead, all eighteen Myrtle Warbler samples were in a group of their own. All the Goldman's Warblers were in another place, also all on their own. Then, in a completely different region of the graph, was another very interesting group. At the top of this region were all the Audubon's Warblers. At the bottom, but adjoining, were all the Black-fronted Warblers. Clearly these two are closely related; I'll tell more of their secrets in a moment. Clearly, the important conclusion of this marvelous study is that Audubon's and Myrtle Warblers are quite different species genetically, even if they do hybridize a bit along their contact zone.

So why do we still lump Audubon's and Myrtle Warblers together as Yellow-rumped Warblers? The genetic evidence is clear. In fact, some ornithologists already refer to them as if they were two species.[10]

But the official American Ornithological Society (AOS) name still is just a lumped Yellow-rumped Warbler. Why? It is because of a tension between biological and genetic species concepts. Observations like those of a Slow Birder, recorded on eBird, can help with the former. Ultimately, though, there has to be a deciding body. It is a committee called the North American Classification Committee (NACC) of the AOS. Its members have the final word, at least in the United States. Most scientific papers on American birds say somewhere that they follow the AOS names.

There are clear guidelines for names. They favor stability of common English names, even if they seem arbitrary. They change names only on the basis of a proposal for a change. They capitalize bird names, as I do here. The names must be unique. When a species is split, they prefer to use new names for both the new and old species, so earlier, more general usage is not confused with later, more narrow usage. More important, names follow the International Code of Zoological Nomenclature. I have named three new bacterial species that follow their own code, and believe me, it is challenging and complicated.

Because the decisions and the discussions are made public after the committee meets, we can learn afterward exactly how they decided on names. I was looking for the room for a talk when I was at the 2019 AOS meeting in Tucson, Arizona, when I was almost physically scooted aside by another scientist. I had inadvertently gotten close to the door of the room where this committee was meeting and was under no circumstances allowed to go in, not that I wanted to. They do not want to be influenced or to have their deliberations made public until afterward.

Nicholas Mason and David Toews, along with Alan Brelsford, proposed to split up the Yellow-rumped Warbler in 2017. They recommended that it be split into three species: Audubon's Warbler, Myrtle Warbler, and Goldman's Warbler. Audubon's would encompass both Audubon's and Black-fronted Warblers, at least for now. Their main evidence was from the study I mentioned earlier that showed the genetic differences so clearly. The evidence seemed overwhelming to me. But the committee again voted no. Why?

It seems that one has to be really conservative to get on this committee. There were five no votes and five yes votes. I guess a tie means no change in the bird world. But there are eleven committee members, so one vote is not seen. A summary of the no votes is that they went with the biological species concept and simply ignored the genetic data. They want to know more about what happens in the hybrid zone. They want to know if the song is different, or exactly what the cost of hybridization is. They mention their own experiences with seeing these birds in the field. Actually, it makes for quite fascinating reading. Clearly they are all professional Slow Birders who pay intense attention to the birds. Here are quotes on both sides of the issue from the written material that came from the discussion.

YES to split of goldmani, given how well-differentiated genetically and morphologically it is. A weak YES to split of coronatus and auduboni (despite the hybrid zone), given the indirect evidence for post-mating isolating mechanisms (which are after all isolating mechanisms), their different calls, and their differing morphology.

YES. A strong yes, in fact. I feel that the weight of the evidence is now strongly in favor of this re-split. The genomic evidence is very strong that (for example) auduboni and coronata are well-differentiated, and that some regions of their genomes are under differential selection. Within the hybrid zone there appears to be no assortative mating (= little prezygotic isolation), but there does appear to be only limited genetic introgression and some form of selection against hybrids (= substantial postzygotic isolation).

NO. Maintain as one species, for now. I'm sorry, but I just can't get past the issue "of little assortative mating in the hybrid zone." If you believe in the BSC [biological species concept from Ernst Mayr] as I do, that's pretty much it. And I'm not sure what the "indirect evidence

for selection against hybrids in the contact zone" means. I can readily
identify these two species groups. They not only look different, both in
alternate and basic plumage, their call notes sound different. I think
songs differ too, but both have a variety of songs . . . I did see several
hybrids in summer along the Stikine River, southeast Alaska, and I
believe there are pretty much all hybrids along one river, I think in
northern BC.

NO*. At the outset, I would like to make it clear that I have always*
"disliked" the Myrtle–Audubon's lump because in my tidy little world-
view, if I can identify two taxa by call note as far away as I can see
them, they "have to be" species. In fact, to this day, I use "Myrtle" and
"Audubon's" in my field notes etc. Also at the outset, I find these ge-
netic data interesting and important to understanding the history and
process of diversification, and I applaud the authors of the recent papers
for making substantial progress. But application of my tidy little
worldview to real world situations is, predictably, not always tidy,
and application of genetic data to taxonomy is not always straight-
forward.

So, the lumped name stands, at least until the next challenge is
brought up. But the AOS is not the only group deciding on bird
names. There is also the International Ornithological Committee
(IOC) with a world bird list of its own. I went to its website and
downloaded its life list (http://www.worldbirdnames.org/new/), free
to anyone who wants it. Guess what? The IOC has already accepted
the proposal to split the Yellow-rumped Warblers into Myrtle Warbler, Audubon's Warbler, and Goldman's Warbler. I wonder why
these two committees cannot get together. Both cover all birds.

If we follow the split, we have the Myrtle Warbler here in St.
Louis. I like this older name better than Yellow-rumped Warbler, for
it points to this bird's secret superpower, which is that it can digest

wax, particularly from the abundant bayberry *Myrica pensylvanica*, a member of the myrtle family. This superpower is one reason for the abundance of the bird in northern climes, even in colder weather. This tiny bird migrates from the southern third of the United States, Mexico, and Central America back north much earlier in the spring than other birds because it can use this unusual food.

For all their commonness, Yellow-rumped Warblers are fairly unstudied. But a classic study features them. If ecology had saints, Robert H. MacArthur would be one. After an undergraduate degree in mathematics from Marlboro College in Vermont and a master's degree, also in mathematics, from Brown University in 1953, he moved to study ecology for his Ph.D., starting right at the top. His Ph.D. advisor was G. Evelyn Hutchinson, the father of modern ecology for his work on aquatic biology and, most relevant to MacArthur, the theory of the niche. MacArthur's every published word has been studied carefully ever since he perished, way too young, of kidney cancer at age forty-two in 1972.

MacArthur did a landmark Ph.D. project on five species of warblers that is now the defining work on how animals divide up their habitat. It is no surprise he chose warblers, since as a teenager he worked in Algonquin Provincial Park and was well aware of the warblers that nested there. He began his Ph.D. observations in 1956 on a 9.4-acre plot of white spruce on Bass Harbor Head on Mount Desert Island in Maine. He then went to his parents' home in Marlboro, Vermont, and resumed his observations, this time on red spruce. The next year he studied a variety of plots in Aroostook County, Maine, until June 5, when he decamped to Mount Desert Island and censused five plots for the remainder of the breeding season. I imagine that today a careful research project design would not allow all this moving about.

MacArthur wondered if five warblers that commonly bred in his area might violate an important principle of ecology first set forth by Joseph Grinnell, whom we met in the Blue Jay chapter, and then by

David Lack in 1954.[11] This is the same David Lack of the optimal number of nestlings, whom we met in the House Wren chapter. Here the proposal that interested Lack was that species must differ in how they use the environment, or one would drive the other to extinction. It is an idea developed under the name "niche theory," in particular by MacArthur's own Ph.D. advisor at Yale, G. Evelyn Hutchinson.

The specific principle that MacArthur famously tested is that for two species to coexist, individuals of the same species should limit the increase of others of its own species more than they limit the other species. This principle actually is quite simple. For example, if a species can eat only strawberries, then members of that species will compete a lot for strawberries. They will not affect another species that eats only raspberries.

Of course, individuals normally do not eat just one thing. They eat a basket of different things. Those baskets will look the most similar among members of the same species, so they will compete with each other the most. This is the principle that MacArthur tested with his five warbler species: How similar are their food baskets? Are the colorful Yellow-rumped, Black-throated Green, Blackburnian, Bay-breasted, and Cape May Warblers eating the same thing at the same place in defiance of niche theory?[12]

MacArthur's test of this idea in warblers was a good one. After all, one tests ideas where they seem most likely to fail. There would be no point in looking for different feeding behavior as a limitation to populations somewhere that the differences were clear. We do not test hypotheses or theories by looking for positive examples. We test them by looking for the most difficult cases, where the theory is most likely to be wrong. Only by understanding those cases are we apt to learn something. And such a case for testing niche theory were the warblers of Maine and Vermont feeding on insects in red, white, and black spruce and balsam fir in those long-ago summers of 1956 and 1957.

To determine whether the five warbler species were actually feeding differently, MacArthur considered the spruces to be divided into sixteen different zones according to height and distance from the tree trunk.

Then MacArthur, with two mathematics degrees in hand, took up his binoculars and watched warblers. Where were they and how did they feed? On paper, he wrote down species, location, and time spent in each zone for each individual. He also noted how the warblers foraged, if they were nervous and moved often, or stayed in one location, or flew out from the tree to catch insects in the air—just like a good Slow Birder.

In a landmark paper, MacArthur presented his data on Christmas tree shapes, with height and closeness to trunk zones indicated and the time the warblers spent in each zone written on the tree diagram.[13] He stippled the areas where the numbers were highest for quick reference.

The Yellow-rumped Warbler used the broadest swath of the tree. It was the only species that spent time in the bottom ten feet of the tree, though they could also be found at the very top and at intermediate zones. MacArthur recorded data on Yellow-rumped Warbler location for 4,777 seconds, or 1.32 hours, including a total of 263 feeding actions. Of these, 28 percent were in the bottom ten feet of the tree, 16 percent were in the next ten feet, closer to the trunk. Up at thirty to forty feet high, this species spent 10 percent of its total time in the middle distance from the trunk. The remaining 46 percent of the time, they were in other parts of the tree. MacArthur noted that it was often hard to see the birds in the dense spruce branches. At the top of the trees, there were few observations closest to the trunk, where the birds would have been hardest to see.

With these observations, MacArthur felt he could explain the co-existence of these five species. Though they were all feeding in the same evergreens, they foraged differently, both according to location in the tree and technique. MacArthur found the Yellow-rumped Warbler to

be present in a lot of areas, but never abundant. The Cape May Warblers were close to the southern limit of their breeding range in Maine
and thrived only in years with outbreaks of spruce budworm. The
Blackburnian, Black-throated Green, and Bay-breasted Warblers differed with respect to feeding zones within the trees.

MacArthur concluded this famous paper with an affirmation of
his original idea. Birds of the same species forage more similarly than
birds of another species, so species are divided. He found that the
population sizes of these warblers were proportional to the volume of
the tree in which they feed. With binoculars, a stopwatch, and a notebook, this young mathematician changed the face of ecology with a
paper that has been cited by other scientific papers 1,919 times (which
is a lot!), including dozens of times even since 2020, more than sixty
years after it was published.

Others have used MacArthur's methods to understand the distributions of these and other birds. In 2004, Enid Cumming published a paper on warblers and other boreal birds in the oldest forests
of Saskatchewan, much deeper into the natural breeding range of
Yellow-rumped Warblers.[14] She did her solitary fieldwork in the late
spring and early summers of 1990 and 1991. In her study plots in
Prince Albert National Park, she first measured tree density using the
area that the base of the tree occupied, so a larger tree would count
for more than a smaller one. By this measure, white spruce made up
nearly half of the total basal area of trees (at 46 percent), followed by
balsam fir (30 percent), trembling aspen (20 percent), and white birch
(4 percent).

Enid talked to me on November 13, 2020, from her sunny home
in Saskatoon before heading out on her cross-country skis to enjoy
the snow. She reminisced about her years watching birds deep in the
old-growth forests. She learned to listen to the warning chatter of
the red squirrels. Paying attention to such chatter once saved her, as
she turned around to see a black bear stalking her. Her screaming,

waving of her arms to appear large, and banging of sticks convinced the bear to leave.

At night in her trailer, she sometimes heard the howls of wolves. Their favorite prey in Prince Albert National Park were the elk, but they also hunted moose, which were harder to catch. No wolf stalked the mother moose and her baby that Enid startled one morning. She held absolutely still and the moose did not locate her and moved off in another direction. Such encounters and others with pine martens, badgers, foxes, beavers, and the all-important red squirrels made this a memorable time in her life.

Enid told me that she did not use a notepad, for that would have meant taking her eyes off the birds. Instead, she hung a cassette recorder around her neck. She then recorded her data by voice, following a bird with binoculars and estimating foraging height to within three meters and verifying the estimates with a clinometer. She had the undistracted focus of the ultimate Slow Birder, making me want to try her tape recorder technique.

Many of the insects that attracted the warblers in such number themselves were attracted to Enid. She said that she could slap herself and leave an imprint of dead mosquitoes, black flies, and midges. Sometimes the warblers were hard to hear above the whining of the mosquitoes. She could not wear a veil, for that would make it hard to see the birds. Insect repellent strong enough to work made her face peel, so she relied on the repellent fumes descending from her well-soaked hat brim to keep the insects off her face. Another challenge was the hummocky surface under the towering trees. The ground in this oldest of forests consisted of a tangle of downed trees, some three feet in diameter, and dense thickets filling areas where a tree had fallen. She said:

> *Everything was covered in moss and* Lycopodium *and the ostrich ferns were taller than I was. The canopy was alive with birds—as well*

as mosquitoes and blackflies! Sometimes, you could hear as many as six
Tennessee Warblers counter-singing from the same point-count location!

    Because it [is] a national park, it was also alive with large mam-
mals: black bears, wolves, red fox, moose, elk, deer, beaver, otter, fisher,
pine marten, snowshoe hare . . .

    At night sometimes I would hear the wolves howling—it is eerie
and amazingly cool at the same time. Other nights, I fell asleep listen-
ing to the wails/yodels of loons and the weird donkey-like calls of Red-
necked Grebes.

Enid analyzed her recordings back in her tiny trailer parked deep
in the forest at the end of a dirt road. She used a stopwatch to quantify
how long each bird was at a specific location as she listened to the
tapes. This tedious work took much longer than the actual observations and had to be done every day so that she could reuse the tapes
the next day. This method had the advantage of great accuracy, since
her observations were never interrupted by writing.

She also made the Christmas-tree-shaped plots of her data, like
MacArthur did, but the bird locations were different in this ancient
forest because no birds foraged in the dark bottom ten feet. Yellow-
rumped Warblers foraged most thirty to forty feet up and in the outer
branches, though they also foraged closer in and in the ten food zones
above and below that one. Cumming made 198 observations of the
locations of Yellow-rumped Warblers, finding them most often in
white spruce and least in trembling aspen. Just as MacArthur, she
found that Yellow-rumped Warblers used more of the tree than the
other species did. In the spruce and fir, she found that Yellow-rumped
Warbler zones overlapped with those of Magnolia Warblers and Boreal Chickadees by 95 percent. Even the most different species' zones
overlapped by more than 80 percent. In the aspen and birch, she
found that the foraging zones of Yellow-rumped Warblers overlapped
with those of Blackburnian Warblers by 88 percent.

She also noted what trees they used and found that Yellow-rumped Warblers were in white spruces preferentially, particularly avoiding trembling aspen. But they also foraged in the greatest diversity of trees and locations, though they did not use the low branches that MacArthur found them in. Cumming ends her paper with a plea for the conservation of old-growth boreal forests and their unique assemblages of birds.

The Yellow-rumped Warblers that I secretly call Myrtle Warblers that I see in my St. Louis circle don't stick around long. From late May until September they will be much farther north, tending their young. October and April are the months I can count on this lovely warbler, though some stick around all winter, probably feasting on bayberries.

YELLOW-RUMPED WARBLER ACTIVITIES FOR SLOW BIRDERS

1. **Record their presence.** Yellow-rumped Warblers are so common for so much of the year in many parts of the country, the first thing one can do is simply note where they are and what they are doing. Log your observations on eBird so we can all track them in their migrations. Why, on October 11, 2020, I saw dozens in the willows near the Mississippi.

2. **Watch their foraging behavior.** Yellow-rumped Warblers forage broadly through trees. If you are fortunate enough to live somewhere they breed, see if you can map out their use of the spruce trees by height and closeness to the trunk. Compare them with the other birds also using the trees for food. Researchers say Yellow-rumped Warblers use more of the tree than other warblers, going high, low, close to the trunk, and out on the branches. They even

hawk insects by flying out from a perch. You can also watch them on wintering or migration grounds, for birds never stop eating.

3. **Watch a nest.** If you are far enough north to have breeding birds, watch them. How often do the parents come and go? Has the nest been parasitized by a cowbird? If so, you might see a nestling much larger than either parent. See if you can take notes like Margaret Morse Nice did on her Yellow-rumped Warbler nest.

4. **Look for hybrids.** If you happen to live along the contact zone of Audubon's and Myrtle Warblers, then you can hunt for and watch nests of Audubon's-Myrtle hybrids. The main difference is that Audubon's Warbler males have a yellow throat. A hybrid might have that yellow outlined in white.

White–Throated Sparrow

Can It Really Have Four Sexes?

An easy way to remember the song of the White-throated Sparrow is to hum the words "Pure sweet Canada, Canada, Canada." This reflects a song nearly as haunting as the loon's and isn't heard only in the far north, for White-throated Sparrows winter all through the southern United States. For me, these clear, slow notes capture my longing for the north, wrapped up in my yearning for youth, friends, nature, and the awakening I experienced on the shores of Michigan's Douglas Lake as a young field biologist taking classes at the University of Michigan Biological Station.

White-throated Sparrows have an extremely unusual characteristic that observers were blind to until astonishingly recently, something even Audubon missed entirely, causing him to paint an erroneous illustration of the species, but I'll discuss that further on.

White-throated Sparrows are not rare. Along with Dark-eyed Juncos, they define winter in St. Louis and many other places in the United States. I see both nearly every day from November to March, eating seeds that fall from the feeder in my backyard, or pecking around in the grasses of Flynn Park or Tyson Research Center. The juncos seem really different from the sparrows, but they are actually very closely related, and at least once even produced a hybrid.

Behavior near feeders may be our most common observation of White-throated Sparrows, so I'll start with it and the work of a rising star in biology, Professor Emilie Snell-Rood of the University of Minnesota. As an undergraduate at the College of William & Mary, Emilie Snell-Rood wondered about who got the most seeds among wintering White-throated Sparrows.[1] In particular, she wondered if those that arrived first got the best seeds and continued to dominate even after the others showed up.

Emilie did her research in a woodlot right on the William & Mary campus, in Williamsburg, Virginia. A cemetery was on one side of the plot, and a not-yet-mature forest was on the other side. She joined Professor Dan Cristol, who had been studying White-throated Sparrows in this population for years, banding them with unique color bands since 1998.

Snell-Rood and Cristol did an experiment in which she captured birds and nourished them in captivity before releasing them. This meant they would be late arrivers at the feeding plots but not in poor condition. Would they have a lower rank than those that got there earlier? She released them on January 14, 2002, and watched them interact with the uncaptured birds for twenty-nine hours over thirteen days between January 20 and March 29, 2002. Would their earlier arrival have a lasting impact on competition for seeds?

Snell-Rood and Cristol made sure to conduct this experiment blind, meaning that they did not know which birds had been held in captivity and which had not. Not knowing which bird was in which group when taking down observations is important in just about any scientific study to avoid the danger of inadvertently seeing a pattern rather than what is really there. This was easy for them to do by simply not learning the color bands of the two classes of birds.

The behaviors that they looked for were dominance interactions. If one bird moves to a spot and the bird that was there moves away, the first bird is dominant to the second one. If one is eating and raises its feathers or wings when another approaches so the newcomer leaves, that is dominance. If one lunges at another, that is dominance. It is one of the best-studied aspects of animal behavior, going back to early studies of chickens and paper wasps.

One of the good things about these sparrows is that the dominance interactions seemed to be stable. If a bird won an interaction one time, it won all the interactions the researchers observed with that particular opponent. So they could assign dominance rank even to birds that did not interact very often.

The result of the experiment was clear. Birds that arrived earlier were dominant. Those that had been kept in captivity deferred to the earlier arrivals.

The experiment matched what they saw as they watched unmanipulated birds and also saw that later arrivals were less dominant. In that part of the study there were two ways to be early. One was by having been at the site the year before. The other was by arriving earlier in the current year. Snell-Rood and Cristol looked at both. What they discovered is that birds that had been at the study site for the winter the year before were more likely to dominate newcomers. Among the newcomers, those that arrived earlier in the given year also dominated those that arrived later.

Besides their arrival time, Snell-Rood thought that larger or fatter birds might win encounters, so they measured size by wing-bone length and visually estimated fat when they trapped the birds. They figured out the sex of birds with blood tests, because sex might also influence winning. Interestingly, size did not seem to matter. Another thing did not matter that will come up later: whether they were of the white or tan form. Just wait for this story!

It is common that individuals that have simply been at a place first should win contests. It is called the bourgeois effect and is puzzling because presumably a given resource would be equally valuable to the newcomer. So why should the one already there be the one to fight the hardest for it and win? Why shouldn't strength have a role? The usual argument is that the individual that has already been there knows the site better and can more easily find the best resources, in this case seeds and sheltered places for night, but this is still an active area of research.

Emilie Snell-Rood told me that this work was her undergraduate honors thesis. Snell-Rood was unusual in that she chose her undergraduate college according to the presence of one masterful biology teacher, Daniel Cristol. She knew that at the College of William & Mary, with Dan, she could begin research in her very first year. She particularly liked a lot of things about this project. She loved watching banded birds. When birds are banded, she can get to know them, understand their individual personalities, and welcome them back each winter, especially the rare few that came five winters in a row. As she put it:

> *I saw not only differences in dominance and aggression between individuals, but also site preferences, slight differences in foraging behavior, exploration, timidity, and all the other behavioral traits now folded into behavioral syndromes/personality. I am not sure it was surprising to me as much as a wonderful window into their individual lives because I could tell them apart.*

Snell-Rood also got into the theory, understanding how the behavior of sparrows on their wintering ground benefited each individual. But she loved the personal side of it. Here is what she said:

> *I have so many fond memories of solitude during this work. My senior year I felt comfortable enough to do a lot of the banding, and most all of the observations, by myself. I got a single dorm room so I could get up at 5:00 a.m. every day without disturbing a roommate, hop on my bike, and head over to the . . . field site, [which] was a wooded area adjacent to a cemetery. And to get to one of the blinds, I would trek through the often fog-laden field of graves at dawn . . . I would sit in the blinds for a few hours in the morning before hopping on my bike and heading back to campus for class.*
>
> *One last random memory . . . every year right after Christmas, Dan would head to tree lots around Williamsburg to get discarded trees. We would use these in the aviary and around the feeder and trap areas as cover. All of this work is thus interlaced in my memory with the smell of spruce/fir trees. And getting one of these trees in December always makes me think of White-throated Sparrows.*

Besides their foraging behavior, White-throated Sparrows have other marvels. Their haunting song has not escaped the researchers' ears. To me it is one of the most entrancing things about White-throated Sparrows, at least until I learned their crazy secret that I'll write about soon. It turns out that recently their song changed abruptly in Alberta, Canada. The birds shortened "Canada" to simply "Cana."[2] To some ornithologists this did not seem like a huge surprise because variation in birdsong in other species was known from the work of people like Peter Marler and Margaret Morse Nice. But the speed with which this song variant spread was astonishing.

By 2004 over a hundred birds in the Alberta–British Columbia area had shortened "Canada" in their song. Remember, it is usually "pure, sweet, Canada, Canada, Canada." The modern birds shortened it to "pure, sweet, Cana, Cana, Cana." And then in 2005 the mutant song appeared in a long-term study population at Cranberry Lake Biological Station in Adirondack Park, New York, thousands of miles east of Alberta. How had this rapid change happened? And furthermore, how did this mutant song spread so that now all of the West has the new song as does Michigan, Ohio, and the rest of the Midwest?

The first requirement for a song to spread is that other birds hear it. But where might a western Canadian bird contact a New York bird? Ken Otter and his collaborators figured that might happen in the winter when the birds move south. So they put geolocators on fifty Alberta males to figure out where they wintered. Geolocators are devices that detect light patterns. If the bird is recaptured, then reading the geolocator tells where the bird was by the diurnal cycles it recorded. They recovered nine of the fifty birds the next spring on their breeding territories, and all but one of them had wintered between Iowa and East Texas. (The lone exception went to San Francisco.) Since eastern birds also wintered in the southern plains, they could have learned the new song from the western birds on these wintering grounds.

But why would the new song have become so popular and spread so fast? Otter suggests that maybe females tired of the old song and went for these snappy birds singing the latest hit, but whether that is true will have to await further research. And we may have to wait a while. After all, the report of the new song transmission area is from August 2020, when COVID-19 was sweeping the world.

By the way, much of this research was done by citizen scientists. The authors relied on people who uploaded just two things, location and a song recording, to places like Merlin, eBird, or xeno-canto. Perhaps somewhere is a recording that predates these tools and that might tell us more exactly when that first bird dropped a syllable. I, myself, will start paying closer attention to all the syllables, for St. Louis is in an area where the birds that shortened the song should occur in winter.

Watching White-throated Sparrows strive for dominance under your feeder and listening for new songs is rewarding. But there is something else worth knowing about White-throated Sparrows, something that would have surprised John James Audubon. If you pull up his print of this lovely bird, you can see he does a careful job of painting it. The yellow spot on the lores in the white stripe just above the eye is clear. So are the faint wing bars. The leaves and blossoms on the dogwood, *Cornus florida*, look just like the ones in my backyard, so I imagine Audubon found this bird while it was still on its wintering grounds. And that may have been the origin of his mistake.

It was a rather big mistake, quite unlike him. In the painting, the lower bird is numbered 1 and the upper bird is numbered 2. The legend indicates that these are male and female.

But this is a mistake. There is no telling which sex the birds in the painting are. Instead they simply indicate the two different color patterns that occur in both sexes of the White-throated Sparrow. Audubon's upper bird is of the tan form, while the lower one is of the white form. In the tan form, the chin, the stripe above the eye, and the stripe down the crown of the head are tan. In the white form, these areas are pure white along with a bright yellow spot in the white by the eye.

I had both forms in the little flock foraging under my feeder. They did not behave in ways that let me tell if they were males or females on their wintering grounds. I guess Audubon's mistake is easy to make, since many species have females that are duller than the males.

The truth about color was not discovered until the 1960s. James K. Lowther of the University of Toronto figured it out.[3] He must have had an inkling that there was a problem when he asked six museums to lend him bird skins that had collecting dates from places and times the birds were breeding, between May 15 and July 15 of the collection year. These skins had the bird's sex indicated on their labels, something that had been determined by dissection as the skins were prepared. He received 134 from the Royal Ontario Museum, 81 from the National Museum of Canada, 57 from the United States National Museum of Natural History, 6 from the Royal British Columbia Museum, 4 from the Royal Saskatchewan Museum, and 4 from the Manitoba Museum. In addition to these dead samples, Lowther and his team caught, inspected, and banded 199 adults on their territories in Canada's Algonquin Provincial Park. He determined the sex of the living birds by whether their cloacae bulged out, a sign of maleness that shows up only during breeding season. With all these samples, Lowther then determined the relationship between sex and coloration.

The living birds Lowther studied fell into two categories, white and tan, determined primarily by the stripe that went right through the crown. He determined that there was no overlap between the two colors and so they were true different types, though at that time he did not know what caused the differences, just that it wasn't sex. Or so he thought. It turned out that it was a new kind of sex entirely.

Out of the 110 mated pairs that Lowther and his team observed in Algonquin Provincial Park, only 4 pairs were of the same stripe, and these 4 pairs were all tan. There were no white-white pairs. He also found that in the 15 cases where a bird switched partners during the season, in all but 1 case they chose a mate of the same color pattern as their previous mate.

This was quite a discovery! It is as if White-throated Sparrows have four sexes. An individual must find a mate of both the opposite sex as we usually think of it, but also of the opposite color pattern, although strictly speaking, two tan birds can mate. This means that finding a mate is quite a bit more difficult, since only a quarter of the available birds will be of a sex and color appropriate for one to choose as a mate, and this is assuming they are all equally abundant in the population. There is lots of evolutionary theory about why nearly all organisms have only two sexes, and it is based on increased difficulty in finding mates, so this is a big finding indeed.

Lowther then went on to try to understand the basis for the differences. It reminds me a bit of Charles Darwin trying to explain heredity before any idea of genetics, genes, or chromosomes. First Lowther determined that the differences are not developmental, or associated with age. Once a bird is white, it stays that way for its life and the same goes for the tan bird, through all its molts. The colors were not necessarily extremely different though, and there could be some overlap between them, especially in winter. Ever the careful scientist and a true Slow Birder, Lowther based this on recaptures of banded birds, twenty-eight banded in 1959 and recaught in 1960. Finally he concluded there was a color polymorphism in White-throated Sparrows that was genetically controlled.

How quickly would other ornithologists accept Lowther's careful work? At least one person challenged it. In a study published in 1971, Linda Donaldson Vardy disputed the bimodality of the crown stripe and other color features that Lowther used to sort the birds into two morphs.[4] Her opinion was based on her research on birds that she trapped at Kalbfleisch Field Research Station on Long Island, New York.

Vardy's work was careful. She did an operation, a laparotomy, to determine the sex of the birds by peeking directly at their gonads. She also determined whether the birds were young of the previous year by making an incision on their heads to look at how ossified their skull was. Don't worry—she treated the birds humanely and held them in a cage until they had recovered from these procedures and could be let go. She also took careful measures of the median and lateral crown stripes and other color measures and did not find the two categories of Lowther. Instead she found a continuum.

Vardy used her data to challenge Lowther's finding that there is a polymorphism in White-throated Sparrows. She also challenged specific ideas about the genetic nature of the differences. She thought it was more likely that there were gradual genetic differences in multiple genes and not absolute genetic differences.

It turns out that her interpretation was simply wrong. This location gives a clue as to why she did not agree with Lowther. Since White-throated Sparrows do not breed on Long Island, all her samples were winter residents or migrants collected at a season when color differences are not as strong.

The next challenge was to figure out what caused the color polymorphism. H. Bruce Thorneycroft solved this question in an elegant study he did for his master's thesis at the University of Toronto and published in the top journal *Science* in 1966.[5] Thorneycroft worked with Klaus L. Rothfels and J. Bruce Falls, the former a chromosome expert and the latter a bird behavior expert. Perhaps his advisors suggested that the secret to the color polymorphism and the near requirement of mating with the opposite morph lay in the chromosomes. A likely candidate would be an inversion, a piece of a chromosome that had flipped and was reinserted backward.

Thorneycroft carefully prepared the chromosomes of thirty-five White-throated Sparrows. Chromosomes are where the DNA is. The DNA is all wound up tightly and protected by a tight sheath of proteins, mainly histones. They are in the nucleus of all cells. Thorneycroft cultured out chromosomes from kidney tissues, whole embryos, or feather pulp at the base of the feathers. He numbered the chromosomes by size, as is standard. The surprising thing Thorneycroft found was in the second- and third-largest chromosomes. Some were what we might call normal, with a large first chromosome pair. The next two largest chromosomes were two pairs with acentric centromeres, a constricted part of the chromosome that separates the two arms and where the spindle attaches during chromosome copying. But other individuals seemed to have only one second chromosome. They had another chromosome Thorneycroft called the M chromosome, which had a central centromere, and it had no partner, the way all chromosomes are supposed to. All White-throated Sparrows had four chromosomes that would make up the second and third pairs, but some had this M chromosome and some did not. But what is important for us is that the ones with the M chromosome, the unusual one with the centromere in the middle, are the white morph and they can be male or female, as seen by the fourth chromosome pair, where there is either a ZW pair (female) or a ZZ pair (male). This fourth pair is the sex chromosomes. In a way, the white-tan difference is very similar chromosomally to the actual sex chromosomes.

Thorneycroft's masterful work was a revolutionary step toward understanding the genetics behind white and tan individuals, something that ultimately led to perhaps the best demonstration of the genes behind behavioral traits in any organism.

Sadly, Bruce Thorneycroft died by suicide on May 22, 1969, three years after the publication of this landmark work and right after receiving his Ph.D. for more extensive work on the system. Anyone who might have speculated on what troubled Thorneycroft is now also gone. But I was able to speak with one important person connected to the story. It was the person who brought Thorneycroft's Ph.D. work to publication while claiming no credit for himself. This person is Gerald F. Shields, currently holding an endowed professorship at his alma mater, Carroll College, in Helena, Montana. Now he mostly works on blackflies.

Gerry, as he likes to be called, took Thorneycroft's data and thesis, crafted it into a remarkably complete story, and published it in *Evolution*.[6] Klaus Rothfels particularly wanted to see this happen and thought it was important that his student Thorneycroft be the only author. Shields agreed and is mentioned only in a footnote to the title of the paper. Bob Montgomerie, also from the University of Toronto, gave me the connections necessary to put together this story.

There are stories of selfishness and competition in academia, so it is enriching to also hear of stories like this one. I would imagine Gerry Shields, having just finished his own Ph.D. on the chromosomes of juncos, was anxious to publish his own work and make that most difficult transition from student to professor. What must he have thought when Rothfels asked him to write up someone else's thesis? What Gerry told me was that he was happy to for many reasons. It was reading Thorneycroft's 1966 paper in *Science* that set Gerry on a path to study cytogenetics, the structures of chromosomes. It is what motivated him to apply to the University of Toronto and to embark on his own work on Dark-eyed Juncos, in which he discovered a number of chromosomal inversions, work that initiated an illustrious career as an evolutionary geneticist. So Gerry had a personal connection to the work. But he also believed in the importance of making information public, no matter how the credit was given.

Once it was clear there was a chromosomal inversion in White-throated Sparrows, we can ask when in evolutionary time the inversion happened. Since both forms still exist in the population, it is likely that it was not too long ago, at least on the evolutionary scale of thousands of years. Elaina Tuttle and her team tried to figure this out.[7] It is likely to have happened only once, in a single bird, that then passed on the trait to all its descendants, an ancestral Eve or Adam. One single bird. It is astonishing. There are also human genes that trace back to a single individual, as David Reich's book *Who We Are and How We Got Here* makes clear.[8]

Elaina Tuttle wanted to figure out when the chromosomal inversion arose. The way to figure that out is to see if related species also have it. So the Tuttle group obtained DNA sequences from six related species, either from public databases or by sequencing the DNA from birds themselves. They then generated a tree of evolutionary relationships among species, a phylogeny. This branching tree puts the most closely related species together.

A phylogeny does not have to include all the DNA. It can be made with just one gene, and in this case it is called a gene tree or gene phylogeny. What they wanted to do was to compare the gene trees on the inverted region of the M chromosome with those not on the M chromosome. Comparing them would tell when the M chromosome arose, when the first White-throated Sparrow with a truly white stripe and throat first flew the earth.

The Tuttle group made such trees and included close relatives of the White-throated Sparrow. The closest relatives of the White-throated Sparrow are Harris's Sparrow, Golden-crowned Sparrow, White-crowned Sparrow, and Rufous-collared Sparrow. More distant relatives are Dark-eyed Juncos and Song Sparrows.

Tuttle found that the closest relative of genes of the tan birds in the uninverted region was in the same region in the Harris's Sparrow. Furthermore, this region was even closer to that in Harris's Sparrow than to the equivalent region on the inverted M of the white form of the White-throated Sparrow. The white-inverted region, by contrast, is equally distant from the tan region in the White-throated Sparrow and the same region in the Harris's Sparrow, Golden-crowned Sparrow, and White-crowned Sparrow. However, none of these other species have the inversion.

Exactly where the inversion happened and how it got into White-throated Sparrows is something we probably won't figure out exactly. The Tuttle group suggests that the evidence supports the theory that the inversion occurred in another species that is now extinct and got into the White-throated Sparrow by hybridizing. This might seem surprising, but hybridizing is known to happen, and once the inversion was in the White-throated Sparrows, those with a copy of the inverted chromosome could do quite well.

Besides white and tan making an additional pair of sexes, it turns out there are also behavioral differences in both the males and the females according to color. Those differences are not only interesting themselves, but they also led to the discovery of the gene in the inverted region behind the differences.

Elaina Tuttle was a leader in the behavioral work. From 1988 to 1995 she studied White-throated Sparrow behavior at Cranberry Lake Biological Station in the Adirondack Mountains, in a park that is one of our country's earliest conservation victories. Her main study plot was seventy-five acres and had between twenty-five and thirty-five breeding pairs of White-throated Sparrows in a season.[9] She set up nets in late April along stream edges and other habitats favored by the birds. The stream bisected a meadow created by beavers and then ran into a bog, a place that must have been magical even with black-flies, no-see-ums, and mosquitoes. Year after year, Tuttle and her coworkers methodically built a dataset of over a thousand birds that could be used to answer many questions.

Tuttle found that the tan males spent their time guarding their females by staying within fifteen feet of them. White males did not guard their females. She also found that the tan females spent less time soliciting copulation from their mates than did the white females.

Early on this could be as much as 12 percent of their time. But much less time was spent actually mating, which involved only 2 percent of their time.

What was the consequence of different behaviors in guarding one's own female or chasing after others for the white and tan males? Twin sisters Andrea and Melissa Grunst used the breeding data from 1998 to 2014 to answer this question.[10]

This amounted to an astounding 1,532 nestlings from 412 White-throated Sparrow pairs. Of these young, only 16 percent did not belong to the father of the nest. Which fathers, tan or white, were most likely to have one of these chicks from another father? It turns out that 83 percent of the extra-pair young were in nests of tan females mated to white males.

I bet that they were fathered by white males because white males are the most likely to court other females, the tan females in particular. After all, there is little point in courting white females, because the chicks would get two copies of the inversion, which is usually lethal.

It is a lot easier to see which chicks do not belong to the parents tending a nest than it is to determine which other male those chicks might belong to. The latter requires good sampling of the entire population. So I wondered if the study was comprehensive enough to tell us who fathered those 241 babies? The Grunst team discovered that many nearby males had been genotyped, giving them hope that they would be able to figure out who fathered the chicks in nests tended by a male not their genetic father. In fact, they were able to assign an amazing 127, or 53 percent, of these young to neighboring males. And over 90 percent of them were white males. So a tan male mated with a white female is relatively safe from cuckoldry. And white males give what they get, though the same males are not necessarily gaining from extra-pair copulations as they are losing to invasions by others. This careful work shows that the chromosomal inversion causes behavioral differences in the males. Now if only the researchers could discover exactly what genes in the inverted area had caused these changes.

When a region is first inverted, the genes on it are the same as before. But the inversion links all the genes in the inverted area together, allowing them to evolve together, something that can have new effects. Exactly which genes might be most important is something that can be discovered because there are not as many genes in one inverted region as in the whole set of chromosomes. This inversion contained about 1,100 genes though, so it was still challenging to figure out which ones conferred the behavioral differences.

Jennifer Merritt and her team in Atlanta figured out one of the genes important for driving the behavioral differences between tan and white males in a tour de force paper.[11] Merritt looked hard at the inverted region of the white males and studied the genes in the area to see if there was a gene that was already known to make behavior more aggressive and promiscuous. Merritt knew that territorial aggression is typically caused by steroid hormones. She also knew that white males had higher levels of testosterone and estradiol than tan males, so this was a start. But when tan birds were treated with testosterone, their aggression did not increase to the level of that of the white birds, so something else had to be at play.

Maybe the white males were more sensitive to testosterone, perhaps because of a more sensitive hormone receptor. A receptor is what links testosterone to the behavioral response through the nervous system. There is a candidate gene she had in mind, called *ESR1*, or estrogen receptor alpha. It turns out that the gene behind this receptor is in the region that is inverted in white birds, so her hunch was right. Also in that region were genes that control how the brain perceived testosterone.

A big dose of testosterone makes the white birds more aggressive but does not have the same effect on tan birds. To see if they had identified the right gene, that estrogen receptor *ESR1*, Merritt and her team used modern genetics to interfere with the gene to see if the experimentally treated white birds would behave more like tan birds. And they found they were right. When the white birds had that gene blocked, they no longer responded to testosterone.

So this and a lot of other fancy techniques showed that they had found the gene that was important. Because *ESR1* was in that inversion area and could not recombine with the gene on the other chromosome, this region could help the birds evolve different behaviors with more aggression, really an entirely different behavioral plan, compared to the tan males.

All told, there is nothing common about the behavior, color, or genetics of this common winter bird. Even the name is a mistake, for only the white form has a white throat. Teams of scientists took over half a century and the latest techniques to figure out this intriguing story.

I love knowing all this about White-throated Sparrows. I listen to how many times they sing "Canada." When I see them, I look at their throats and eye stripes to see if they are tan or white. I feel like I am peering into their private lives and know which are faithful males and which are doing their best to mate with a neighbor. But these are birds, so it is pointless to be judgmental. They are behaving as they have evolved to behave, and in this species there are two different behaviors that are both successful.

Now, I may know about the genetic basis to some of their behaviors, but what I most love is how they signal a St. Louis winter. I see White-throated Sparrows scuttling into the dry grasses around the buildings at Tyson Research Center. I see them jostling for seeds under my feeder. And I listen to their haunting melody, which draws me north as winter begins to turn to spring.

WHITE-THROATED SPARROW ACTIVITIES
FOR SLOW BIRDERS

1. **Look for the birds.** Divide your backyard or wherever you are watching White-throated Sparrows into different habitats. You might divide the habitat by height above ground, type of vegetation, availability of seed, or bare soil, grass, or concrete. Then take a scan every few minutes to just log where the birds are. Then you can make a drawing that shows your results.

2. **Check the number of white and tan birds.** What are the numbers of white and tan birds that you see? Try to note which color they are when you log this bird in eBird. Do the two forms generally behave differently? But be careful—the differences are not so clear in the winter.

3. **Look at color-pattern variation in behavior.** See if you notice any behavioral differences between the tan and white birds. Do the white birds dominate in competition for food?

4. **Observe dominant behavior.** How do White-throated Sparrows interact on their wintering grounds, where they are in small flocks? Scatter sunflower seeds for them somewhere you can watch them. It might be easiest near some vegetation, since they can be timid. Then choose a certain amount of time, perhaps ten minutes, and simply see what they do. Do some peck the others? If the seeds have a denser and less dense area, does one bird keep others out of it? Or do they defend an area near shelter?

5. **Listen to the song of White-throated Sparrows.** As you know, the song can be verbalized as "pure, sweet, Canada, Canada, Canada." But as Ken Otter and his colleagues report, sometime be-

tween 1960 and 2000, the western birds took a shortcut. They repeat, "Cana, Cana, Cana." What is it in your area? Are there any other differences? You can easily save songs to xeno-canto and record them using methods on the Cornell Lab of Ornithology's webpage, or just click save when you record using BirdNET. This will help the scientists pursue the change and makes you a citizen scientist as well as a Slow Birder.

6. **Observe migration arrival and departure.** There are only a few places in the Northeast where White-throated Sparrows stay year-round. Everywhere else they migrate—south in fall and north in spring. If you use eBird to record what you see in your yard or a nearby place each day, you will be contributing to our knowledge of where the birds are and how it changes with the years. If you note if they are white or tan, then you could also document any differences between these two.

7. **Look at the color patterns of paired birds.** If you are somewhere where White-throated Sparrows nest, see if you can find some pairs. They might be near their nests on the ground in thickets of pine, for example. How many pairs can you find? Are they all made up of one white and one tan bird? Which one is the female? She will be the one building and sitting on the nest most of the time.[12]

Riverlands

To understand St. Louis's birds is to understand its rivers, for along their shores are the great migrations and thousands of egrets, herons, and sandpipers in the wet; warblers, vireos, and orioles in the trees; and sparrows and bobolinks in the grasslands. Where the Mississippi flanks the Arch, the Missouri has already joined it seven miles upstream. Farther upstream still, the Illinois River joins in. In my twenty-mile circle are miles of riverbanks, marshes, and horseshoe lakes to explore. I began with the conservation areas along the Missouri, starting with the Cora Island Unit of the Big Muddy National Fish and Wildlife Refuge.

On May 1, 2020, I visited the Cora Island Unit with Patrizia, my husband, Dave, and our pups, Coton de Tulear Zeus and long-haired Chihuahua Gioia. At the end of the trail the muddy water flowed fast, carving into the sandy bank. Cora Island Unit and Boone's Crossing are the only Big Muddy refuges in my area. The Audubon Center at Riverlands, just a few miles north of the Cora Island Unit, has fields, marshes, and lakes along the Mississippi. Other great places in the area are Columbia Bottomlands, on the southwest side

of the rivers, and the state park that sticks out into the actual confluence, though it is often flooded.

These are my main riverside parks, but farther south along the
Mississippi, still nearby, is Cliff Cave County Park. The Meramec
River joins the Mississippi a few miles south, but following it north
are parks along tangled waterways, including George Winter St.
Louis County Park and George Winter Jefferson County Park. Farther north along the Meramec are Possum Woods Conservation Area
and Emmenegger Nature Park. Flanking the Meramec, following it
upstream to the west, are Lone Elk Park and Castlewood State Park,
but these are more forest than river.

Up the Missouri River from Cora, we come to Boone's Crossing,
another Big Muddy National Wildlife Refuge Unit, mostly on an
island. Then there is Howell Island Conservation Area. Follow our
rivers on either shore as closely as you can, and you will find marvelous wetlands and preserves too numerous to count even within my
area.

I haven't yet mentioned ancient loops of the Mississippi like
Horseshoe Lake State Park to the east, with Cahokia Mounds to its
south. To the north is Marais Temps Clair Conservation Area. To the
west is Creve Coeur Marsh.

The great rivers crossing my twenty-mile circle have been drain-
ing the central United States for more than one hundred thousand
years, meandering slowly across the landscape in the flatter areas. But
that does not mean they have been the same even for the last two
hundred years.

February 16, 1764, is the date fourteen-year-old Auguste Chouteau
set ax to trees on a site Pierre Laclède had recently chosen for his new
warehouse and surrounding village.[1] Laclède chose it because it had a
limestone foundation, lifting the land above the flooding Mississippi.
Most of the shore was either limestone cliffs or alluvial soils, prone to
flooding. It also did not hurt that it was on the French side of the river.

But another date changed the rivers much more: the arrival of the first steamboat, the *Zebulon M. Pike*, which arrived in St. Louis on August 2, 1817. By 1854, steamboats lined the St. Louis waterfront for more than a mile. Anyone close to the rivers could smell the smoke coming from their boilers. Steamboats had transformed travel on the rivers, west up the Missouri, east up the Illinois and the Ohio Rivers, and, most important, south to New Orleans. Steamboats transformed the culture all along the rivers and far inland from them. They also changed the landscape, seemingly forever.

The first steamboat, the *New Orleans*, coming out of Pittsburgh in 1811 started a huge new trade, so that by 1860 there were 735 river steamboats. In St. Louis alone there were 22,045 steamboat visits between 1845 and 1852.

The great boilers that produced the steam to move the paddles needed fuel. That fuel was wood. Terry Norris calculates that most of the wood cut from the Mississippi floodplain ended up burned in the insatiable fuel boxes of steamboats.[2] One measure of the lost trees is in the witness trees that bordered the river. More than half of them had been cut down by 1826. Witness trees are a good measure of the earliest forests because they are large trees that mark the edges of properties, so their identity and location are recorded.

Steamboats burned between 12 and 75 cords of wood a day, where a cord is 4 by 4 by 8 feet of lumber, about 1,536 board feet (1 foot wide, 1 inch thick). It takes two trees that are fifty years old to make a cord of wood. Terry Norris puts the consumption of large steamboats in terms of houses to show how much more damaging to the forest steamboats were. If a modest framed house is 32 feet square, it would take 7,500 board feet. A large steamboat burning 75 cords of wood would therefore be the equivalent of 15.4 houses, burned in just one day. He goes on to argue that in 1861, over seven hundred steamboats were on the Mississippi near St. Louis, which were likely to be burning wood enough in a year to build four houses per person each year. As the nineteenth century waned, all the mature trees anywhere close to the Mississippi's banks were gone between the Illinois and Ohio Rivers, a stretch of 180 miles.[3]

This devastation did more than remove the forests along the river. It changed the river itself, as the banks eroded, slumping into the river that was already fairly flat around St. Louis. The river widened by 50 percent and became shallower, causing hundreds of steamboats to founder, so the river became scattered with their carcasses. The Mississippi also shifted course creating new islands, cutting into formerly wooded banks, and generally shifting, especially during floods.

The Missouri River was also affected by the flaming maws of steamboats. Already shallower, with more bends and snags, the Missouri was particularly susceptible to deforestation. Captain Joseph M. LaBarge ran steamboats on the Missouri from 1831 to 1896, covering most of the period. The first boat up the Missouri followed the *Zebulon M. Pike* by only three years. The *Independence* navigated up the Missouri from St. Louis and docked in Franklin, Missouri, thirteen days later, then continued to the mouth of the Chariton River, removing the trees as it went.

Why all this about the sorry history of the forests along our great rivers? Only to remind myself that any forests I see along them are new. The islands and riverbanks not scoured into farmland, or paved and groomed into structures, look more like they did 200 years ago than they did 100 or even 150 years ago. The birds then had acres of forests away from the river. Now the flood-prone riverbanks make some of the best available habitat.

RIVERLANDS ACTIVITIES
FOR SLOW BIRDERS

1. **Watch the water's edge.** Find a spot where you can sit quietly by a creek, river, pond, lake, or sea where you are hidden from the water's edge. Choose a place with vegetation down to or in the water if you can. What birds do you see and what are they doing?

2. **Document how birds are distributed near the water.** Are they spread out evenly? Are they clumped in groups? If clumped, do the same species stick together?

3. **See how birds fly into the wet areas.** Do they approach in groups or on their own? Do they circle? What exactly do they do before landing in the water or nearby?

4. **Find a rookery in spring if possible.** This is a place where birds come together to nest, though each nest is independent. Often they are near water. Choose a nest to watch and see if larger chicks monopolize the food parents bring back. What else can you observe?

American Coot

Whose Chicks Are These?

A quick sketch of an American Coot might consist of an all-black bird with a white beak sitting on the water like a duck. A more careful artist might make the head darker than the body and put in the little line of white pointing to the tip of the tail, from the white along the tips of the secondary feathers. They might even add the shield bulging over the beak and color it brick red to brown.

American Coots were among the first birds my children learned about, watching them from the fishing pier on the 40-Acre Lake at Brazos Bend State Park, near our home in Houston, before we moved to St. Louis and before the kids grew up. They learned to distinguish coots from the two other most common water birds they saw, Black-bellied Whistling Ducks and Common Moorhens, now called Common Gallinules. These are not hard birds to tell apart, so they are perfect for very young children whose soft hands and sharp eyes have not yet learned to coordinate binoculars.

When my youngest son, Philip, needed a science fair project in third grade, I suggested something outside. He chose alligators, which would mean trips to Brazos Bend State Park. With his friend Alex, Philip looked at the interaction of alligators and American Coots.

Alligators are usually in the water alone. We see their eyes first, then more of their geometrically scaled body as they surface. Or we see them on the bank, apparently sleepy and often with a draping of water plants covering their long bodies. We walk around them carefully or back away if it is a mother with her yellow-and-black-striped babies.

Coots that are not nesting are usually in the water in groups eating vegetation. Being in a group can help them avoid being grabbed by an alligator or other predator. They can take turns feeding so someone is always attentive and can alert the others. But what size should those groups be? This is something Philip and Alex could study. They could count the coots in the water. They could count the alligators in the water. They could see if coots near alligators are in larger groups.

We took Philip and Alex to Brazos Bend State Park on more than one weekend, and they counted coots and alligators in Pilant Marsh, Hale Lake, and the 40-Acre Lake. They counted multiple groups in these three lakes, fulfilling the other key element of hypothesis testing: that there be replicates. If they had counted only one group with alligators and one without, they would not be able to say that presence of alligators caused the difference. The more groups they counted with and without alligators, the more likely they were to find a pattern. I wish I could locate that old science fair poster and show their careful hand-drawn graphs of group size and alligator presence. I know just where it would have been in our old Houston home: in the attic. I do have a photo I like of the two of them sitting on the bank with clipboards looking at the water. Now, twenty years later, both are in grad school studying biology.

Why do I love coots so? They are unexpected since they are in the rail family, along with soras and black rails, but they act like ducks. The other species of rails usually lurk in the reeds and marshes rather than float duck-like on lakes and ponds. But a glimpse of their feet might reveal that they are relatives. Their feet are not webbed but toed. These toes have been shaped for water life for a long time and have evolved phalanges that fold going forward and spread when pushed backward, just what a swimmer needs. And they are green.

Coots are just about anywhere there is a bit of water. If you don't know birds, this is one you can easily learn, for no others have white beaks and plump black bodies. But coots need more than water to breed. They need a bit of reedy vegetation in which to build their nests and teach their young to dip down for plants to eat.

If you see just adult coots, you are missing one of the mysteries of nature. In 1948, H.J. Boyd and Ronald Alley, who may have been the first to publish a description of newly hatched coot chicks, put it this way:

> *Most striking is the reddish head, almost bald on the crown and tinged blue above the eyes, with brilliant red papillae around the eyes and at the base of the bill, and the bill itself banded vermilion, black, and white. Long yellow-tipped filaments are thickly scattered among the down of the back of the head and neck, and extend across the mantle and along the wings. The rest of the body appears sooty black.*[1]

The coot they studied was the Eurasian Coot, *Fulica atra*. The American Coot, *Fulica americana*, is even brighter, with a cape of vermilion. Boyd and Alley wondered about the colors but knew they were not to scare off predators. After all, if a predator is near, baby coots crawl out of their nest and seek cover, sticking their heads deep into the leaves as if they know they are too bright. If they cannot leave the nest, they bury their heads into its floor. A few days older, when they can swim, they dive upon the approach of a predator and surface only with their bill and eyes. Boyd and Alley surmised that the color had to do with attracting parental attention during the first few days of life, when the chicks are dependent on the parents for food. And this is exactly true, but there is more to it, as Bruce Lyon discovered.

Bruce is a professor at University of California, Santa Cruz. When I talked to him on April 28, 2020, he was following a Peregrine Falcon with his camera until it went out of sight over the ocean and then returned with a Red-necked Phalarope in its talons. Bruce studied American Coots for his Ph.D. at Princeton, but his love of biology came from earliest childhood when he watched Barn Swallows nesting in the carport from his toddler playpen in Richmond, British Columbia, just south of Vancouver.

He was in British Columbia working with John Eadie on Common Goldeneyes while he looked for his own project. Bruce said:

> John took an afternoon off to play baseball, and I passed the time exploring local marshes. I heard a noise I did not know, waded into the vegetation, and found my first coot chick, and it was shocking . . . The main reason I went to BC is because I knew there were coots there and the vegetation structure of the wetlands—a thin fringe of reeds along the shores—was ideal for watching families.

Bruce wanted to test some ideas of Mary Jane West-Eberhard on parental choice and figured the red-headed coot chicks might be a good option. But first he needed to find a bigger population of breeding coots, preferably in his beloved British Columbia. So he turned to the local experts, the folks at Ducks Unlimited, who were managing thousands of acres of land for ducks, some in collaboration with the local landowners and some of their own land. They helped Bruce discover what he calls Coot Paradise. It is Riske Creek, about seven hours north of Vancouver. Bruce could work on a natural wetlands with as many as 160 nests. But the next year there was a drought and the wetlands dried out. Again Bruce turned to Ducks Unlimited, and they let him work on wetlands near Williams Lake that they managed with dikes to keep wet, and his Ph.D. was saved. These sites had names like Beecher Prairie, Jaimeson Meadow, and the Chilco West marshes near Hanceville.

But Bruce did not do a Ph.D. on parental care and clutch size after all. Within a week of his first year, Bruce realized: "Brood parasitism was rampant and hosts were rejecting eggs. I knew about the topic from Eadie's thesis work—not yet finished—and realized I had stumbled on a gold mine, so I decided then and there to change the focus of my dissertation research. Talk about lucky." Parenting is never easy. In birds there are ways to reproduce without taking the trouble to parent. Males can do this by mating with someone not their mate, so another male will help rear the chicks. Females avoid parenting by laying eggs in another female's nest. This behavior is called brood parasitism and is surprisingly common in coots.

This is an unusual part of Canada, a plateau over three thousand feet high with meadows and forests, cattle-ranching country. Nights were chilly. Coots were easy to study because the reed edges to the waters were thin, making nests simple to find and reach. But Bruce already knew of this area from *Grass Beyond the Mountains*, which his father had read to him when he was little. One of his field site landladies even knew the character Panhandle Phillips.[2]

Bruce Lyon began with brood parasitism, but we will begin with those bright chick heads and capes. Why do the chicks have such bright heads, necks, and upper backs? Bruce started with the simplest of techniques. He found American Coot nests, caught the parent coots at night and put yellow collars with numbers around their necks, and watched them. It is more normal to band bird ankles, but on coots they would be hidden under the water. Chicks he identified with beads put on the head with a harmless safety pin that fell off after a few months.

Now that Lyon and his team had marked the chicks so they could recognize them individually, they could discover whether chicks had evolved that brightness to get more parental attention than their nestmates. But first a bit of background on coot families.

In the spring, coots pair up and fight to defend a bit of marsh or lake that has the reedy growth they need. Gordon Gullion estimated that near Berkeley, California, on Lake Temescal, the coots needed at least 2,600 square feet of reedy vegetation and 470 linear feet of lakeshore to rear their young.[3] Lyon's British Columbia territories were much smaller. Acquiring and defending that territory is likely to involve lots of drama—fights, running across the water at each other, and much calling. But once they have it, the parents build a simple nest of dead reeds. The female lays an egg every day or two in the nest. After the first one or two eggs have been laid, both parents take turns incubating the eggs, which ultimately number between eight and twelve. It takes about twenty-three days of incubation before the chicks hatch. There is on average a five-day spread between the first and last hatched chick, which sets up the competitive asymmetries that define coot family life.

When the last egg hatches in a coot nest, some chicks already will be out of the nest and in the water, and the oldest of these chicks could be over a week old. There is a nest, a brooding platform, and chicks everywhere bobbing up and down in the water among the reeds, peeping incessantly for food and thrusting their gaudy heads at the parents. Knowing whom exactly to feed are life-and-death questions in the coot world. These little chicks are precocious because they can get about by themselves as soon as their feathers dry after hatching, but they depend on the food parents give them for at least a month after hatching. Coots have large territories in which they nest and feed their chicks that they defend aggressively. The chicks stay on their parents' territory until they are about fifty days old.

Why should they be so brightly colored upon hatching? Bright colors are usually associated with mating, with females choosing the brightest males, not with the bright, bare head and brilliant feathers of a newborn chick who is usually intent on hiding, not displaying. What survival advantage do bright feathers on chicks serve? Were Boyd and Alley right that it has something to do with the family? Do parents feed bright chicks more? Are there too many chicks, so many that parents choose to feed some and neglect others? If so, the bright colors might be a way that chicks compete with one another for their parents' attention.

Bruce Lyon, John Eadie, and Linda Hamilton traveled to their field site in central British Columbia in 1992 to do an experiment that would determine if parents preferred their brighter chicks. They found ninety pairs of coots in three small marshes, each marsh only ten to forty acres. If they muted the bright feathers of chicks, would parents shun them? They wanted to manipulate the brightness of the chicks to see if that changed the parents' behavior. Dying them would not work, since it took the waterproofing off their feathers. So the researchers simply trimmed the bright tips off some of the feathers, making chicks that were mostly black with little orange remaining, a coloration like other rail species, essentially bringing the chicks the ancestral coloration and not the bright new coloration.[4] This would let them test the idea that the parents favored bright chicks.

The researchers put the chicks back in their nests and waited to see what the parents would do. Sure enough, the chicks that kept their orange feathers were the ones that the parents picked as favorites to be fed. But this depended on hatch order. There was no difference in survival of orange and black (orange feathers trimmed away) oldest chicks, with both having over 80 percent survival odds. Second- and third-hatched chicks did better if they were orange rather than black, but even the black ones had survivorships over 60 percent. But for the youngest chicks, there was a huge difference between orange and black, with the orange chicks surviving as well, or better, as the firstborn chick, and the black ones plummeting to between 55 and 38 percent survival. Clearly a young black chick was not going to become the favorite and get food from mom or dad, whereas an orange one might.

This careful team of scientists considered two other possibilities for the reduced feeding of the black chicks. One was that perhaps the chicks with their orange feathers trimmed off begged less. But that was not the case. The second worry was that the black chicks appeared smaller without the orange plumes. But that should have caused them to be fed more, not less, and so was not an explanation.

Why did chicks evolve these bright colors that make them so much more visible to predators that they have to tuck their heads away when parents give alarm calls? Why do parents divide up the brood and favor younger chicks? Clearly there are lots more questions. Some of the answers go back to the reason Bruce Lyon originally began studying coots: brood parasitism.

Lyon discovered the extent of brood parasitism by checking many nests every day or two and numbering the eggs with black ink. The nests were not hard to find, because adults became agitated as he approached a nest. He could tell when there was an egg laid by another because birds do not lay more than one egg a day and sometimes two showed up in a nest on the same day. The parasite egg had enough of a subtle patterning difference that Lyon could often tell exactly which egg did not belong. Furthermore, some eggs were laid after the parents were done laying. Mothers usually laid eight eggs in their own nest, varying between six and thirteen.

Bruce Lyon found that in his population of American Coots in British Columbia, 41 percent of nests had eggs in them laid by other females, accounting for 13 percent of all eggs.[5] This percentage was no estimate. He based it on watching 417 coot nests on sixteen lakes across four years, from 1987 to 1990. A quarter of the parasitic eggs were from females who never had their own nest. But most of the parasitic eggs were from females who did have their own nests. They laid eggs in other females' nests before laying their own nests.

Lyon wondered if the parasitism rate was high enough that some females simply eschewed rearing their own young for the sneaky parasite habit, a kind of within-species cuckoo. But this was not a great strategy. Lyon found that it produced only 6 percent of the number of young of natural parents. This was for two main reasons. First, parents often rejected parasitic eggs. Of the 163 parasite-laid eggs that Bruce identified, the host nest parents rejected 38 percent of them. The other reason depended on the behavior of the coots toward the last-produced chicks in their nest. Sometimes the last-laid eggs did not hatch because the parents stopped incubating them. Sometimes they died because the parents did not tend to the newborn chicks in the nest. The adults might have already left the nest with their favorite chicks, younger but not that young.

So if floater females who are only brood parasites do worse, why ever be a floater? Maybe because it might be better than no reproduction at all. It requires only that the female has a mate to fertilize the eggs. Why not just nest and rear young? It turns out that floaters are probably in worse condition than nesting females, so they may be unable to find and defend a territory. Bruce also found that the floaters snuck in their eggs on average ten days later in the season, and those eggs were smaller.

It is understandable that floaters sneak eggs into others' nests, but this is not the only source of foreign eggs. It turns out that a quarter of all females with their own cozy nests also pop eggs into a neighbor's nest. Overall, these females sneak out three or four eggs, as Bruce found from following ninety-eight females over the four years. Bruce observed 394 such eggs and found that the females laid most of them (84 percent) before beginning their own nests. It seems odd because these coots had functional nests that they had not yet laid in.

Anyway, a coot nest can be built in a day, as reconstructions after nest predation indicated. And they parasitized their immediate neighbor's, so it isn't spreading any risk from predators very far away.

The eggs that nesting mothers laid in others' nests were in addition to their own eggs. They did not lay fewer eggs in their own nest when they laid in others' nests, but those other eggs were only a quarter as successful as their own eggs. I suppose that even a quarter success is a bonus since it doesn't come at a cost to their own laying.

Coots act as if eggs are cheap. They lay more than they usually rear in their own nest and in others' nests. Once they have laid six eggs, the chances that any subsequent eggs will make it are below half, even just to fledging. Mostly the chicks that come from those late eggs die by starvation. The dead chicks Bruce found out of the nest were lighter than the living ones. The last chicks to hatch died only a couple of days after hatching. They often had peck marks and bruises on the tops of their heads. Who did it was hard to say, but odds are these were the young of females who laid in others' nests, since Bruce never saw a parent peck their own chick. They may have tousled them, but they did not peck them.

In the water though, parents sometimes shook non-preferred chicks until the chicks stopped displaying their colors for food. Without food, they died, though the ones that died were most likely to be from the parasitic egg layers, because it makes little sense to produce too many young in one's own nest.

One of the delights about being a professor is that every now and then we get someone even more obsessed than ourselves, a student who is not only wicked smart but fabulously dedicated to a project. Such a student for Bruce Lyon was Daizaburo Shizuka, and because of this, he made discoveries that would have been hidden from a less fanatical scientist. Here is what Bruce says about the early days of working with Dai in the field.

In the first year Dai did some exploratory cross-fostering experiments [moving eggs from one nest to another] to try to alter hatching patterns—experimentally reduce the degree of hatching asynchrony. Of course the whole assumption about the validity of cross-foster experiments is that the parents cannot tell. Dai came to me one day after the results were in from the pilot study. He had good and bad news.

The bad news was that the foster chicks had significantly worse survival than the hosts' own chicks, which meant we could not use cross-foster to study hatching patterns. The good news, which Dai recognized immediately, was that this suggested that these birds might be able to recognize parasitic chicks. If this were true, it would be amazing, given that all of the hosts of interspecific brood parasites are unable to recognize the cuckoo chicks in their nests that look nothing like their own chicks and are often substantially larger than the host parents.

Dai came up with the right experiment completely on his own, also after a freak natural history occurrence. I was watching a pair of coots with newly hatched chicks, and during my observation they suddenly turned on their own chicks and killed them all. This was completely crazy, and we had never seen anything like it. After this observation I returned to Santa Cruz [and] one of the field assistants suddenly remembered that this pair of coots had adopted their neighbor's chicks while they were sitting on their own eggs. Dai suddenly realized from this observation that the coots might imprint on the first chicks they encounter in a season—normally the chicks in their own nest but in this case, due to a dumb error, the pair imprinted on their neighbor's kids—and then used this information to decide that their own kids were brood parasites, and treated them accordingly.

. . . These cross-fostering experiments were crazy difficult in terms of logistics, and I have never seen anybody work as hard as Dai did to pull this off. We pulled pipped eggs [eggs about to hatch] from nests and hatched them in incubators at the field house, and during peak hatch

*we often had several hours of work processing chicks before going into
the field. It was really complicated keeping track of where chicks came
from, where they were going, and in some cases whether the chicks got
a haircut to dull the plumage color.*

So how can we summarize the result of Lyon and Shizuka? First,
they discovered that the parents do not necessarily keep the chicks
together or even feed them together. During the first ten days of life,
there is a free-for-all, with each chick trying to get as much food as
possible. After about the tenth day of life, each parent takes some of
the chicks and feeds them, a kind of friendly divorce in which each
parent gets a kid or two. Shizuka and Lyon discovered that at this
point it is the youngest of the chicks a parent gets that is fed the
most.[6] When they beg for food, they swim up to the parents and
display their bright colors. Could the researchers show that the parents
are judging the chicks according to brightness and will then feed
the brightest ones more?

Another cool thing that Lyon and Shizuka asked was if the parents
learned which chicks were their own. We already know the parents
each pick a favorite chick and feed it preferentially. How do they
know they are picking one of their own chicks and not one of the
all-too-frequent parasitic chicks from eggs laid by another? This is a
harder question to answer than it might seem. Here is what Dai Shizuka
says about this study:

*Not only is this a hard question to answer—it was not even a question
we had originally thought to ask. If host species typically don't reject
cuckoos or cowbirds, why would we expect coots to reject a parasite that
is the same species—and likely harder to distinguish from their own?
The full story is long, but one key moment was when Bruce videotaped
an actual instance of infanticide on the lake one day, and I found the
chick near the shore later that day—it had a nape tag, so we could tell*

it was the same chick. And later, when we looked at our notebooks, we realized that the chick was a parasite in that nest. In another instance, we realized that two parasitic chicks had been adopted by the pair in the neighboring territory—which we later figured out were actually their biological parents. Anecdotes like that kept piling up until we came up with the right experiment to figure it all out . . . We wouldn't have even come up with the study without hours and hours of watching the same birds.

Clearly Dai and Bruce are true Slow Birders.

To recognize one's own chicks, first there has to be variation among chicks that relate to family identity. We know there is variation in egg patterns, and Lyon was able to pick out the egg that did not match the others and therefore was laid by a different mother, the parasite. He showed that the birds did this too.[7] It is also important that parents recognize the chicks that hatch from those eggs and discriminate their own eggs from the foreign ones.

It turns out that parents learn to recognize their own chicks by forming a recognition template based on their first-hatched young. This works because parasites don't start laying their eggs until after the parent does.[8] This means that learning to identify chicks that hatch on the first day and then using that information for keeping or rejecting subsequent chicks is a good system. About three chicks usually hatch on the first day and can be used as a template, since only about 15 percent of first-day chicks are from the parasites. But how did Shizuka and Lyon show that this is what actually happened?

They took the eggs that were beginning to hatch from nests and kept them in captivity until they finished hatching. Then they added back a first chick, either the parents' own or one from a different female. This would be the chick that the parents imprinted on. If Shizuka and Lyon were right, the parents receiving a chick not their own would prefer that chick's siblings, hatching in the next days, and not their very own chicks. And that is exactly what they found. Parents imprinted on the chicks that hatched on day one and preferentially accepted future chicks that matched them. It is no wonder that Dai got the top prize of the Animal Behavior Society, the Allee Award, in 2009.

I see coots in almost every marsh, impoundment, or lake I visit. They are the most reliable bird in the water and by far the most visible rail. They breed from Texas through Missouri and Michigan and up into Canada, particularly in the West. But the ones I have seen breeding most commonly were in the lake by our home in the year we spent in Berlin, though those were European Coots. My home in Villa Walther was on a channel between two artificial lakes, drainage from the construction of Grunewald villas in the preexisting swamp. This meant that I could hear coots calling and fighting from my bed at night. In the morning as I walked our dog, I could see them crashing along the water, chasing away intruders.

The winter had more coots than the summer, migrants from even farther north, I suppose. I also saw coots in Grunewaldsee, darting among the reeds. By spring each pair of coots in the two lakes had about five hundred feet of shoreline in which to rear their chicks. And I could see these red-headed chicks and imagine all the things Bruce Lyon and Dai Shizuka had figured out. I saw that each parent seemed to feed one chick in particular and that it was very red. I also saw other chicks, though I never saw parental aggression on chicks.

AMERICAN COOT ACTIVITIES
FOR SLOW BIRDERS

1. **Locate the coots.** Be on the lookout for coots whenever you are near water. How many are there? What size group are they in? If

two groups swim near each other, do they fuse or keep separate? If there are predators nearby, coots will form larger groups.

2. **Watch a coot feed.** American Coots eat underwater vegetation, and they eat a lot of it. But sticking their head underwater makes them vulnerable to predators. What do they do about it? Watch coots feeding to see how often they check for predators. Do they do it more when they are in small groups than in large groups?

3. **Find nesting coots.** Coots breed mostly in northern regions but also breed in Texas marshes. If you have breeding coots near you, watch them. Maybe you will get to see red-headed babies and parental preference for feeding one chick. If the chicks look different enough for you to tell them apart, you could keep track of exactly how much one parent feeds them by simply keeping track of the activities of one parent. Watch it for a while and then watch the other if you can see both. It can be challenging to do so, as they are likely to mostly keep to the reedy edges of a water body.

Great Egret

Will the Chick from the Third-Laid Egg Survive?

The Great Egret is an iconic bird of the wetlands. It stands tall, white, and thin, patiently waiting for fish. Most of the time I see them alone, hunting quietly. But during migration dozens aggregate in the marshes of Riverlands, just north of St. Louis along the Mississippi.

This is a good bird for a beginner because it is hard to mistake for anything else. The Snowy Egret is much smaller and has black legs and yellow feet. The white morph of the Great Blue Heron is larger, has a thicker bill and pale legs, and is common only in the Florida Keys. The white morph of the Reddish Egret is smaller and has a yellow bill with a black tip and is rare. The white morph of the Little Blue Heron is much smaller and has paler legs. I don't suppose anyone would mistake a White Ibis for a Great Egret, since the ibis has a long, curved red bill and red legs.

The Great Egret is often the first bird I see on a trip to Riverlands. After I cross the Missouri River, Highway 67 is elevated and the roadsides are wet. In these ditches, I might see the first Great Egret of the day, standing motionless and as impossibly elegant as the ladies whose desire for feathered hats nearly annihilated Great Egrets about a century ago. But just because I see a Great Egret standing still does not mean she is unoccupied. She is waiting for a fish to come near; then she will strike and swallow, then freeze again, waiting for the next fish, storing the first in her crop. In nesting season she'll fly home with as many as thirty one- or two-inch-long fish in her crop to feed her young.

I've never been a fan of birding from the car, so we keep driving past these motionless birds to the watery basins along the Mississippi. Great Egrets are in the shallower waters, not out in the great rivers. One Sunday toward the end of the day, looking across Alton Slough, I saw a Great Egret and then another. But the third white figure was simply a post. Above it flew a Bald Eagle.

We are lucky to have Great Egrets at all, because Americans more than a century ago nearly exterminated them. It was the feather trade. The feathers women most liked on their hats were those of egrets in breeding plumage. Millions of birds were killed in the breeding season, leaving millions more chicks to starve in their nests.

As William Hornaday said, "The whole earth is a poorer place to live when a colony of exquisite egrets or birds of paradise is destroyed in order that the plumes may decorate the hat of some lady of fashion, and ultimately find their way into the rubbish heap."[1]

It was not just a few feathers either. Though collection was banned in the United States in 1901, a piece from the London Feather Sale of February 1911 gives an idea of the scale of feather collection. At that one sale, four companies—Hale and Sons; Dalton and Young; Figgis & Co.; and Lewis and Peat—sold a total of 6,346 ounces of egret feathers. Six egrets are killed for one ounce of feathers, so this represents 38,000 birds. In a nine-month period, it came to 129,168 egrets killed just for London. New York was similar, and Paris, Berlin, and Amsterdam had even more.

Some women organized to fight feathered hats and their terrible consequences. In Boston in 1896, Harriet Hemenway founded the Massachusetts Audubon Society to protect birds from feather hunters and other aggression against birds. She and her cousin Minna Hall urged women away from feathered hats. But it took time to change minds, time the egrets almost did not have.

By 1912 there were fewer than 3,000 Great Egrets nesting in only thirteen colonies in the American southeast and California.[2] In the years since the ban on feather collection, their numbers have slowly increased so that there are now around 360,000 Great Egrets in the United States.

Another approach to saving the egrets was to preserve nesting colonies themselves, forbidding the massacre at single places at a time. One such reserve was that on Avery Island, Louisiana, where the McIlhenny family makes Tabasco sauce. Here is what Edward A. McIlhenny said:

> *In some recent publications I have seen statements to the effect that you believed the egrets were nearing extinction, owing to the persecution of plume hunters, so I know that you will be interested in the enclosed photographs, which were taken in my heron rookery, situated within 100 yards of my factory, where I am now sitting dictating this letter.*
>
> *This rookery was started by me in 1896, because I saw at that time that the herons of Louisiana were being rapidly exterminated by plume hunters. My thought was that the way to preserve them would be to start an artificial rookery of them where they could be thoroughly protected. With this end in view I built a small pond, taking in a wet space that contained a few willows and other shrubs which grow in wet places.*
>
> *In a large cage in this pond, I raised some snowy herons [egrets]. After keeping the birds in confinement for something over six months I turned them loose, hoping that they would come back the next season,*

as they were perfectly tame and were used to seeing people. I was re-
warded the next season by four of the birds returning, and nesting in
the willows in the pond. This was the start of a rookery that now cov-
ers 35 acres, and contains more than twenty thousand pairs of nesting
birds, embracing not only the egrets but all the species of herons found
in Louisiana, besides many other water birds.

To commemorate the importance of egret conservation, both for
itself and for the origin of the conservation movement, the Great
Egret is now the symbol of the National Audubon Society.

I could dwell more on this painful period that inspired the Lacey
Act of 1900, prohibiting trade in illegally gathered wildlife, fish, or
plants. In 1901 water birds were specifically protected from the feather
trade. Then eighteen years later, the Migratory Bird Treaty Act was
passed, protecting eight hundred migratory bird species from harvest
of any kind, dead or alive. In other countries, though, plumes continued to be harvested.

Every bird has a story it tells best. For the Great Egret the story
is in the rookery, where the chicks are raised. A rookery is a magical
place, one where hundreds of birds of different species build their
nests often only a few feet apart. The squawks and calls come from all
directions in a cacophony. The branches and grounds below the nests
are white with droppings. Predators like snakes—or in the South,
alligators—may lurk under these nests waiting for a nestling to fall.

If I look at eBird, it seems there should be Great Egret rookeries
in my twenty-mile St. Louis circle. But I did not know of any, so I
asked local bird expert Bill Rowe if he did. It turns out there is a
rookery right in midtown St. Louis, around 4100 Olive Street. The
Olive Street rookery, which I visited early in the spring, has cross
streets North Sarah Street and Vandeventer Avenue. The rookery extends north to Washington Boulevard. Last summer there was a lot
of concern when some of the rookery trees were trimmed, destroying

some of the nests. Lisa Saffell organized a survey and found 40 Great Egret nests among 147 Little Blue Heron, 24 Black-crowned Night Heron, 8 Snowy Egret, and 18 unidentified nests.

Nesting birds avoid predators in two ways. The first way is choosing a safe place to nest, called a rookery. Rookeries are generally in trees in a swamp or on a small island, a place somewhat protected from predators, like foxes or coyotes. The second way comes from nesting in a group in the rookery, which provides further protection. Nests on the edge are more likely to be discovered by predators than nests in the center of the colony. Living in dense rookeries is possible only because the nesting adults can fly far from them in search of food for their young. Where to nest and where to eat is a trade-off they do not have to make.

But there is another cruel gamble that Great Egrets take, one I think of whenever I see an elegant Great Egret fishing patiently, whether for herself or for her chicks. It was a question asked by Doug Mock, who, alternating with his assistants, spent the summers in the late 1970s and early 1980s in tiny blinds for days at a time to figure out who gets fed and ultimately who survives.

The fish that Great Egrets depend on are not a predictable resource. Some years they will be much more plentiful than others. This makes it hard for the birds to judge how many eggs they should lay. So they hedge their bets. They lay more eggs than they are likely to be able to see to adulthood, hoping for plenty of food so they can rear all the chicks. But in years when fish are less abundant, they have evolved a way to jettison just one chick without starving all of them.

The way they do it is by being unfair and not feeding all chicks equally. They do this with an evolved system that takes the choice out of the parents' beaks. They begin to incubate their eggs after the first one is laid instead of doing what most birds do and waiting until all eggs, or all but one egg, are laid. Great Egrets have a hatching hierarchy. The third Great Egret egg will hatch when the chick from the first laid egg is two to four days old. It will be no match for its older siblings, which not only have hatched earlier but also have already received several days of food. So the older chick could take food from its parents first, leaving the smaller, younger chick with less food. Does this happen? Do the parents interfere? These are questions Doug Mock wanted to work out. He figured the parents would intervene, partly from personal experience, since he was the fourth-born son and his own parents intervened frequently in antics with his brothers.

I have known Doug Mock since April 1984, when he came through Houston on his way to setting up the field project in Lavaca Bay. We went to my social wasp field site at Brazos Bend State Park along with Tim Lamey and my husband, David. We saw wasps. We saw a Bald Eagle from the tower over Pilant Marsh. We have been friends ever since.

Doug has always been an obsessive scientist. Where others might watch nests or colonies for an hour at a time, Doug decided the nests needed to be watched from first light to dark. He did this on islands in Lavaca Bay from 1979 to 1984. From a blind forty feet from the nests, he could record everything going on in over a dozen nests at a time. He worried about the disturbance that a person going into or out of the blind might cause, so he or his assistants slept in the blind, changing people only once a day in the middle of the afternoon. They even had a portable toilet in the blind, carrying out their own waste in a blue plastic bag at shift's end. Watching during all daylight hours made for more than fifteen thousand nest hours in 1980 and 1981.

But they had to come out of their blinds and get close to mark the chicks with feather dye when they hatched in order to tell the hatching order of a chick, where rank comes from birth order. They used yellow, black, and no color, marking the top of the head and down the neck so that the color could be seen from any angle. Over the years they changed who got what color in case the color itself biased the birds. They did not capture and mark the adults, since it would be very disruptive and was not necessary for the study, as the adults tended only their own nests.

Mock and team recorded fights, feeding, and mortality. They formally defined fights as starting with the first blow and ending with the last blow. They counted the number of blows and their outcome. They considered a chick to have lost when it crouched or fled, or when the fight was interrupted by a feeding. If these didn't happen, they called it a tie. They recorded what fish the chicks received when they were visible and how big the prey fish were.

They called the chicks A, B, and C, with A being the firstborn.

Fights within the family are no rarity, as some of our own origin stories tell. Biologists explain this conflict as based on scarce resources combined with different genetic interests. Though family members are closely related, no one is as related to anyone else as much as they are to themselves. So if resources are limited, conflict will ensue. Just as siblings will differ in their views for how food should be divided, so should parents differ with those children.

This is a huge area of biology. Conflict within families can explain things like the structure of the mammalian placenta, where the fetus plunders more from the mother than she might optimally give. It is a kind of conflict that can explain the squawks at a nest as each baby asks for more food than the next one. It is a kind of conflict that explains runts, the last pup on the last teat, surviving only in the best of circumstances. It goes to the very roots of all the struggles within families, at least from a biological perspective. And Great Egrets might be the very best place to understand family conflicts, because they are exaggerated and visible.

First- and second-born chicks relentlessly attacked their siblings, sometimes even killing them. An attack could last for minutes. Third-born chicks inevitably managed to get less food, which could end up killing them. Young that fell out of the nest were soon eaten by alligators waiting under the nests. But still some third chicks survived.

Some attacks included as many as 127 consecutive blows with the
bill to the loser's nape and base of the skull.[3] Surely, Doug reasoned,
this was excessive. The parents should stop this aggression when they
could. Would it not be sufficient for the differences in food availability to work their harsh effects on younger chicks? After all, this was
how it was in Great Blue Herons. They also laid more eggs than they
could usually rear. They also began incubating from the first egg.
They also lost third chicks. But in the Great Blue Heron case, it was
to starvation, not aggression.

But it turned out that the parents did not stop the aggression.
Mock looked at fights according to whether the parents were present.
In broods with three chicks, for example, he recorded an astonishing
2,932 fights in the first month of the chicks' lives, and of those, one
or both parents were present for 2,829 of them. Of these fights, parents did something that ended the fight, usually brooding, feeding, or
tripping over the chicks, only 23 times. Clearly the parents were not
helping the smaller chicks.

But maybe the presence of the parents reduced the severity of the
fights. Doug coded fights as severe if the victim subsequently went to
the edge of the nest or draped its head far off the nest to avoid blows
to the head. This latter posture, a chick in the nest, its head draped
far out, I found particularly heartbreaking. Doug recorded as less
severe any fight where the victim simply crouched in the nest, or the
perpetrator stopped before the victim did anything.

I was not the only one to find the fights hard to take. Doug Mock
told me:

> Once a local newspaper reporter visited the colony (my group was a
> colorful addition to Port Lavaca) and was horrified to see the aggres-
> sion. She asked, "Why don't you do something to stop it?" And I an-
> swered, "There are 500 nests on this island. You take 250 and I'll fix
> the others!" She saw my point . . . this has been going on for millions of

years. So she asked, "How can you stand it?" And I replied, "The first step in studying siblicide is that your soul has to die." I was being flippant, of course (as usual), but it really is pretty harrowing to watch . . . until you habituate.

Mock then compared fights and found that there were fewer severe fights when the parents were present, but it did not seem to be the result of anything the parents actively did, just more that the parents were a source of food and so a distraction. In Great Egrets, sibling aggression accounted for between a third (from a sample of 145 nests) and a half (from observation on 21 nests) of all deaths.

Brood reduction does not have to involve the murdering of siblings. It does not in Great Blue Herons. Death-of-chick rates were similar in the two species. Mock found that in 145 Great Egret nests with three or four chicks, 61 percent had chicks that died. About half of those deaths were because of siblicide. In Great Blue Herons of 41 nests with three or four chicks, 66 percent had chicks that died. But only one was because of overt aggression.[4]

Why do they fight when the last-born chicks are the ones most likely to die anyway? Great Egret chicks can monopolize the food more easily because it is small and they can get it right out of the parent's bill, but why should this change things?

Experiments are the closest biology gets to truth. Observations can tell us a lot, but ultimately you do an experiment that actually changes the conditions you think are important. This is hard in the field, and laboratory experiments have their own problems of unnaturalness.

I thought of the things important to the story so far and realized I could predict the experiments Doug did. They are simply to manipulate the variables he thinks are important.

First is what if there was enough food so all could eat? Would there still be so much aggression? Doug looked at this along with students Tim Lamey and Bonnie Ploger in a sample of one hundred nests in

1985 by comparing fifty nests they supplemented with double the normal fish with fifty that were unsupplemented.[5] This was not easy to do. Doug said, "The food-supplementation was the hardest experiment, since we had to visit each nest every day bringing chopped fish and delivering it from the end of a four-foot section of house guttering (place food in gutter's end, extend gutter over the nest, invert gutter . . .)."

The parents continued to provision both kinds of nests normally. Surprisingly, getting double the normal amount of food did not reduce fighting among the chicks. It seems from these results that Great Egrets fight no matter what, that this is not a flexible behavior that can change with conditions. But there was good news. The third-born C chicks from the nests that got food supplements weighed 61 percent more than those that were unsupplemented. There were 41 percent fewer chick deaths in the supplemented nests, so they fought as before, but the consequences were not as dire.

The second experiment Doug could have done was to change the ability of chicks to monopolize food. What if Great Egrets brought in huge fish and flopped them in the nest the way the Great Blue Herons do? Doug had a clever way of going about this one. It was impossible to get Great Egrets to start bringing in larger fish. So he put nature to work for him and simply transplanted newly hatched Great Egret chicks into Great Blue Heron nests. How would the chicks respond to the food of the others? Doug and his team of three then watched the nests during all daylight hours for twenty-five days. The parents didn't seem to notice that their eggs had been switched out for another species'.[6]

Did the fostered Great Egret chicks become less aggressive when they could not monopolize food? The answer is no. They kept hammering their youngest sibling at the same rate as in natural nests where food could be monopolized.

Doug wanted to do one more kind of experiment. He wanted to

remove the size advantage of the first-hatched chicks. He could do this simply by manipulating the eggs so that they all hatched on the same day. Would there be an aggressive free-for-all with everyone suffering lethal wounds? Or would they calm down, reducing aggression when no one had the advantage?

For this one, Doug and his student Bonnie Ploger turned to a closely related species that also nested on the islands and also had siblicide. Cattle Egrets are a lot more abundant, are a bit easier to manipulate, and have the same general system of nesting.[7] They had four treatments. In one they left the nests untouched. In another treatment, they switched the eggs around but preserved the average natural spacing between hatching of one and a half days. They did this mixing instead of just leaving the natural nests in case the manipulation or the differences in the eggs mattered. There were two experimental treatments. In one, the eggs were all set up to hatch on the same day. In the other, the intervals were about double the natural ones. They marked the alpha chicks with a head patch of yellow picric acid, marked the second ones with black Nyanzol-D, and left the third chicks unmarked. In the synchronous broods, they did the coloring haphazardly to be able to distinguish the chicks, but there was no first or last. In these three kinds of broods, with a total sample size of 134 nests, the percentages of siblicide was 12 percent in the control chicks, 13 percent in the chicks with exaggerated intervals, and 17 percent in chicks from nests where chicks hatched simultaneously. Fight number and severity was the highest in the broods where everyone hatched at the same time. But the fights diminished over time as the chicks set up a hierarchy, with the lower ones deferring to the more dominant ones. It just took longer in the nests where everyone hatched at the same time.

There was another thing going on that made the first-laid chick fight and win those fights. It turns out that the third-laid egg got less testosterone in its yolk.[8] This translates ultimately into a less aggressive chick.

Fights were not the only thing that hurt the lowest-ranked chick. It also got less food. Like Great Egrets, Cattle Egrets scissor the bill of the parent to get the food deposited directly in their bills. In the simultaneously hatching broods, the top-ranked chick got 49 percent more food than the bottom-ranked chick. In the control broods, the top-ranked chick got 65 percent more food than the bottom-ranked chick. In the broods where the hatch-time difference was extended, the top-ranked chicks received 153 percent more than bottom-ranked chicks.

So when I look out at a wetland graced by Great Egrets, as I did yesterday at St. Stanislaus Conservation Area, I see a flock of elegant birds. I see birds nearly driven extinct for their feathers. I see the Audubon Society's emblematic bird. But I also know that most of them are first- or second-born chicks. I wonder which ones are the lucky third chicks that survived and how that has affected them. This is also a question that Doug Mock would like to answer.

GREAT EGRET ACTIVITIES
FOR SLOW BIRDERS

1. **See where Great Egrets are close to home.** Great Egrets migrate through much of the United States and breed in wetland areas scattered around, including both my Texas and Missouri homes. Determine what your exposure to these great birds is.

2. **Observe a rookery.** If you are fortunate enough to have a rookery nearby, watch it. When do the Great Egrets start to breed? How are their nests spaced? Can you observe nest behavior, including how often the chicks attack the smallest? Draw a map of the rookery, showing how different species are distributed.

3. **Observe a Great Egret foraging.** Watch a Great Egret hunt. How long does it stand in one place? Does it leave after swallowing a fish or wait for another? How close to other egrets is it?

4. **Watch the migration.** In migration Great Egrets often form large groups. How big is the group you see? How many are vigilant looking up, not eating, and how many are looking down? Does vigilance behavior differ according to group size?

Snow Goose

Arctic Dreams

When I observe Snow Geese in long, bent lines streaming north over the confluence of the Mississippi and Missouri Rivers, heading to the Arctic to raise their young, I feel a longing for wilderness. I gaze at line after line as they cross over Missouri in astounding numbers in February. I pick out the other species that travels with them, Ross's Goose, a little more than half as large but keeping up apparently effortlessly.

These Snow Geese are at the northeastern edge of my twenty-mile circle, around the Audubon Center at Riverlands, along the Mississippi River sloughs just north of its confluence with the Missouri River. I sometimes see Snow Geese fly right over my home, but Riverlands is where I go to see them.

February 8, 2020, felt bitterly cold when we met at Teal Pond for the St. Louis Audubon Society birding trip, led by the incomparable Bill Rowe. I say "bitterly cold" because long underwear, sweaters, and coats did not seem to take the edge off the chill wind, though the thermometer indicated we were not breaking any records. We did not know this would be the last field trip for a long time, as COVID-19 isolated all of us.

We watched the Snow Geese in awe. Could they really be flying north already when there was no sign of spring? Where were they going and when would they get there? The Snow Geese did not stop. We watched bent V after bent V. We watched straight lines. We saw them lift from the waters and move up into the rain-heavy sky. We saw Snow Geese in the soggy meadows planted with winter wheat along Wise Road. All told, we estimated that perhaps six thousand Snow Geese flew overhead that day, but it could have been more. A check back at eBird tells me that February is the big month for Snow Goose migration through Missouri.

A Snow Goose on land is an unassuming bird, white with a mostly pink bill and pink legs.[1] A Snow Goose's dark eye is unadorned in an otherwise white head, giving it a friendly and innocent look. However, that white head is sometimes stained orange-brown from grubbing for food in iron-rich mud. Its wingtips are dipped in black. There is another form, at one time called the Blue Goose, which is a dark blue-gray except for the head. Where the blue form came from is a story I tell a bit later. When Snow Geese take flight, who can help pausing as the magnificent birds wheel overhead calling to one another, raising and lowering their wings in line, yet somehow never running into each other in confusion as the entire line turns? They head far north to their huge colonies in Nunavut, Greenland, and Alaska, so much farther north than I have ever been.

What is a goose, I wonder? There are seventeen species of geese worldwide, seven in North America, and these can be divided into two genera, *Anser* and *Branta*. Snow Geese are in the *Anser* group, and Canada Geese are in *Branta*. You know Canada Geese, the ones eating grass on the lawn. They are brownish of body with a black neck and head, a white chin strap, and white under the tail. Besides eating grass, I think of them flying low and calling to their group members.

Geese are most closely related to swans and together make up the subfamily Anserinae.[2] People domesticated the ancestor of the Gray-lag Goose (in *Anser*) for food in the New Stone Age, eleven thousand to four thousand years ago in southeastern Europe. Now Germans cherish a meal of goose for Christmas, a winter tradition that goes back longer than the holiday itself. Indeed, we had a meal of goose at a park-like restaurant the last winter I lived in Berlin.

I chose Snow Goose as my last bird for this book because they tie me to the past and to the future. In my mind, they bring me south to my former home on the Gulf Coast, where Snow Geese winter in coastal marshes and rice fields, and they bring me north to the remotest shores of the Arctic Ocean, where I have never been. I dream of the Arctic more easily from my childhood Michigan home, though it is still thousands of miles from the Arctic Ocean. I let the Snow Geese make the trip for me.

There are other reasons to write about Snow Geese. They may be more like us than any other bird, because they live in groups and are paired with a single mate; because their numbers are exploding, devastating the environments where they occur; and because they suffer from some highly contagious diseases. But I will now tell the story of Snow Goose life.

A Snow Goose first sees the world when it pecks its way out of an egg near the ocean's edge in the high Arctic. It is usually one of five chicks in the nest.[3]

The nest is soft from downy feathers the mother has plucked from her own breast, and it is warm from that same mother's body. If the chick hatches from the first or last egg its mother lays, it will start out smaller, since these eggs are smaller, but the chick catches up to its siblings very quickly. That the first or last egg might not hatch at all is another sad truth.[4] Surprisingly, some chicks are unrelated to the mother that warms them, the result of egg dumping done by a female who sneaks an egg into another's nest (also called brood parasitism).

The eggs take about twenty-four days to hatch. Half the chicks in the whole colony hatch within a day or two of each other, and almost all hatch in the same week. Colonies that are farther north produce young later. Synchronous egg laying and hatching within a colony floods the local predators with food, increasing the chance that any given chick will survive. A fox stalking the colony for a meal will have many chicks to choose from, though each will be defended by fierce goose parents. If there is another chick between you and the fox, it is more likely to be eaten. No doubt this is why there is such competition to nest in the middle of the colony.

By the time the chicks are three weeks old, they grow new feathers, and by six weeks have large enough wing feathers to fly, just when the adults will have finished changing out their own worn feathers, readying the whole family for the long flight south. During this annual molt, none of the geese in a colony can fly, so it gives researchers a chance to herd them into enclosures and put identifying bands around their legs and necks.

Many Snow Geese fly south along the Mississippi flyway. They first fly a bit west from their breeding colonies in the eastern Canadian Arctic, then southeast through North Dakota, South Dakota, and Iowa before joining up with the Mississippi flyway, which takes them straight down to the Gulf Coast where hundreds of thousands winter in Anahuac National Wildlife Refuge, just an hour and a half east of my former Houston home.

During winter the birds grub for plant roots but also discover rice, an abundant delicacy that has caused the Snow Goose population to explode. By February, when the azaleas are blooming in nearby Houston, the Snow Geese will have already begun their trip north, flying over St. Louis. They will reach their breeding grounds by late May or early June, and there they will keep eating. Snow Geese have such a fast digestive system that their vegetarian diet stays in their digestive tract only an hour or two before they defecate, something they do about every ten minutes, making them a kind of pooping machine.

Once they arrive back on their Arctic breeding grounds, yearling Snow Geese still stay close to their parents, but the parents will be busy getting another clutch laid, incubated, and hatched. All will go through another molt and then fly south, back to the same place as before.

When the time comes to fly north together, the male forsakes his natal grounds and his family to follow her to hers. Birds of any species that find their life partner away from their nesting ground have evolved for one sex or the other to set the breeding destination. If they were humans, they would be called matrilocal, since the female's home is where they go.

Once at the breeding ground, the female builds a nest and then both rear the brood. But these two-year-olds are inexperienced and will not be very good at it. They will not score a great spot to nest since they will not compete well with the older geese. Two-year-olds have nests at the edge of the colony. Or they may find places in the middle of the colony that are damp or otherwise less desirable.

If Snow Geese have not found a mate in their second winter, they try again the third winter and most likely succeed. After all, there are about as many males as females, so there should be someone for everyone.

If two-year-olds manage to bring a few goslings into the world and fly south with them, they often skip breeding the next year, instead strengthening themselves on their wintering grounds by eating and remaining with their yearlings. The three-year-olds that breed are those that did not breed in their second year. By the time they are four years old, they will all have paired up, built a nest, laid eggs, and attempted to see their chicks through to adulthood.

It used to be that ornithologists thought there were two species, a Snow Goose and a Blue Goose, the latter named *Chen caerulescens* by

Carl Linnaeus in 1758. The blue is more sooty gray than blue and
has a white head. The populations were distinct. The Blue Goose
wintered along the Gulf Coast in Louisiana, making the Sabine
River a true boundary between the Snow Goose of Texas and the
Blue Goose of Louisiana.[5]

But the breeding grounds of the Blue Goose were unknown until
the early part of the twentieth century. Along the shores of Hudson
Bay and on the known breeding grounds above the Arctic Circle,
only the Snow Goose was found.

We all take on our own challenges, for reasons known or unknown even to ourselves, and these challenges enrich our lives. For a
famous ornithologist, J. Dewey Soper, the personal challenge was to
find the breeding grounds of the Blue Goose.[6] Soper was born on
May 5, 1893, near Rockwood, Ontario. He went to Alberta College
and then the University of Alberta. Thoreau's *Walden* inspired him,
though Soper yearned for true wilderness, northern wilderness.
Through naturalist connections, he managed to get a position as a
naturalist on a number of Canadian Arctic explorations. Ultimately,
he worked for the Victoria Memorial Museum, traveling the far
northern areas of Canada with Inuit guides. They explored for years,
mostly by boat, places on Baffin Island like Nettilling Lake and Foxe
Basin.[7] His official tasks involved Arctic plants and animals, but his
passion was Blue Geese. He wanted to discover where they nested.
Like many discoveries by Europeans and their descendants, discovering meant connecting with the right Native people who knew all
along where something was, and so it was with Soper.

One of Soper's bases was Pangnirtung in Cumberland. In August
1926 from this field base Soper learned from an Inuit hunter from the
Tikoot Islands that the Blue Geese nested in Bowman Bay, northeast
of Foxe Peninsula.

Anxious as Soper was to set straight across or around the southern
end of Baffin Island to the Blue Goose breeding grounds, he could

not go that same year because it was late in the season. But he returned in 1928. He began at Cape Dorset, on the southwest shore of
Baffin Island. There another Inuit, named Salia, drew a map from
memory that also pointed to Bowman Bay. By mid-May Soper, five
Inuit, and forty-two dogs pulling sleds crossed to Bowman Bay. On
June 2 one flock of Blue Geese flew over, and by June 6 thousands
appeared.

Dewey Soper was the first European to see where the Blue Goose
breeds.

Soper and his team stayed in Bowman Bay through July, studying
the natural history of the Blue Goose. Now the place is memorialized
as the Dewey Soper (Isulijarnik) Migratory Bird Sanctuary. It is a
world heritage site that has more than a million nesting birds. Besides
Snow Geese, there are Canada Geese, Atlantic Brent, Long-tailed
Ducks, and King Eider. Caribou also use the area.

I suppose the breeding grounds of the blue form of the Snow
Goose is a place I will never go. But as these birds pass by, I can dream
of this distant land, this rolling tundra of lakes and puddles, snow-free
only in the short summers.

So what brought Blue Geese and Snow Geese together across the
Louisiana–Texas border? As rice-growing regions in Texas and Louisiana increased after the Civil War and continued to increase to the
present, Snow Geese also increased, expanding their feeding areas
until they overlapped. Looking at the Audubon Christmas counts
from 1979 to 1984, it is clear that Louisiana still had mostly Blue
Geese, but they also occurred along the Texas coast mixed in with the
white ones, all the way to Brownsville.[8]

The plumage difference occurred as the result of a chance mutation that made a goose blue. It was not a huge mutation comprising
many genes. It turns out that the blue form is just a tiny change of one
DNA codon that changed one amino acid in a single protein. That
gene has the complex name of melanocortin-1 receptor, or *MC1R*,

and works in the cells that regulate color in the feather buds of all birds.[9] The Blue Geese have a mutation that changes the building blocks of this protein slightly, at a particular location, number 85 along the protein. At this location the amino acid is valine in white geese, the ancestral form, and methionine in blue geese. If a goose gets two copies of the blue mutation, the methionine, then it is darker than if it got a blue copy from one parent and the white copy from the other.

You may have heard of the *MC1R* gene before. This is the same gene that when mutated in a different way causes red hair in humans. The mutations are different in redheads than in Snow Geese. The mutation that causes red hair and freckles is a mutation from amino acid asparagine to amino acid histidine at location 294. I pay attention to redhead genes because my hair used to be red and my two sons are redheads.

There is another impact of color in the Snow Geese. They usually choose a mate that shares their color, though there is no actual advantage to doing so that scientists have yet discovered. Why then do they care? The best guess is that their color preference is part of a spillover from behaviors that keep individuals from mating with individuals from another species.

In birds, as in all species, it is an excellent idea to mate with someone of one's own species. It may be the most basic of all mate choice rules, more important than that a mate be in good health or a good provider. This is because hybrids between two species often have genetic problems that mean they have fewer babies or that their babies survive and reproduce poorly or not at all. But this would not be the case for white and blue Snow Geese, since they have been breeding apart for only about ten thousand years. The gene for color in Snow Geese is not indicative of any overall genetic similarity, just that one thing that happens to be highly visible and therefore gets picked up by others' visual systems.

The best hypothesis is that matching colors is a side effect of matching species. Fred Cooke, retired from Queen's University, Kingston Ontario, Canada, and his team have an idea as to how this works. They surmised that it might be easier to match someone that matches one's family than one's self. After all, animals do not have mirrors and may not know what they look like. But they do know what their family members look like. And it turns out that Snow Geese are likely to choose mates based on their family, not on themselves, shown with an ingenious experiment.[10]

Cooke and his team, which included Bob Montgomerie back when he was an undergrad, tested this in a clever way, using pink geese and artificial families.[11] No, pink geese are not natural. Cooke and his team dyed some families of white geese pink so that the goslings around them saw pink as their natural color. Would the goslings then tend to choose pink over white or blue? Indeed they did, though these trials were of maturing young and whom they wanted to associate with immediately. Cooke makes the argument that these early choices reflect later mate choices.

I suppose it is challenging to study Snow Geese in their breeding colonies, because they are on delicate tundra edging the Arctic Ocean, with major colonies on Baffin Island, Bylot Island, and Southampton Island. But the most famous study of all was conducted quite a bit farther south, at a latitude of 58.7°, forty kilometers east of Churchill. The population Cooke studied built their nests along La Pérouse Bay off Hudson Bay in what is now Wapusk National Park.

Fred Cooke and Ken Ross, both then of Queen's University in Canada, began to study this population in 1968, that terrible year of Martin Luther King Jr.'s assassination, followed by Robert F. Kennedy's assassination, and then the Olympic riots, and Tlatelolco massacre in Mexico City. But none of those human tragedies impacted the Snow Geese beginning their nests, rearing their brood, surviving the flightless molting period, and then heading south in

that same year, some with bands from the budding champions of
Snow Goose research.

Snow Geese did not always nest in La Pérouse Bay. According to
Cooke and collaborators, others found no Snow Geese there in the
late 1940s and early 1950s. In 1962 Harold Hanson, working for the
Illinois Natural History Survey, searched around La Pérouse Bay and
found no nests.[12] The very next year there were 5,623 birds nesting in
the sedge meadows there. Fred Cooke speculates the origin of the
breeding colony came from very cold spring weather that stopped the
geese from traveling farther north. Then the resulting chicks viewed
this comparatively southern place as home and returned there year
after year. Or at least the females did, trailed by their mates acquired
on their wintering grounds.

As a graduate student, George Finney started the camp that would
be used for decades on an island in the Mast River that flows into the
southwest corner of La Pérouse Bay. It was relatively secure from polar
bears, but meant the researchers had to begin their days walking across
the river in waders. Or maybe it wasn't that secure, since Bob Montgomerie has scary memories of sudden encounters with the huge bears.
Researchers came in late April, before the geese, and stayed until late
July, when the molting geese could be gathered and banded.

Just about everything we know about Snow Geese on their nesting grounds comes from this colony. We know how they nest and
how their young feed on their own. We know what predators take
Snow Geese and their eggs. We know how females return to their
birth colonies. We know that some polar bears are saved from starvation by eating Snow Geese. We know about the plants that Snow
Geese eat. We know so much and yet there is more to learn.

Despite all the valuable results, research at La Pérouse has ceased,
not only because researchers do not last forever but also because of
what the geese have done. Snow Geese have largely destroyed the
plants they eat in La Pérouse Bay itself, so the research and the geese

have moved farther east along the Hudson Bay coast in Wapusk National Park. It seems that this is what Snow Geese do. They find a place to nest, nest there for a few decades, during which they destroy the local food supply, making it unsuitable for further use as a nesting colony, and then move on. As their numbers increase, one wonders if there will be a place to move on to or if they will slowly destroy all the vulnerable Arctic habitat for both themselves and other less numerous Arctic breeders.

What can we do about the surfeit of geese? My friend Bob Zink at University of Nebraska in Lincoln posted a photo of slabs of goose meat covered in salt and spices and announced on Facebook he was putting up twenty-one Ross's Geese and thirteen Snow Geese. He made pastrami and breakfast sausage, and left pieces of the Ross's Goose whole because he said they made an excellent stir-fry. This might make famous biologist Zink look like a poacher extraordinaire, especially since these were from a springtime hunt, but actually nothing could be further from the truth.

Zink's posting was my first intimation of exactly how critical the goose situation has become. The legal and encouraged hunts outside the usual fall season are part of a conservation order by the US Fish and Wildlife Service. These spring hunts generally run from February 11 to April 15 and have no limit as to the number of birds that a hunter can take, so long as nontoxic (not lead) shot is used and the hunter has the necessary hunting permits. Spring hunting is a desperate effort to stop the destruction of fragile Arctic tundra from millions of geese whose numbers are increasing each year.

For people who like to hunt, spring hunts are also a challenge. Bob Zink wrote:

> *The birds got very smart very quickly [after spring hunts began] and instead of gliding low across the edges of fields to land and feed, they seem now to drop straight down from on high, and are very wary.*

Hunters went to huge decoy spreads (1,000+) and electronic callers (legal during spring hunt), but the geese have seen all the decoys and heard all the tapes of goose flocks 100s of times. So they often approach a decoy spread, and then veer 90 degrees; they detect any movement you make when they're on approach. Some of these geese are 15 years old and have been hunted 9 months a year their entire lives.

I suppose hunters take the place of the predators they once faced on feeding and migration grounds before humans were on the scene, so the geese had in their repertoire cautious behaviors.

When I think of the importance of Slow Birding, killing the birds is about the last thing I imagine. Could I bear to see one of those marvelous birds planning to fly north to the farthest reaches of Canada come tumbling out of the sky and onto my dinner plate? It reminded me of other catastrophic hunts, like that of Passenger Pigeons and Great Auks. How could there be a wrong so great that such hunting puts it right? Is the US Fish and Wildlife Service correct? How can I explain a problem so big that unlimited hunting is the solution?

The answer lies in what is happening in the Arctic. One image keeps coming to mind. That of a muddy field, entirely ground up, as if it were an overused soccer pitch. In the middle of that field is a lone patch of lush grasses and sedges, improbably green against the black mud. It is a picture of a goose exclosure at La Pérouse Bay in the subarctic. A fence keeps the geese out, thereby demonstrating what they do to the breeding grounds that they and many other migratory birds depend on. The geese destroyed or severely degraded 700 miles of coastline along the James Bay and the west coast of the Hudson Bay—more than 260,000 acres.

Similar pictures might be taken in Texas, in Anahuac or the San Bernard National Wildlife Refuge, where the geese remove the plants by their roots and stolons, letting the salt water come in. Has this damage become so intense and widespread, so unnatural that we turn to hunters for answers? Yes, and even intense hunting is not sufficient to solve the Snow Goose problem.

There are too many Snow Geese. Before the 1960s, Snow Geese numbered fewer than a million birds. There are now over fifteen million. The increase has come from artificially increased food in the wintering grounds, mainly rice left in fields in California and along the Gulf Coast. The geese have also proven adept at moving to where they can find these grains.

Other factors also reduce Snow Goose numbers, though even these are not sufficient to avoid habitat degradation. One of the most important is avian cholera. In geese, cholera is a disease caused by a bacterium called *Pasteurella multocida*, isolated by Louis Pasteur in 1881.[13] He also discovered that a small inoculation scratch could protect domestic fowl, one of the first vaccines ever. The disease causes fever, loss of appetite, mucous discharge, diarrhea, and pneumonia. It is caught from other birds, not from water sources. Originally a European disease, it was first found in North America in 1943. Now it is widespread in wild birds and is also a threat to chickens, turkeys, and other domestic fowl.

The bacterium that causes Snow Goose cholera is not at all the same as the one that causes cholera in humans, *Vibrio cholerae*. The two bacteria are not even particularly closely related, and the illness is different. In humans, the most extreme symptom is diarrhea, while in birds it could be described as hemorrhagic septicemia.

Here is an image: A dead male Snow Goose lies on its back next to a small nest containing three eggs. The eggs are cushioned on downy feathers plucked from his mate's own breast. But she is nowhere to be seen. This photograph stays with me as I think of all the potential in those eggs, eggs that will never hatch, never produce proud goslings that learn to root out tubers, eat sedges and grasses, and ultimately fly south with their parents. The photograph is from Egg River Valley on Banks Island in Canada's Northwest Territories, taken in 1995, the year of a huge cholera outbreak in Snow Geese.[14] Banks Island is far north of the Arctic Circle and is a major nesting ground for the Snow Geese that winter mainly in California's Central Valley and Texas's Gulf Coast.

That 1995 outbreak in the Egg River colony killed about thirty thousand Snow Geese.[15] Unfortunately, there was nothing unusual about this outbreak, as there were huge outbreaks in the Mississippi and central flyways in 1979 and 1980.[16] As the Snow Geese flew south, there were outbreaks near Manitou, Manitoba, and in Iowa, Nebraska, and Missouri along the Missouri River. The deaths continued through the winter at the Aransas and Brazoria National Wildlife Refuges, and in the Texas Panhandle's Playa Lakes region, where over five thousand Snow Geese died. As the Snow Geese flew north the following spring, in 1980, cholera came with them.

Even healthy-looking Snow Geese can be carriers of cholera, spreading the disease to other birds and other places, as Michael D. Samuel and coworkers discovered in a study of apparently healthy birds in the Playa Lakes region.[17] Even though fewer than 5 percent of birds were carriers of the disease, that was enough to introduce the cholera pathogen to entire susceptible populations of this and other species of water birds.

Of the millions of Snow Geese that grace our planet, between 5 and 15 percent die every year because of cholera. One of the issues with dense nesting and group migration is that diseases can be easily transmitted from bird to bird. In the Egg River colony, more than 20 percent of the 121,000 birds nesting in the densest part of the colony died of cholera. In that area there were about 49 birds per acre. By contrast, in the low-density area only about 1 percent of birds died of cholera.

One might wonder why more birds did not simply nest in low-density areas where death rates were lower, just as we tried to maintain a six-foot distance from others during the COVID-19 pandemic. The answer is that there are more things that threaten Snow Geese than cholera. Arctic foxes, Herring Gulls, and many other predators go after the nests and take more eggs and nestlings from the edges than from the dense center. And anyway, cholera is a new disease, one they are unlikely to have yet evolved defenses against.

When I look up at Snow Geese migrating north along the Mississippi, I still feel awe. I wonder where this particular flock spent the winter and if it was in the wildlife refuges I most often visited, Anahuac and Brazoria, near Houston. I also wonder where in the Artic North this group will breed. Will they be one of the few that breeds along the Hudson Bay coast near Churchill, or will they go right on up to Baffin Island and beyond, to the other northernmost islands in the Arctic Ocean? I look at the eBird map of where they might be at any given season and dream.

Snow Geese are winter birds for me. According to eBird, Riverlands has Snow Geese from November through March. My favorite time to see them is February, when they are already migrating north. I like them then because of all the activity, the excitement of seeing line after line fly off, destined for the farthest Arctic shores.

But now that I know more about them, I see trouble in those numbers, troubles we humans know all too well. There is the torment of a new disease that can cause them to fall dead from the sky, one that they did not have any exposure to eighty years ago. Avian cholera is a disease of density, passed from one bird to another, with the potential of killing nearly a tenth of the population every year, creating goose heartbreak when one's partner for life dies. Ten percent is an enormous number of birds, and yet still the population expands, feeding on the remnants of our own population's most important grain worldwide: rice. Snow Geese find comfort and safety in numbers. Those nesting most centrally on their breeding grounds suffer less predation. Those feeding in denser winter flocks will be less likely to be hunted according to the inexorable geometry of the selfish herd.

Disease, crowding, habitat destruction, and death are part of the Snow Goose world. I know this, and yet still they inspire as they fly ineluctably north for another short breeding summer at the top of our planet.

SNOW GOOSE ACTIVITIES
FOR SLOW BIRDERS

1. **Observe group size.** If you have Snow Geese in your twenty-mile circle, it will be either during the winter or during migration, unless you live in the Arctic. Check out eBird to see what people are noticing if you are not sure. Snow Geese may be found in a nearby marsh or along a river. Go to such a place and see if you can count the numbers of Snow Geese in the groups that pass overhead. How many are in each group?

2. **Watch group flight dynamics.** Is it in a line or a V? If the latter, how many birds are in each leg of the formation? Does the bird at the point of the V stay at the front? After all, that first bird takes more of the wind while the others draft off the one in front, just the way cyclists do.

3. **Observe Snow Geese on land.** Like all geese, Snow Geese spend a lot of time eating. Can you see what they are eating? How big are the groups in which they feed? How often do they move to a new patch of vegetation, and do they walk or fly?

4. **Identify vigilance.** Snow Geese are always in groups. In a group, one or more stay vigilant, looking about for predators, while the others feed. Spot the one that is vigilant. How long does it keep looking up, protecting the group and not feeding? How does a

vigilance turnover happen? Does the vigilant one start eating and then another takes on the role, or does it wait for a replacement sentinel before feeding?

5. **Watch the family groups.** Young geese stay with their parents during the first winter and then fly back north with them, hanging about while the parents begin a new breeding season. Can you see groups of four to six birds that might represent these family groups? How many are in the smallest groups?

6. **Study the blue and white color forms.** Do you see both blue and white Snow Geese? Count them. Are they mixed together in the same group, or do they stay separate? Do you see some birds that look like hybrids between blue and white?

7. **Hunt Snow Geese in the spring.** If you are a hunter, consider hunting Snow Geese in the spring, when the meat tastes better, since they have been eating grain in the South. About 750,000 Snow Geese have been banded. Of those, an astonishing 118,000 bands have been recovered, nearly all from hunters. If you are hunting geese or happen to find a dead one with a band, please report that band number. You can do so at the US Geological Survey's Bird Banding Laboratory website: https://www.pwrc.usgs.gov /BBL/bblretrv/. You can still keep the actual band as a memento.

Conclusion

When I go out to watch birds, I remember Sarah Kocher, who studied American Robins in a Christmas tree plantation as she fell in love. I think of Karen Wiebe climbing high into rotting aspens to saw a window into a Northern Flicker nest. I remember Bruce Lyon's stories of trimming away the red feathers of baby American Coots and watching to see if they got less parental care. I remember my grad student Debbie Morález DeLoach patiently watching Northern Mockingbirds, ten minutes on each territory. I imagine being on Baffin Island with Dewey Soper and learning where the blue form of Snow Geese nest from the patient local people who always knew.

The stories of these researchers, the ultimate Slow Birders, make it easy to spend time watching a few birds for a morning instead of racing around and just counting them. A stool, a notebook, a sketchpad, and maybe a camera become important tools. As I look more carefully, I see what the birds are doing. A Blue Jay calls from an oak, and I look up to see it hammering away at an acorn. I'm not close enough to see if it is breaking into the flesh or simply removing the cap before it flies on. In another tree is a group that looks like a family because of their proximity to one another, though no one is begging. Northern Cardinals shelter in pairs in an elderberry in my back garden. I feel glad they are in a native bush and not tricked by a honeysuckle. American Robins are up in the trees eating fruit at this waning time of year. Their bright bellies are also fading, but I often hear their shriek that reminds me of my mother when she feared we would hurt ourselves.

Each of these birds and the others that I have described in this book seem to call out to me, making me wonder what about them I have missed and what more I can see. Besides watching birds carefully on given days, I can compare my notes across the year.

I can look back at my notes of exactly a year ago at this same place and see what I saw and how it made me feel, just as I used to read journal entries that my young son wrote. He wrote them as a kind of letter to me for several years until teenagerhood increased his need for privacy. At bedtime I read last year's entry to him, then the one from the year before, ultimately going back as many as five years. He grew over that time, but many of his interests stayed the same, and he has never lost his empathy for others or his love of writing.

Have there been changes here in St. Louis? I might be seeing fewer hawks this year, or more, for there is a natural variation in the tides of nature. Which patterns are real and which are imagined, and can they even be separated? I will keep watching the local birds, hoping to deepen my connection to the spot on the globe were I find myself. I am a Slow Birder and I delight in the birds others might pass over. When someone asks what new or exciting birds I have seen on my morning walk, I smile and answer with delight as I name the commonest birds.

Acknowledgments

For a long time I have known that I wanted to write a book and that it would be entitled *Slow Birding*. But I did not know how to write a book. I did not know how to embody a message in the flesh of story, anecdote, and scientific truth. I knew that I wanted to encourage everyone to pay attention to the birds all around us, for they are our best connection to wildness. I also wanted to coax birders who run from one bird to the next to slow down and watch the birds they treasure. I know how to teach people to observe, for I have been a professor who concentrates on animal behavior for decades. But I did not want to write a textbook, and I could not invite everyone to the animal behavior laboratory where I used to teach. How could I move forward?

Frans de Waal encouraged me to take the first formal step at a meeting in Arizona at the end of March 2012 when I told him I wanted to write a book entitled *Slow Birding*, with the same philosophy as the Slow Food movement. He suggested I contact his agent, Michelle Tessler. And I am so glad she took me on. Michelle helped me solidify a plan for this book. But still I stalled. Apparently I had to have a full outline of all the chapters, and I could not imagine how to do that. A year as a fellow at the Wissenschaftskolleg zu Berlin in 2018–2019 introduced me to an international group of scholars who regularly brought books to life. Daniel Schönpflug, the Wiko head of academic programs at Wissenschaftskolleg zu Berlin—Berlin's Institute for Advanced Study—helped a lot. He read my early writings and told me that I could write a much better book than I imagined. I hope he was right.

Ultimately, I decided a book that would accomplish my goals would cover just a few common birds and places within twenty miles of home. The bird chapters would meld my own experiences with the discoveries of ornithologists and the stories of how they made those discoveries. Each chapter would end with some ideas of how to really watch birds. Michelle Tessler was enthusiastic and found a publishing home and introduced me to Sara Carder, the most thoughtful and supportive editor, who, along with Ashley Alliano, has helped me through the confusing final stages. Thank you to copy editor Maureen Klier for her insights and clarifications.

This book is a pandemic baby, so much of the time it took was carved from travel I did not do and weekends with few museums and friends and no theater or restaurants. But my own laboratory group (we work on social interactions of microbes) had to be more patient than usual with me, waiting for guidance and comments on their work, and for that I thank Debbie Brock, Laura Walker, Margaret Steele, Tyler Larsen, Trey Scott, James Medina, Shreenidhi P.M., Israt Jahan, and Calum Stephenson and the undergraduates who worked with them. I also thank Kim Medley and her great team for making Tyson Research Center a welcome home and my wildest place in my circle.

Every teacher says they learn from their students. Watching my students discover birds in the class on bird behavior that I taught for about twenty years at Rice University gave me a lot of ideas of what one could see with careful watching. Later with Dave Queller and

Cin-Ty Lee, I taught a bird field biology class, and I learned so much from Cin-Ty, who is the best at field observations, seeing and hearing everything around us.

I could not have written this book without my husband, David Queller, and his expert reading of many chapters. He often found better ways to say what I really meant. But more than reading and commenting, Dave came along on countless explorations of natural areas around St. Louis, picking up binoculars and going out to explore each new area we discovered. He also supported me in countless ways through the hardest periods of book writing.

I thank all the bird biologists who shared their time and expertise and saved me from many mistakes, though of course all that remain are my responsibility. During the more than forty-five years I have been a biologist, I have studied behavior intensely. But my subjects have been social wasps, stingless bees, and microbes, not birds. I have depended on the help of ornithologists.

Bob Montgomerie, expert ornithologist, has encouraged this project from when we first discussed it at the meeting of the American Ornithological Society in Tucson, Arizona, in 2018. His consistent enthusiasm for the project and belief that I could do it saw me through the most difficult chapters.

Professionals shared their stories of specific birds, which brought the drama of field research alive. Bob Montgomerie, Patrick Weatherhead, and Sarah Kocher shared their stories of American Robins. Charlie Thompson, Cara Krieg, Scott Johnson, and Scott Sakaluk told me of their work on House Wrens. Ellen Ketterson shared her life's work on Dark-eyed Juncos. Karen Wiebe helped me feel what it was like to study Northern Flickers in the British Columbia forests. Bob Rosenfield is the world's expert on Cooper's Hawks and told me of his adventures with them. Dustin Rubenstein told me of African Starlings. Doug Mock and Trish Schwagmeyer shared their stories of work on House Sparrows. Sylvia Halkin helped me understand

Northern Cardinals. My graduate student Debbie Morález DeLoach and Dave Gammon helped with the intricacies of Northern Mockingbirds and their song. Enid Cumming made the boreal forests come alive for me, not only with Yellow-rumped Warblers. Emilie Snell-Rood, Gerald Shields, and Andrea Grunst gave valuable insight on their work on White-throated Sparrows. Bruce Lyon and Daizaburo Shizuka set me straight on the family life of American Coots. Doug Mock shared the dark side of Great Egret family life.

Each chapter benefited from careful reading and comments, saving me from both mistakes and confusing writing. For Blue Jay, I thank Dave Queller, Bob Montgomerie, and Maude Babington. For American Robin, I thank Dave Queller and Bob Montgomerie. For House Wren, I thank Charlie Thompson and Scott Johnson. For Dark-eyed Junco, I thank Dave Queller and Ellen Ketterson. For Northern Flicker, I thank Karen Wiebe. For Cooper's Hawk, I thank Dave Queller and Bob Rosenfield. For Cedar Waxwing, I thank Bob Montgomerie and Karin Gastreich. For European Starling, I thank Dave Queller and Dustin Rubenstein. For House Sparrow, I thank Trish Schwagmeyer, Doug Mock, and Maude Babington. For Northern Cardinal, I thank Sylvia Halkin and Bob Montgomerie. For Northern Mockingbird, I thank Dave Queller and Dave Gammon. For Yellow-rumped Warbler, I thank Bob Montgomerie and Bob Ricklefs. For White-throated Sparrow, I thank Andrea Grunst. For American Coot, I thank Bruce Lyon and Daizaburo Shizuka. For Great Egret, I thank Doug Mock and Maude Babington. For Snow Goose, I thank Dave Queller, Bob Montgomerie, and Patrizia d'Ettorre.

I thank the members of the St. Louis Audubon Society for welcoming me and for leading many field trips, particularly Bill Rowe, currently president of St. Louis Audubon Society.

Most of all I thank my family. My parents encouraged me in just about everything and taught me to love nature. My father gave me my first pair of binoculars and tried to teach me to sketch and to write.

My sisters, Beverly and Diana, shared my earliest birding experiences, and Diana taught me how to use eBird Mobile. My children, Anna, Daniel, and Philip, also love birds and are patient with their slow mother as I pause for another bird along the trail. There would have been no book without the support of my husband.

Notes

PREFACE

1. C. Petrini, *Slow Food: The Case for Taste* (New York: Columbia University Press, 2003).

BLUE JAY

1. C.S. Sargent, *Sixteen Maps Accompanying Report on Forest Trees of North America* (New York: Bien, 1884).

2. J.G. Schuetz and A. Johnston, "Characterizing the Cultural Niches of North American Birds," *Proceedings of the National Academy of Sciences* 116, no. 22 (2019): 10868–73.

3. L.P. Brower, J. Van Brower, and J.M. Corvino, "Plant Poisons in a Terrestrial Food Chain," *Proceedings of the National Academy of Sciences* 57, no. 4 (1967): 893.

4. G. Petschenka and A.A. Agrawal, "Milkweed Butterfly Resistance to Plant Toxins Is Linked to Sequestration, Not Coping with a Toxic Diet," *Proceedings of the Royal Society B: Biological Sciences* 282, no. 1818 (2015): 1865.

5. Brower, Van Brower, and Corvino, "Plant Poisons in a Terrestrial Food Chain."

6. J. Grinnell, "Up-Hill Planters," *The Condor* 38, no. 2 (1936): 80–82.

7. D. Palacios et al., "The Deglaciation of the Americas During the Last Glacial Termination," *Earth-Science Reviews* 203 (2020): 103–13.

8. W.R. Farrand, "Postglacial Uplift in North America," *American Journal of Science* 260, no. 3 (1962): 181–99.

9. M.W. Pedersen et al., "Postglacial Viability and Colonization in North America's Ice-Free Corridor," *Nature* 537, no. 7618 (2016): 45–49.

10. P. Anderson et al., "Climatic Changes of the Last 18,000 Years: Observations and Model Simulations," *Science* 241, no. 4869 (1988): 1043–53.

11. G.L. Jacobson Jr., T. Webb III, and E.C. Grimm, "Patterns and Rates of Vegetation Change During the Deglaciation of Eastern North America," *North America and Adjacent Oceans During the Last Deglaciation* 3 (1987): 277–88.

12. J.S. Clark, "Why Trees Migrate So Fast: Confronting Theory with Dispersal Biology and the Paleorecord," *American Naturalist* 152, no. 2 (1998): 204–24.

13. S. Darley-Hill and W.C. Johnson, "Acorn Dispersal by the Blue Jay (Cyanocitta cristata)," *Oecologia* 50, no. 2 (1981): 231–32.

14. P.A. Callo and C.S. Adkisson, "Recovery of Cached Food by Blue Jays (Cyanocitta cristata)," *Bird Behavior* 13, no. 2 (2000): 85–91.

15. A.T. Pietrewicz and A.C. Kamil, "Search Image Formation in the Blue Jay (Cyanocitta cristata)," *Science* 204, no. 4399 (1979): 1332–33.

AMERICAN ROBIN

1. C.C. Rega, C.H. Nilon, and P.S. Warren, "Avian Abundance Patterns in Relation to the Distribution of Small Urban Greenspaces," *Journal of Urban Planning and Development* 141, no. 3 (2015): A4015002.

2. R. Montgomerie and P.J. Weatherhead, "How Robins Find Worms," *Animal Behaviour* 54, no. 1 (1997): 143–51.

3. N.T. Wheelwright and B. Heinrich, *The Naturalist's Notebook: An Observation Guide and 5-Year Calendar-Journal for Tracking Changes in the Natural World Around You* (North Adams, MA: Storey Publishing, 2017).

4. N.T. Wheelwright, "The Diet of American Robins: An Analysis of US Biological Survey Records," *The Auk* 103, no. 4 (1986): 710–25.

5. D.J. Levey and W.H. Karasov, "Digestive Modulation in a Seasonal Frugivore, the American Robin (Turdus migratorius)," *American Journal of Physiology: Gastrointestinal and Liver Physiology* 262, no. 4 (1992): G711–18.

6. E.N. Vanderhoff et al., "American Robin (Turdus migratorius)," version 1.0, in *Birds of the World*, ed. P.G. Rodewald (Ithaca, NY: Cornell Lab of Ornithology, 2020).

7. K.M. Rowe and P.J. Weatherhead, "Social and Ecological Factors Affecting Paternity Allocation in American Robins with Overlapping Broods," *Behavioral Ecology and Sociobiology* 61, no. 8 (2007): 1283–91.

8. P.A. English and R. Montgomerie, "Robin's Egg Blue: Does Egg Color Influence Male Parental Care?," *Behavioral Ecology and Sociobiology* 65, no. 5 (2011): 1029–36.

9. R. Croston and M. Hauber, "A Recoverable Cost of Brood Parasitism During the Nestling Stage of the American Robin (Turdus migratorius): Implications for the Evolution of Egg Rejection Behaviors in a Host of the Brown-Headed Cowbird (Molothrus ater)," *Ethology Ecology and Evolution* 27, no. 1 (2015): 42–55.

10. J. Altmann, "Observational Study of Behavior: Sampling Methods," *Behavior* 48 (1974): 227–65.

HOUSE WREN

1. M.J. Newhouse, P.P. Marra, and L.S. Johnson, "Reproductive Success of House Wrens in Suburban and Rural Landscapes," *Wilson Journal of Ornithology* 120, no. 1 (2008): 99–104.

2. L.S. Johnson, "House Wren (Troglodytes aedon)," version 1.0, in *Birds of the World*, ed. A.F. Poole (Ithaca, NY: Cornell Laboratory of Ornithology, 2020).

3. J.G. Cooper, "Nesting Habits of the California House Wren (Troglodytes aedon var. parkmanni)," *Bulletin of the Nuttall Ornithological Club* 1 (1876): 79–81.

4. S.C. Kendeigh, "In Memoriam: Samuel Prentiss Baldwin," *The Auk* 57, no. 1 (1940): 1–12.

5. S.P. Baldwin, "The Marriage Relations of the House Wren (Troglodytes a. aedon)," *The Auk* 38, no. 2 (1921): 237–44.

6. S.C. Kendeigh and S.P. Baldwin, "Factors Affecting Yearly Abundance of Passerine Birds," *Ecological Monographs* 7, no. 1 (1937): 91–123.

7. M.A. Finke, D.J. Milinkovich, and C.F. Thompson, "Evolution of Clutch Size: An Experimental Test in the House Wren (Troglodytes aedon)," *Journal of Animal Ecology* 56 (1987): 99–114.

8. E. VanderWerf, "Lack's Clutch Size Hypothesis: An Examination of the Evidence Using Meta-Analysis," *Ecology* 73, no. 5 (1992): 1699–705.

9. C. Hodges et al., "Cascading Costs of Reproduction in Female House Wrens Induced to Lay Larger Clutches," *Journal of Evolutionary Biology* 28, no. 7 (2015): 1383–93.

10. E.K. Bowers, S.K. Sakaluk, and C.F. Thompson, "Experimentally Increased Egg Production Constrains Future Reproduction of Female House Wrens," *Animal Behaviour* 83, no. 2 (2012): 495–500.

11. L.S. Johnson et al., "Extra-Pair Young in House Wren Broods Are More Likely to Be Male Than Female," *Proceedings of the Royal Society B: Biological Sciences* 276, no. 1665 (2009): 2285–89.

12. E.K. Bowers et al., "Increased Extra-Pair Paternity in Broods of Aging Males and Enhanced Recruitment of Extra-Pair Young in a Migratory Bird," *Evolution* 69, no. 9 (2015): 2533–41.

13. L.S. Johnson et al., "Evidence for a Maternal Effect Benefiting Extra-Pair Offspring in a Songbird, the House Wren Troglodytes aedon," *Journal of Avian Biology* 40, no. 3 (2009): 248–53.

14. L.S. Johnson and L.H. Kermott, "Effect of Nest-Site Supplementation on Polygynous Behavior in the House Wren (Troglodytes aedon)," *The Condor* 93 (1991): 784–87.

15. L.S. Johnson, J. Brubaker, and B. Johnson, "How Males in the House Wren, a Cavity-Nesting Songbird, Discover That Eggs Have Hatched and Transition to Provisioning Nestlings," *Behaviour* 145, no. 12 (2008): 1781–96.

16. N.S. Dubois, E.D. Kennedy, and T. Getty, "Surplus Nest Boxes and the Potential for Polygyny Affect Clutch Size and Offspring Sex Ratio in House Wrens," *Proceedings of the Royal Society B: Biological Sciences* 273, no. 1595 (2006): 1751–57.

17. L.S. Johnson and L.H. Kermott, "Structure and Context of Female Song in a North-Temperate Population of House Wrens (Estructura y contexto de la canción de una población norteña de hembras de troglodytes aedon)," *Journal of Field Ornithology* 61, no. 3 (1990): 273–84.

18. C.A. Krieg and T. Getty, "Not Just for Males: Females Use Song Against Male and Female Rivals in a Temperate Zone Songbird," *Animal Behaviour* 113 (2016): 39–47.

DARK-EYED JUNCO

1. G. Friis et al., "Rapid Postglacial Diversification and Long-Term Stasis Within the Songbird Genus Junco: Phylogeographic and Phylogenomic Evidence," *Molecular Ecology* 25, no. 24 (2016): 6175–95.

2. E.D. Ketterson, "Environmental Influences upon Aggressive Behavior in Wintering Juncos," *Bird-Banding* 49, no. 4 (1978): 313–20.

3. R.L. Holberton, K.P. Able, and J.C. Wingfield, "Status Signalling in Dark-Eyed Juncos, Junco hyemails: Plumage Manipulations and Hormonal Correlates of Dominance," *Animal Behaviour* 37 (1989): 681–89.

4. E.D. Ketterson and V. Nolan Jr., "Geographic Variation and Its Climatic Correlates in the Sex Ratio of Eastern-Wintering Dark-Eyed Juncos (Junco hyemalis hyemalis)," *Ecology* 57, no. 4 (1976): 679–93.

5. E.D. Ketterson, "Aggressive Behavior in Wintering Dark-Eyed Juncos: Determinants of Dominance and Their Possible Relation to Geographic Variation in Sex Ratio," *The Wilson Bulletin* 91, no. 3 (1979): 371–83.

6. E.D. Ketterson and V. Nolan Jr., "Overnight Weight Loss in Dark-Eyed Juncos (Junco hyemalis)," *The Auk* 95, no. 4 (1978): 755–58.

7. J.C. Wingfield et al., "Testosterone and Aggression in Birds," *American Scientist* 75, no. 6 (1987): 602–8.

8. E.D. Ketterson et al., "Testosterone and Avian Life Histories: The Effect of Experimentally Elevated Testosterone on Corticosterone and Body Mass in Dark-Eyed Juncos," *Hormones and Behavior* 25, no. 4 (1991): 489–503.

9. E.D. Ketterson et al., "Testosterone and Avian Life Histories: Effects of Experimentally Elevated Testosterone on Behavior and Correlates of Fitness in the Dark-Eyed Junco (Junco hyemalis)," *American Naturalist* 140, no. 6 (1992): 980–99.

10. D.A. Enstrom, E.D. Ketterson, and V. Nolan Jr., "Testosterone and Mate Choice in the Dark-Eyed Junco," *Animal Behaviour* 54, no. 5 (1997): 1135–46.

11. Ketterson et al., "Testosterone and Avian Life Histories: Effects of Experimentally Elevated Testosterone on Behavior and Correlates of Fitness in the Dark-Eyed Junco (Junco hyemalis)."

12. Enstrom, Ketterson, and Nolan, "Testosterone and Mate Choice in the Dark-Eyed Junco."
13. Enstrom, Ketterson, and Nolan, "Testosterone and Mate Choice in the Dark-Eyed Junco."
14. G.C. Cardoso and J.W. Atwell, "Shared Songs Are of Lower Performance in the Dark-Eyed Junco," *Royal Society Open Science* 3, no. 7 (2016): 160341.
15. E.D. Ferree, "White Tail Plumage and Brood Sex Ratio in Dark-Eyed Juncos (Junco hyemalis thurberi)," *Behavioral Ecology and Sociobiology* 62, no. 1 (2007): 109–17.
16. D.J. Whittaker et al., "Bird Odour Predicts Reproductive Success," *Animal Behaviour* 86, no. 4 (2013): 697–703.
17. D.J. Whittaker et al., "Experimental Evidence That Symbiotic Bacteria Produce Chemical Cues in a Songbird," *Journal of Experimental Biology* 222, no. 20 (2019): jeb202978.

NORTHERN FLICKER

1. K.L. Wiebe and W.S. Moore, "Northern Flicker (Colaptes auratus)," version 1.0, in *Birds of the World*, ed. P.G. Rodewald (Ithaca, NY: Cornell Laboratory of Ornithology, 2009).
2. F.E.L. Beal, *Food of the Woodpeckers of the United States* (US Department of Agriculture, Biological Survey, 1911).
3. E.O. Wilson, "Causes of Ecological Success: The Case of the Ants," *Journal of Animal Ecology* 56, no. 1 (1987): 1–9.
4. E.J. Fittkau and H. Klinge, "On Biomass and Trophic Structure of the Central Amazonian Rain Forest Ecosystem," *Biotropica* 5 (1973): 2–14.
5. B. Hölldobler and E.O. Wilson, *The Ants* (Cambridge, MA: Belknap Press of Harvard University Press, 1990).
6. Beal, *Food of the Woodpeckers of the United States.*
7. E.A. Gow, K.L. Wiebe, and R.J. Higgins, "Lack of Diet Segregation During Breeding by Male and Female Northern Flickers Foraging on Ants," *Journal of Field Ornithology* 84, no. 3 (2013): 262–69.
8. K.L. Wiebe, "Microclimate of Tree Cavity Nests: Is It Important for Reproductive Success in Northern Flickers?," *The Auk* 118, no. 2 (2001): 412–21.
9. E.A. Gow, A.B. Musgrove, and K.L. Wiebe, "Brood Age and Size Influence Sex-Specific Parental Provisioning Patterns in a Sex-Role Reversed Species," *Journal of Ornithology* 154, no. 2 (2013): 525–35.
10. J. DeWoody et al., "'Pando' Lives: Molecular Genetic Evidence of a Giant Aspen Clone in Central Utah," *Western North American Naturalist* 68, no. 4 (2008): 493–97.
11. Wiebe, "Microclimate of Tree Cavity Nests."

12. K. Martin, K.E. Aitken, and K.L. Wiebe, "Nest Sites and Nest Webs for Cavity-Nesting Communities in Interior British Columbia, Canada: Nest Characteristics and Niche Partitioning," *The Condor* 106, no. 1 (2004): 5–19.

13. A.C. Bent, "Life Histories of North American Woodpeckers: Order Piciformes," *Bulletin No. 23 of the United States National Museum* (Washington, DC: Smithsonian Institution Press, 1939).

14. E.A. Gow, K.L. Wiebe, and A.B. Musgrove, "Nest Sanitation in Response to Short- and Long-Term Changes of Brood Size: Males Clean More in a Sex-Role-Reversed Species," *Animal Behaviour* 104 (2015): 137–43.

15. A.R. Sherman, "At the Sign of the Northern Flicker," *The Wilson Bulletin* 22, no. 3/4 (1910): 133–71.

16. K.L. Wiebe, "Division of Labour During Incubation in a Woodpecker Colaptes auratus with Reversed Sex Roles and Facultative Polyandry," *Ibis* 150, no. 1 (2008): 115–24.

17. C.L. Elchuk and K.L. Wiebe, "Ephemeral Food Resources and High Conspecific Densities as Factors Explaining Lack of Feeding Territories in Northern Flickers (Colaptes auratus)," *The Auk* 120, no. 1 (2003): 187–93.

18. E.A. Gow and K.L. Wiebe, "Determinants of Parental Care and Offspring Survival During the Post-Fledging Period: Males Care More in a Species with Partially Reversed Sex Roles," *Oecologia* 175, no. 1 (2014): 95–104.

19. R.J. Fisher and K.L. Wiebe, "Effects of Sex and Age on Survival of Northern Flickers: A Six-Year Field Study," *The Condor* 108, no. 1 (2006): 193–200.

20. K.L. Wiebe, "Local Recruitment in Northern Flickers Is Related to Environmental Factors at Multiple Scales and Provides Reproductive Benefits to Yearling Breeders Settling Close to Home," *The Auk* 137, no. 2 (2020).

21. Fisher and Wiebe, "Effects of Sex and Age on Survival of Northern Flickers."

22. Fisher and Wiebe, "Effects of Sex and Age on Survival of Northern Flickers."

23. K.L. Wiebe and B. Kempenaers, "The Social and Genetic Mating System in Flickers Linked to Partially Reversed Sex Roles," *Behavioral Ecology* 20, no. 2 (2009): 453–58.

24. Wiebe and Kempenaers, "The Social and Genetic Mating System in Flickers Linked to Partially Reversed Sex Roles."

25. Wiebe and Kempenaers, "The Social and Genetic Mating System in Flickers Linked to Partially Reversed Sex Roles."

26. D.T. Flockhart and K.L. Wiebe, "Absence of Reproductive Consequences of Hybridization in the Northern Flicker (Colaptes auratus) Hybrid Zone," *The Auk* 126, no. 2 (2009): 351–58.

27. L.L. Short, "Hybridization in the Flickers (Colaptes) of North America," *Bulletin of the American Museum of Natural History* 129, art. 4 (1965).

COOPER'S HAWK

1. R. Carson, *Silent Spring* (Boston: Houghton Mifflin Harcourt, 2002).
2. N.F. Snyder et al., "Organochlorines, Heavy Metals, and the Biology of North American Accipiters," *BioScience* 23, no. 5 (1973): 300–305.
3. O.H. Pattee, M.R. Fuller, and T.E. Kaiser, "Environmental Contaminants in Eastern Cooper's Hawk Eggs," *Journal of Wildlife Management* 49, no. 4 (1985): 1040–44.
4. R.N. Rosenfield, *The Cooper's Hawk: Breeding Ecology & Natural History of a Winged Huntsman* (Surrey, BC, Canada: Hancock House, 2018).
5. L. Pérez-Camacho et al., "Structural Complexity of Hunting Habitat and Territoriality Increase the Reversed Sexual Size Dimorphism in Diurnal Raptors," *Journal of Avian Biology* 49, no. 10 (2018): e01745.
6. H. Meng, "Food Habits of Nesting Cooper's Hawks and Goshawks in New York and Pennsylvania," *The Wilson Bulletin* 71, no. 2 (1959): 169–74.
7. Meng, "Food Habits of Nesting Cooper's Hawks and Goshawks in New York and Pennsylvania."
8. R.N. Rosenfield, J. Bielefeldt, and J. Cary, "Copulatory and Other Pre-Incubation Behaviors of Cooper's Hawks," *The Wilson Bulletin* 103, no. 4 (1991): 656–60.
9. Rosenfield, Bielefeldt, and Cary, "Copulatory and Other Pre-Incubation Behaviors of Cooper's Hawks."
10. R.N. Rosenfield et al., "High Frequency of Extra-Pair Paternity in an Urban Population of Cooper's Hawks," *Journal of Field Ornithology* 86, no. 2 (2015): 144–52.
11. R.N. Rosenfield et al., "Do British Columbia Cooper's Hawks Have Big Feet?," *British Columbia Birds* 30 (2020): 10–14.
12. Rosenfield et al., "Do British Columbia Cooper's Hawks Have Big Feet?"

CEDAR WAXWING

1. M.C. Witmer, D.J. Mountjoy, and L. Elliot, "Cedar Waxwing (Bombycilla cedrorum)," version 1.0, in *Birds of the World*, ed. A.F. Poole (Ithaca, NY: Cornell Lab of Ornithology, 2020).
2. J.M. McPherson, "A Field Study of Winter Fruit Preferences of Cedar Waxwings," *The Condor* 89, no. 2 (1987): 293–306.
3. J.M. McPherson, "Preferences of Cedar Waxwings in the Laboratory for Fruit Species, Colour and Size: A Comparison with Field Observations," *Animal Behaviour* 36, no. 4 (1988): 961–69.
4. M.M. Nice, "Observations on the Behavior of a Young Cedar Waxwing," *The Condor* 43, no. 1 (1941): 58–64.
5. M.C. Witmer, "Annual Diet of Cedar Waxwings Based on US Biological Survey

Records (1885–1950) Compared to Diet of American Robins: Contrasts in Dietary Patterns and Natural History," *The Auk* 113, no. 2 (1996): 414–30.

6. A. Monroy-Ojeda et al., "Winter Site Fidelity and Winter Residency of Six Migratory Neotropical Species in Mexico," *Wilson Journal of Ornithology* 125, no. 1 (2013): 192–96.

7. B. Jacobs and J.D. Wilson, *Missouri Breeding Bird Atlas* (Jefferson City: Missouri Department of Conservation, 1997).

8. L.S. Putnam, "The Life History of the Cedar Waxwing," *The Wilson Bulletin* 61, no. 3 (1949): 141–82.

9. R. White, *The Burt Lake Band: An Ethnohistorical Report on the Trust Lands of Indian Village* (1986).

10. D.L. Lack, *Ecological Adaptations for Breeding in Birds* (London: Methuen, 1968).

11. B.D. Peer and S.G. Sealy, "Correlates of Egg Rejection in Hosts of the Brown-Headed Cowbird," *The Condor* 106, no. 3 (2004): 580–99.

12. S.I. Rothstein, "Cowbird Parasitism of the Cedar Waxwing and Its Evolutionary Implications," *The Auk* 93, no. 3 (1976): 498–509.

13. S.I. Rothstein, "High Nest Density and Non-Random Nest Placement in the Cedar Waxwing," *The Condor* 73, no. 4 (1971): 483–85.

14. Rothstein, "Cowbird Parasitism of the Cedar Waxwing and Its Evolutionary Implications."

15. Rothstein, "High Nest Density and Non-Random Nest Placement in the Cedar Waxwing."

EUROPEAN STARLING

1. I.J. Lovette and D.R. Rubenstein, "A Comprehensive Molecular Phylogeny of the Starlings (Aves: Sturnidae) and Mockingbirds (Aves: Mimidae): Congruent mtDNA and Nuclear Trees for a Cosmopolitan Avian Radiation," *Molecular Phylogenetics and Evolution* 44, no. 3 (2007): 1031–56.

2. P.R. Cabe, "European Starling (Sturnus vulgaris)," version 1.0, in *Birds of the World*, ed. S.M. Billerman (Ithaca, NY: Cornell Lab of Ornithology, 2020).

3. S. Lowe et al., "100 of the World's Worst Invasive Alien Species: A Selection from the Global Invasive Species Database," in *Aliens* 12 (Auckland, NZ: Invasive Species Specialist Group, 2000).

4. Cabe, "European Starling (Sturnus vulgaris)."

5. E.M. Boyd, "A Survey of Parasitism of the Starling Sturnus vulgaris L. in North America," *Journal of Parasitology* 37, no. 1 (1951): 56–84.

6. B. Kessel, "A Study of the Breeding Biology of the European Starling (Sturnus vulgaris L.) in North America," *American Midland Naturalist* 58, no. 2 (1957): 257–331.

7. C.M. del Rio and B.R. Stevens, "Physiological Constraint on Feeding Behavior: Intestinal Membrane Disaccharidases of the Starling," *Science* 243, no. 4892 (1989): 794–96.

8. Rio and Stevens, "Physiological Constraint on Feeding Behavior."

9. K.L. Wiebe, "Delayed Timing as a Strategy to Avoid Nest-Site Competition: Testing a Model Using Data from Starlings and Flickers," *Oikos* 100, no. 2 (2003): 291–98.

10. W.D. Koenig, E.L. Walters, and P.G. Rodewald, "Testing Alternative Hypotheses for the Cause of Population Declines: The Case of the Red-Headed Woodpecker," *The Condor* 119, no. 1 (2017): 143–54.

11. D.J. Ingold, "Influence of Nest-Site Competition Between European Starlings and Woodpeckers," *The Wilson Bulletin* 106 (1994): 227–41.

12. D.J. Ingold, "Nesting Phenology and Competition for Nest Sites Among Red-Headed and Red-Bellied Woodpeckers and European Starlings," *The Auk* 106, no. 2 (1989): 209–17.

13. R. Pinxten et al., "Extra-Pair Paternity and Intraspecific Brood Parasitism in the European Starling, Sturnus vulgaris: Evidence from DNA Fingerprinting," *Animal Behaviour* 45, no. 4 (1993): 795–809.

14. P. Evans, "Intraspecific Nest Parasitism in the European Starling Sturnus vulgaris," *Animal Behaviour* 36, no. 5 (1988): 1282–94.

15. H.W. Power et al., "The Parasitism Insurance Hypothesis: Why Starlings Leave Space for Parasitic Eggs," *The Condor* 91, no. 4 (1989): 753–65.

16. D.R. Rubenstein, "Superb Starlings: Cooperation and Conflict in an Unpredictable Environment," in *Cooperative Breeding in Vertebrates: Studies of Ecology, Evolution, and Behavior*, eds. W.D. Koenig and J.L. Dickinson (Cambridge, UK: Cambridge University Press, 2016): 181–96.

17. I.J. Lovette et al., "Phylogenetic Relationships of the Mockingbirds and Thrashers (Aves: Mimidae)," *Molecular Phylogenetics and Evolution* 63, no. 2 (2012): 219–29.

18. A.E. Goodenough et al., "Birds of a Feather Flock Together: Insights into Starling Murmuration Behaviour Revealed Using Citizen Science," *PloS ONE* 12, no. 6 (2017): e0179277.

19. M. Ballerini et al., "Interaction Ruling Animal Collective Behavior Depends on Topological Rather Than Metric Distance: Evidence from a Field Study," *Proceedings of the National Academy of Sciences* 105, no. 4 (2008): 1232–37.

20. M. Ballerini et al., "Empirical Investigation of Starling Flocks: A Benchmark Study in Collective Animal Behaviour," *Animal Behaviour* 76, no. 1 (2008): 201–15.

HOUSE SPARROW

1. G.P. Sætre et al., "Single Origin of Human Commensalism in the House Sparrow," *Journal of Evolutionary Biology* 25, no. 4 (2012): 788–96.

2. Q.D. Atkinson, R.D. Gray, and A.J. Drummond, "mtDNA Variation Predicts Population Size in Humans and Reveals a Major Southern Asian Chapter in Human Prehistory," *Molecular Biology and Evolution* 25, no. 2 (2008): 468–74.

3. M. Ravinet et al., "Signatures of Human-Commensalism in the House Sparrow Genome," *Proceedings of the Royal Society B: Biological Sciences* 285, no. 1884 (2018): 1246.

4. J.D. Summers-Smith, "The Decline of the House Sparrow: A Review," *British Birds* 96, no. 9 (2003): 439–46.

5. M.P. Moulton et al., "The Earliest House Sparrow Introductions to North America," *Biological Invasions* 12, no. 9 (2010): 2955–58.

6. W.B. Barrows, *The English Sparrow (Passer domesticus) in North America: Especially in Its Relations to Agriculture* (US Department of Agriculture, Division of Economic Ornithology and Mammalogy, 1889): 17.

7. Barrows, *The English Sparrow (Passer domesticus) in North America*.

8. C.H. Merriam and W.B. Barrows, "Barrows's Report on the English Sparrow in North America," *The Auk* 6, no. 4 (1889): 326–328.

9. D.W. Mock and P. Schwagmeyer, "Not the Nice Sparrow: The 2007 Margaret Morse Nice Lecture," *Wilson Journal of Ornithology* 122, no. 2 (2010): 207–16.

10. T. Burke and M.W. Bruford, "DNA Fingerprinting in Birds," *Nature* 327, no. 6118 (1987): 149–52.

11. L. Brouwer and S.C. Griffith, "Extra-Pair Paternity in Birds," *Molecular Ecology* 28, no. 22 (2019): 4864–82.

12. P. Schwagmeyer and D.W. Mock, *How to Minimize Sample Sizes While Preserving Statistical Power* (Cambridge, MA: Academic Press, 1997).

13. P. Schwagmeyer and D.W. Mock, "Parental Provisioning and Offspring Fitness: Size Matters," *Animal Behaviour* 75, no. 1 (2008): 291–98.

14. P. Schwagmeyer, D.W. Mock, and G.A. Parker, "Biparental Care in House Sparrows: Negotiation or Sealed Bid?," *Behavioral Ecology* 13, no. 5 (2002): 713–21.

15. D.W. Mock, P. Schwagmeyer, and G.A. Parker, "Male House Sparrows Deliver More Food to Experimentally Subsidized Offspring," *Animal Behaviour* 70, no. 1 (2005): 225–36.

16. Mock, Schwagmeyer, and Parker, "Male House Sparrows Deliver More Food to Experimentally Subsidized Offspring."

17. M.B. Dugas, "House Sparrow, Passer domesticus, Parents Preferentially Feed Nestlings with Mouth Colours That Appear Carotenoid-Rich," *Animal Behaviour* 78, no. 3 (2009): 767–72.

NORTHERN CARDINAL

1. K.L. Borgmann and A.D. Rodewald, "Nest Predation in an Urbanizing Landscape: The Role of Exotic Shrubs," *Ecological Applications* 14 (2004): 1757–65.

2. A.D. Rodewald, D.P. Shustack, and T.M. Jones, "Dynamic Selective Environments and Evolutionary Traps in Human-Dominated Landscapes," *Ecology* 92 (2011): 1781–88.

3. S.L. Halkin et al., "Northern Cardinal," in *Birds of the World,* eds. P.G. Rodewald and B.K. Keeney (Ithaca, NY: Cornell Lab of Ornithology, 2021).

4. S.M. Johansen, D.J. Horn, and T.E. Wilcoxen, "Factors Influencing Seed Species Selection by Wild Birds at Feeders," *Wilson Journal of Ornithology* 126 (2014): 374–81.

5. U.S. Fish and Wildlife.

6. Johansen, Horn, and Wilcoxen, "Factors Influencing Seed Species Selection by Wild Birds at Feeders."

7. M.E. McDermott and L.W. DeGroote, "Long-Term Climate Impacts on Breeding Bird Phenology in Pennsylvania, USA," *Global Change Biology* 22 (2016): 3304–19.

8. Halkin et al., "Northern Cardinal."

9. D.D. Dow and D. Scott, "Dispersal and Range Expansion by the Cardinal: An Analysis of Banding Records," *Canadian Journal of Zoology* 49 (1971): 185–98.

10. R.E. Lemon, "How Birds Develop Song Dialects," *The Condor* 77 (1975): 385–406.

11. M.E. Anderson and R.N. Conner, "Northern Cardinal Song in Three Forest Habitats in Eastern Texas," *The Wilson Bulletin* 97 (1985): 436–49.

12. D.L. Narango and A.D. Rodewald, "Urban-Associated Drivers of Song Variation Along a Rural–Urban Gradient," *Behavioral Ecology* 27 (2016): 608–16.

13. S.L. Halkin, "Nest-Vicinity Song Exchanges May Coordinate Biparental Care of Northern Cardinals," *Animal Behaviour* 54 (1997): 189–198.

14. J.R. Vondrasek, "Social Factors Affect the Singing Rates of Female Northern Cardinals Cardinalis cardinalis," *Journal of Avian Biology* 37 (2006): 52–57.

NORTHERN MOCKINGBIRD

1. M. Pauli, "Harper Lee Tops Librarians' Must-Read List," *The Guardian*, March 2, 2006.

2. G. Farnsworth et al., "Northern Mockingbird (Mimus polyglottos)," version 1.0, in *Birds of the World*, ed. A.F. Poole (Ithaca, NY: Cornell Lab of Ornithology, 2020).

3. J. Hodge, "Darwin, the Galápagos and His Changing Thoughts About Species Origins: 1835–1837," *Proceedings of the California Academy of Sciences* 61, no. 2 (2010): 89.

4. D.M.L. DeLoach, "Breeding Success, Mating Success, and Mating Strategies of the Northern Mockingbird, Mimus polyglottos" (Ph.D. diss., Rice University, 1997).

5. C. Hughes and D.M.L. DeLoach, "Developing Microsatellites When They Are

Rare: Trinucleotide Repeat Loci in the Northern Mockingbird Mimus polyglottos," *Molecular Ecology* 6, no. 11 (1997): 1099–102.

6. K.C. Derrickson, "Yearly and Situational Changes in the Estimate of Repertoire Size in Northern Mockingbirds (Mimus polyglottos)," *The Auk* 104, no. 2 (1987): 198–207.

7. N.S. Thompson et al., "Variation in the Bout Structure of Northern Mockingbird (Mimus polyglottos) Singing," *Bird Behavior* 13, no. 2 (2000): 93–98.

8. Derrickson, "Yearly and Situational Changes in the Estimate of Repertoire Size in Northern Mockingbirds (Mimus polyglottos)."

9. D.E. Gammon and A.M. Corsiglia, "Mockingbirds Imitate Frogs and Toads Across North America," *Behavioural Processes* 169 (2019): 103982.

10. International Union for the Conservation of Nature, *The IUCN Red List of Threatened Species, Version 2019-1* (2019).

11. D.E. Gammon, "Are Northern Mockingbirds Classic Open-Ended Song Learners?," *Ethology* 126, no. 11 (2020): 1038–47.

12. Gammon, "Are Northern Mockingbirds Classic Open-Ended Song Learners?"

13. D.E. Gammon and A.C. Tovsky, "A Cross-Sectional Field Study of Fall Song in Northern Mockingbirds Mimus polyglottos," *Journal of Ornithology* 162, no. 2 (2021): 461–68.

14. F.H. Allen, "The Mockingbird's Wing-Flashing," *The Wilson Bulletin* 59 (1947): 71–73.

15. O.T. Miller, *In Nesting Time* (Boston: Houghton Mifflin, 1888).

16. J.P. Hailman, "A Field Study of the Mockingbird's Wing-Flashing Behavior and Its Association with Foraging," *The Wilson Bulletin* 72, no. 4 (1960): 346–57.

17. R.L. Mumme, "White Tail Spots and Tail-Flicking Behavior Enhance Foraging Performance in the Hooded Warbler," *The Auk* 131, no. 2 (2014): 141–49.

18. C.M. Stracey and S.K. Robinson, "Does Nest Predation Shape Urban Bird Communities?," in *Urban Bird Ecology and Conservation* (Berkeley: University of California Press, 2012), 49–70.

19. D.J. Levey et al., "Urban Mockingbirds Quickly Learn to Identify Individual Humans," *Proceedings of the National Academy of Sciences* 106, no. 22 (2009): 8959–62.

20. M.J. Walters et al., "Urban Background Noise Affects Breeding Song Frequency and Syllable-Type Composition in the Northern Mockingbird," *The Condor* 121, no. 2 (2019): duz002.

21. R. Breitwisch, N. Gottlieb, and J. Zaias, "Behavioral Differences in Nest Visits Between Male and Female Northern Mockingbirds," *The Auk* 106, no. 4 (1989): 659–65.

22. R. Breitwisch, P.G. Merritt, and G.H. Whitesides, "Why Do Northern Mockingbirds Feed Fruit to Their Nestlings?," *The Condor* 86, no. 3 (1984): 281–87.

YELLOW-RUMPED WARBLER

1. A. Brelsford, B. Mila, and D.E. Irwin, "Hybrid Origin of Audubon's Warbler," *Molecular Ecology* 20, no. 11 (2011): 2380–89.

2. E. Mayr, *Systematics and the Origin of Species: From the Viewpoint of a Zoologist* (Cambridge, MA: Harvard University Press, 1999).

3. J. Mallet, "Alternative Views of Biological Species: Reproductively Isolated Units or Genotypic Clusters," *National Science Review* 7, no. 8 (2020): 1401–7.

4. D.P. Toews et al., "Genomic Variation Across the Yellow-Rumped Warbler Species Complex," *The Auk* 133, no. 4 (2016): 698–717.

5. G.F. Barrowclough, "Genetic and Phenotypic Differentiation in a Wood Warbler (Genus Dendroica) Hybrid Zone," *The Auk* 97, no. 4 (1980): 655–68.

6. K. Prüfer et al., "The Bonobo Genome Compared with the Chimpanzee and Human Genomes," *Nature* 486, no. 7404 (2012): 527–31.

7. G. Alexander, "Natural Hybrids Between Dendroica coronata and D. auduboni," *The Auk* 62, no. 4 (1945): 623–26.

8. F.M. Packard, "The Birds of Rocky Mountain National Park, Colorado," *The Auk* 62, no. 3 (1945): 371–94.

9. Toews et al., "Genomic Variation Across the Yellow-Rumped Warbler Species Complex."

10. F.E. Rheindt and S.V. Edwards, "Genetic Introgression: An Integral but Neglected Component of Speciation in Birds," *The Auk* 128, no. 4 (2011): 620–32.

11. D. Lack, *The Natural Regulation of Animal Numbers* (New York: Clarendon Press, 1954).

12. R.H. MacArthur, "Population Ecology of Some Warblers of Northeastern Coniferous Forests," *Ecology* 39, no. 4 (1958): 599–619.

13. MacArthur, "Population Ecology of Some Warblers of Northeastern Coniferous Forests."

14. E.E. Cumming, "Habitat Segregation Among Songbirds in Old-Growth Boreal Mixedwood Forest," *Canadian Field-Naturalist* 118 (2004): 45–55.

WHITE-THROATED SPARROW

1. E.C. Snell-Rood and D.A. Cristol, "Prior Residence Influences Contest Outcome in Flocks of Non-Breeding Birds," *Ethology* 111, no. 5 (2005): 441–54.

2. K.A. Otter et al., "Continent-Wide Shifts in Song Dialects of White-Throated Sparrows," *Current Biology* 30, no. 16 (2020): 3231–35, e3.

3. J.K. Lowther, "Polymorphism in the White-Throated Sparrow, Zonotrichia albicollis (Gmelin)," *Canadian Journal of Zoology* 39, no. 3 (1961): 281–92.

4. L.E.D. Vardy, "Color Variation in the Crown of the White-Throated Sparrow, Zonotrichia albicollis," *The Condor* 73, no. 4 (1971): 401–14.

5. H.B. Thorneycroft, "Chromosomal Polymorphism in the White-Throated Sparrow, Zonotrichia albicollis (Gmelin)," *Science* 154, no. 3756 (1966): 1571–72.

6. H.B. Thorneycroft, "A Cytogenetic Study of the White-Throated Sparrow, Zonotrichia albicollis (Gmelin)," *Evolution* 29, no. 4 (1975): 611–21.

7. E.M. Tuttle et al., "Divergence and Functional Degradation of a Sex Chromosome-Like Supergene," *Current Biology* 26, no. 3 (2016): 344–50.

8. D. Reich, *Who We Are and How We Got Here: Ancient DNA and the New Science of the Human Past* (Oxford, UK: Oxford University Press, 2018).

9. E.M. Tuttle, "Alternative Reproductive Strategies in the White-Throated Sparrow: Behavioral and Genetic Evidence," *Behavioral Ecology* 14, no. 3 (2003): 425–32.

10. A.S. Grunst et al., "Extra-Pair Mating and the Strength of Sexual Selection: Insights from a Polymorphic Species," *Behavioral Ecology* 30, no. 2 (2019): 278–90.

11. J.R. Merritt et al., "A Supergene-Linked Estrogen Receptor Drives Alternative Phenotypes in a Polymorphic Songbird," *Proceedings of the National Academy of Sciences* 117, no. 35 (2020): 21673–80.

12. Snell-Rood and Cristol, "Prior Residence Influences Contest Outcome in Flocks of Non-Breeding Birds."

RIVERLANDS

1. P. Cleary, *The World, the Flesh, and the Devil: A History of Colonial St. Louis* (Columbia, MO: University of Missouri Press, 2011), 357.

2. F.T. Norris, "Where Did the Villages Go? Steamboats, Deforestation, and Archaeological Loss in the Mississippi Valley," in *Common Fields: An Environmental History of St. Louis*, ed. Andrew Hurley (St. Louis: Missouri Historical Society Press, 1997), 73–89.

3. Andrew Hurley, ed., *Common Fields: An Environmental History of St. Louis* (St. Louis: Missouri Historical Society Press, 1997), xiv.

AMERICAN COOT

1. H.J. Boyd and R. Alley, "The Function of the Head-Coloration of the Nestling Coot and Other Nestling Rallidae," *Ibis* 90, no. 4 (1948): 582–93.

2. R.P. Hobson, *Grass Beyond the Mountains* (Toronto: McClelland and Stewart, 1951).

3. G.W. Gullion, "Territorial Behavior of the American Coot," *The Condor* 55, no. 4 (1953): 169–86.

4. B.E. Lyon, J.M. Eadie, and L.D. Hamilton, "Parental Choice Selects for Ornamental Plumage in American Coot Chicks," *Nature* 371, no. 6494 (1994): 240–43.

5. B.E. Lyon, "Conspecific Brood Parasitism as a Flexible Female Reproductive Tactic in American Coots," *Animal Behaviour* 46, no. 5 (1993): 911–28.

6. D. Shizuka and B.E. Lyon, "Family Dynamics Through Time: Brood Reduction Followed by Parental Compensation with Aggression and Favouritism," *Ecology Letters* 16, no. 3 (2013): 315–22.

7. B.E. Lyon, "Egg Recognition and Counting Reduce Costs of Avian Conspecific Brood Parasitism," *Nature* 422, no. 6931 (2003): 495–99.

8. D. Shizuka and B.E. Lyon, "Coots Use Hatch Order to Learn to Recognize and Reject Conspecific Brood Parasitic Chicks," *Nature* 463, no. 7278 (2010): 223–26.

GREAT EGRET

1. W.T. Hornaday, *Our Vanishing Wild Life: Its Extermination and Preservation* (New York: C. Scribner's Sons, 1913).

2. D.A. McCrimmon Jr. et al., "Great Egret (Ardea alba)," version 1.0, in *Birds of the World*, ed. S.M. Billerman (Ithaca, NY: Cornell Lab of Ornithology, 2020).

3. D.W. Mock, "Siblicide, Parent-Offspring Conflict, and Unequal Parental Investment by Egrets and Herons," *Behavioral Ecology and Sociobiology* 20 (1987): 247–56.

4. D.W. Mock, "Siblicidal Brood Reduction: The Prey-Size Hypothesis," *American Naturalist* 125 (1985): 327–43.

5. D.W. Mock, T.C. Lamey, and B.J. Ploger, "Proximate and Ultimate Roles of Food Amount in Regulating Egret Sibling Aggression," *Ecology* 68, no. 6 (1987): 1760–72.

6. D.W. Mock, "Siblicidal Aggression and Resource Monopolization in Birds," *Science* 225, no. 4663 (1984): 731–33.

7. D.W. Mock and B.J. Ploger, "Parental Manipulation of Optimal Hatch Asynchrony in Cattle Egrets: An Experimental Study," *Animal Behaviour* 35 (1987): 150–60.

8. H. Schwabl, D.W. Mock, and J.A. Gieg, "A Hormonal Mechanism for Parental Favouritism," *Nature* 386, no. 6622 (1997): 231.

SNOW GOOSE

1. T.B. Mowbray, F. Cooke, and B. Ganter, "Snow Goose (Answer caerulescens)," version 1.0, in *Birds of the World*, ed. P.G. Rodewald (Ithaca, NY: Cornell Lab of Ornithology, 2020).

2. J. Gonzalez, H. Düttmann, and M. Wink, "Phylogenetic Relationships Based on Two Mitochondrial Genes and Hybridization Patterns in Anatidae," *Journal of Zoology* 279, no. 3 (2009): 310–18.

3. F. Cooke, R.F. Rockwell, and D.B. Lank, *The Snow Geese of La Perouse Bay: Natural Selection in the Wild*, vol. 4 (Oxford, UK: Oxford University Press, 1995).

4. T. Williams, D. Lank, and F. Cooke, "Is Intraclutch Egg-Size Variation Adaptive in the Lesser Snow Goose?," *Oikos* 67, no. 2 (1993): 250–56.

5. F. Cooke, D. Parkin, and R. Rockwell, "Evidence of Former Allopatry of the Two Color Phases of Lesser Snow Geese (Chen caerulescens caerulescens)," *The Auk* 105, no. 3 (1988): 467–79.

6. J.D. Soper, *Canadian Arctic Recollections: Baffin Island 1923–1931* (Saskatoon, SK, Canada: Institute for Northern Studies, University of Saskatchewan, 1981), 141.

7. R. Montgomerie, "The History of Ornithology in Nunavut," in *Birds of Nunavut*, eds. J.M. Richards and A. Gaston (Vancouver: UBC Press, 2018), 45–69.

8. Cooke, Rockwell, and Lank, *The Snow Geese of La Perouse Bay*.

9. N.I. Mundy et al., "Conserved Genetic Basis of a Quantitative Plumage Trait Involved in Mate Choice," *Science* 303, no. 5665 (2004): 1870–73.

10. F. Cooke, G. Finney, and R. Rockwell, "Assortative Mating in Lesser Snow Geese (Anser caerulescens)," *Behavior Genetics* 6, no. 2 (1976): 127–40.

11. F. Cooke, P. Mirsky, and M. Seiger, "Color Preferences in the Lesser Snow Goose and Their Possible Role in Mate Selection," *Canadian Journal of Zoology* 50, no. 5 (1972): 529–36.

12. H.C. Hanson, *Population Characteristics of Three Mainland Colonies of Blue and Lesser Snow Geese Nesting in the Southern Hudson Bay Region* (Ontario, Canada: Fish and Wildlife Research Branch, 1972).

13. M. Harper, J.D. Boyce, and B. Adler, "Pasteurella multocida Pathogenesis: 125 Years After Pasteur," *FEMS Microbiology Letters* 265, no. 1 (2006): 1–10.

14. M.D. Samuel et al., "Avian Cholera Mortality in Lesser Snow Geese Nesting on Banks Island, Northwest Territories," *Wildlife Society Bulletin* (1999): 780–87.

15. Samuel et al., "Avian Cholera Mortality in Lesser Snow Geese Nesting on Banks Island, Northwest Territories."

16. C.J. Brand, "Avian Cholera in the Central and Mississippi Flyways During 1979–80," *Journal of Wildlife Management* 48, no. 2 (1984): 399–406.

17. M.D. Samuel et al., "Avian Cholera in Waterfowl: The Role of Lesser Snow and Ross's Geese as Disease Carriers in the Playa Lakes Region," *Journal of Wildlife Diseases* 41, no. 1 (2005): 48–57.

Index

Mock, Douglas, 154–55, 157–64, 271–78
Mockingbirds, 153. *See also* Northern
  Mockingbirds
molting, 77, 79, 144, 206, 233, 284–85,
  289–90
Monarch butterflies, 24–25
Monk Parakeets, 133
monogamy, 40, 54, 57, 155–56, 193, 283
Monroy-Ojeda, Alan, 116–18
Monteverde, Costa Rica, 38
Montgomerie, Bob, 29, 34–37, 41–45, 175,
  236, 289–90
morphological data, 110, 148, 215
"motor birding," 1–2, 6
Moulton, Michael, 152
Mountain Bluebirds, 93
Mountain Chickadees, 93
Mountain Lake Biological Station, 74
Mount Desert Island, 217
Mourning Doves, 17, 22–23, 73, 89, 128,
  169, 202
Mpala reserve, 140
multiflora rose, 170, 171, 183
Mumme, Ron, 201
murmurations, 141–43, 145
mutations, 47, 287–88. *See also*
  genetic analysis
Myers, Jonathan, 186
Myrmica ants, 89
Myrtle Warblers, 209–14, 216–17, 223–24

Narango, Desiree, 177
Nashville Warblers, 117
National Audubon Society, 169, 270
National Museum of Canada, 232
Native Americans, 10, 12, 187, 286
natural selection, 57–58
Neighborhood Nestwatch, 67
nests and nesting behaviors
  American Coots, 252–64, 265
  American Robins, 35–36, 39–46, 48–49
  Cedar Waxwings, 117–22, 124
  Cooper's Hawks, 103–9, 111–12
  Dark-eyed Juncos, 74–77
  European Starlings, 132–40, 143–45

in Forest Park habitat, 127, 129
Great Egrets, 268–78
and home birding environments, 14–15,
  18, 83, 85
House Sparrows, 147, 149–51, 153–54,
  156–59, 161–64, 165
House Wrens, 51–58, 60–63, 65–66,
  67–68
and microbiomes, 79
Northern Cardinals, 170–72, 178–82
Northern Flickers, 88–97, 99
Northern Mockingbirds, 191–96,
  201–3, 204–7
and riverland habitats, 249
and scope of bird research, 9
Snow Geese, 283–87, 289–91,
  293–95
at Tyson Research Center, 187, 188
White-throated Sparrows, 239, 243
Yellow-crowned Night Herons, 2
Yellow-rumped Warblers, 217–18, 224
NestWatch, 49
Nettilling Lake, 286
New Orleans (steamboat), 247
New Stone Age, 283
New Zealand, 151
Nice, Margaret Morse, 8, 116, 124, 154,
  224, 230
Nolan, Val, 73–74
Norman, Oklahoma, 154
Norris, Terry, 247
North America House Sparrows, 151
North American Breeding Bird Surveys,
  102, 151
North American Classification Committee
  (NACC), 214
Northern Cardinals, 167–83
  and Forest Park habitat, 127–28
  frequency of eBird observations, 23
  and home birding environments, 12,
    14, 83
  and Northern Mockingbird songs, 199
  and predation dangers in urban
    areas, 202
  and scope of bird research, 9

About the Author

JOAN E. STRASSMANN has been a Slow Birder all her life. She is an award-winning teacher of animal behavior, first at Rice University in Houston and then at Washington University in St. Louis, where she is Charles Rebstock Professor of Biology. She has written more than two hundred scientific articles on the behavior, ecology, and evolution of social organisms. She is a member of the National Academy of Sciences and the American Academy of Arts and Sciences, and a fellow of the Animal Behavior Society and the American Association for the Advancement of Science, and has held a Guggenheim Fellowship. She lives with her husband in St. Louis, Missouri.

About the Illustrator

ANTHONY BARTLEY is a multimedia artist currently based out of St. Louis with a passion for science. After having been a member of several different types of research labs from age ten to undergrad, upon graduating he decided to combine his passions into one, becoming a scientific illustrator/graphic designer. He currently works as the scientific graphic designer for Washington University in St. Louis's Center for Reproductive Health Sciences.